ISLAMIC

MW01129186

GOVERNANCE:
THEORY AND PRACTICE

DISPELLING MISUNDERSTANDING AND MISAPPLICATION
OF ISLAMIC LAW AND ITS SYSTEM OF GOVERNANCE

HISHAM M. RAMADAN

ISLAMIC LAW AND GOVERNANCE: THEORY AND PRACTICE

Copyright © 2021 Hisham M. Ramadan

Contents

Introduction

0.1   Book Purpose

Muslims are frustrated by negative views of their religion in the international sphere. Phrases like "Islamic law", "Islamic State" or "Islamic system of governance" trigger a host of negative feelings and thoughts among the majority of the non-Muslim population. Muslims are also frustrated by the current state of affairs in many Muslim-majority states where social injustice, political oppression, and failed economies are a reality. These two issues, the negative views and political oppression with adverse outcomes, are closely related. The negative views of Muslims benefit the authoritarian regimes in Muslim-majority states because these regimes present themselves as the only viable alternative to the "scary" Islamic system of government or the "inhumane" Islamic law that threatens Western societies' existence. Many Western governments, out of the purported belief that Islamic law and the Islamic system of governance are intrinsically evil, support dictatorial regimes in Muslim-majority states.

Some Muslims blame the Western world for their current state of affairs. Others blame themselves and their oppressive regimes. A few Muslims, out of desperation and ignorance of real Islam, join terrorist organizations, seeking to change the status quo and instead eventually, indefensibly commit heinous acts. The response in the West and in Muslim-majority states to the threat of terrorism varies from launching wars and perpetuating massive human rights violations to attempting to re-define Islam. These responses have never been effective in eradicating the problem of terrorism that has emerged in many Muslim-majority states.

Negative views of Islam combined with acts of terrorism committed by misled Muslims has created a general state of Islamophobia and has adversely affected Muslims in Western societies. It is the ignorance of the "other", especially when accompanied by a cloud of negative propaganda, that can generate unjustifiable actions. For example, several States in U.S. and provinces in Canada have passed legislation banning Muslims from implementing and exercising Islamic family law notwithstanding that the proposed Islamic family law codes would be subject to the State's constitution and the Human Rights code. Interestingly, the Muslim family tribunal proposal was either rejected or banned by legislation while similar proposals for other faiths (such as Jewish and Catholic faiths) have been tolerated for years. France banned Muslim headscarves in state schools while it allowed nuns' habits and small Christian crosses. France has refused to grant a Muslim woman French citizenship because she insisted on wearing a veil. Switzerland's Parliament banned the building of mosque cupolas because it is a sign of "Islamization." The collective moral code of Europe as pronounced by The European Court of Human Rights shows a deep fear and hostility toward anything "Islamic." In Leyla Şahin v. Turkey, The European Court of Human Rights upheld a state ban on wearing the Islamic headscarf in public schools suggesting that the Islamic headscarf is a symbol of "extremist political movements." Interestingly the Turkish President, then Prime Minister, Recep Tayyip Erdogan's wife wears an Islamic headscarf. The court seems to suggest that the duly-elected Prime Minister's wife represents "extremist political movements"! Not to mention that Muslims residing in the Western world have experienced substantial fear compared to the typical non-Muslim citizen because Muslims suffer a backlash after every terrorist incident whether immediate or in the long run. They fear physical attacks. They sense ill-treatment, discrimination, and harassment due to religious bias and unfair branding.

The West's Islamophobia motivates not only a so-called "war on terrorism" or a war on "radical Islam" but a war on Islam itself, influencing foreign affairs with Muslim-majority states. Robin Wright, the Los Angeles Times expert on Islam wrote, "the United States and Western government officials were still looking for a strategy to deal with the Islamic challenge....".[1] She quoted an unnamed 'senior Bush administration official' as conceding that "we should have to be smarter in dealing with Islam than in dealing with communism 30 or 40 years ago...".[2] With the arrival of U.S. President Trump's racist dogma, Islamophobia has become a mainstream United States policy. The Trump administration has diligently tried to limit immigration to the United States from Muslim-majority states.

---

[1] Edward Said, Covering Islam: *How the Media and the Experts Determine How We See the Rest of the World*, (Random House 1997),7. See also Maxime Rodinson, *Maxime Europe and the Mystique of Islam* (I.B. Tauris 2002), 79-82.
[2] Id.

Negative views of Islamic law and its system of governance, Islamophobia, support of dictators in Muslim-majority states and sometimes terrorism has been triggered by the enemy of humanity: Ignorance. Nothing can defeat ignorance but true knowledge. It has been truly said: "The greatest enemy of knowledge is not ignorance; it is the illusion of knowledge".[3] Many in the West think that they know about Islamic law and its system of governance while in reality, they are victims of the illusion of knowledge. They have received false information from Islamophobics who refuse to acquire or acknowledge true knowledge. Misapplication of Islamic law and its system of governance in many Muslim-majority states enforces this false knowledge. Misunderstandings must be illuminated with knowledge. Islamic law and its system of governance's misapplication must be clarified. This is the goal of the book.

Because this book utilizes only the most authentic sources of *Sunni* Islam to defeat ignorance by presenting true knowledge, it poses a great challenge to Islamophobia's demagogue. Indeed, I challenge Islamophobics collectively to prove misrepresentation of any concept presented here. This book uproots years of Islamophobic work which has sought to spread ignorance and hatred of Islam.

To be sure, this book is not an apology, propaganda, or a work of advocacy. It aims only to illustrate what *Sunni* Muslims believe of Islamic law and its Ideal system of governance. Readers who hope for a book negatively portraying Islam under the guise of "academic rigor", "a balanced approach" or any other glossy concept to justify biases against Islam will not be happy with this book. Surely those readers will find plenty of books to tell them what they want to hear.

---

[3] This quote is owed to Daniel Boorstin.

Readers who are genuinely interested to learn about Islamic law and its system of governance from a Sunni Muslim viewpoint shall find this book very useful. Neither wrong practices of Islamic law and its system of governance nor the smokescreen of Islamophobia should control our understanding of the subject matter. The following simple analogy may clarify the issue at hand. A distinction ought to be made between the car and the driver.[4] Likewise a distinction must be made between Islamic law and its system of governance on one hand and the common misunderstandings and misrepresentations by Muslim-majority states on the other.

0.2 Methodology Explanation

The thesis of this manuscript focuses primarily on *Sunni* not *Shia'* Islam. *Shia'* discrepancy with *Sunni* interpretation of the *Qur'an* and *Sunnah* as well as *Shia'* beliefs and philosophy of governance render grouping *Sunni* and *Shia'* into one thesis an impossible task. Nevertheless, *Shia'* scholars are invited to review the thesis of this manuscript and endorse it in full or in part as is compatible with *Shia'* belief.

This book depends primarily on authentic Islamic sources to present a true, authentic and reliable picture of Islamic law, and its system of governance. As a result, this book relies heavily on *Sunni* Muslim primary sources of law, i.e. the *Qur'an* and *Sunnah*. To explain these primary sources, this book utilizes the role model practices of the first four *Caliphs*, commonly known as the Islamic state's golden era. When needed, ancillary classical *Sunni* scholarly

---

[4] This metaphor is owed to Yusuf Islam, formerly known as the famous pop singer, Cat Stevens.

work shall be invoked to explain the *Qur'an* or *Sunnah* or to endorse a perspective. Modern scholarly work shall be pointed out in limited arguments that do not involve the core thesis of this book. Notably, various Islamic scholarship in the original Arabic language have been utilized because of their importance in explaining the *Qur'an* and *Sunnah* in *Sunni* Islamic thought. When English translation is available, it shall be mentioned. At times, technical legal discussions take place, which only legal scholars would appreciate, solely to explain a point.

This book's very restrictive sourcing is intentional because utilizing non-*Sunni* Muslims sources in building the theses of this book would undermine its legitimacy. As a result, Western sources will not be part of this book thesis. However, when needed, a comparative analysis to Western sources shall be drawn to help the Western reader understand the issues satisfactorily. Post-colonial analysis will sometimes be drawn when the subject matter warrants. This methodology may be disappointing to some Western scholars. Nonetheless, it is time to see issues related to Islamic law and its system of governance through a Muslim lens. The reader of this book must be prepared to see the Muslim perspective without preordained biases. The Western reader must be ready to accept these facts: Muslims believe that the Western perspective is not the ultimate truth. It is not the criteria for right and wrong. It is only one perspective. Truth is relative; Truth is in the eye of beholder.

CHAPTER 1

The Islamic Law: Sources and Historical Development[5]

꒨ꔫꔫꕤ

1.1   Introduction

One night while the forty-year-old Muhammad Ibn Abd Allah was meditating in a cave near Mecca, the Angel Gabriel appeared before him saying, "Read". Muhammad responded, "I am illiterate". The Angel Gabriel hugged Muhammad very tightly and released him and repeated the order, "Read". Muhammad responded again, "I am illiterate". The Angel Gabriel hugged Muhammad again very tightly, released him and then revealed the first verses of the *Qur'an* (69:19):

> *Read! In the Name of your Lord Who has created (all that exists). He has created humankind from a clot (a piece of thick*

---

[5] Some parts of this chapter have been previously discussed in Hisham M. Ramadan, "Toward Honest and Principled Islamic Law Scholarship", 2006 *MICH. ST. L. REV.*, 1573.

coagulated blood). Read! And your Lord is the Most Generous. Who has taught (the writing) by the pen. He has taught humankind that which he knew not.

These few words marked the initiation of the religion of Islam with its laws and customs. These first verses of the *Qur'an* emphasize the supreme Islamic human rights rule: seeking knowledge through education is a divine command for all humankind, men and women, from birth until death. Over the next 23 years of the Qur'anic revelation, numerous Islamic law rules followed. However, the subsequently revealed Qur'anic Islamic law rules were not as forceful in language and style as these initial verses. Rather, the first portion of the *Qur'an* that was revealed in Mecca focused primarily on rooting the new religion in the hearts and minds of the believers, significantly challenging the contemporary Arabs' way of life. The second part of the *Qur'an*, revealed in Medina, established most of the Islamic law jurisprudence. This method of revealing the *Qur'an* was remarkably effective. Human nature typically resists receiving commands that challenge the established way of life unless such commands are received from a recognizable authority. Even then, some might be tempted to challenge any recognizable authority that attempts to change the social norms. The first portion of the *Qur'an* that was revealed in Mecca attempted to change this equation by employing the pleasure and pain technique. Mankind generally seeks pleasure and attempts to avoid pain. The portion of the *Qur'an* that was revealed in Mecca emphasized the rewards for good deeds and the punishment for bad deeds. Paradise is the reward for the virtuous and hell is for the sinful. The *Qur'an* further described in detail the beauty of paradise with its limitless pleasures and the unbearable suffering in hell. In modern legal terminology, it is very clear that the Meccan portion of the *Qur'an* employed general deterrence to its full extent to persuade people to avoid divine wrongs while offering amazing incentives for good deeds.

Although the *Qur'an* is the fundamental source of Islamic law, it is only the initial step in the study of Islamic law. Many sources of Islamic law have contributed to current Islamic law jurisprudence.

1.2 What is Islamic Law?

According to Islamic beliefs, God (Allah) is the source of law. God's will has been transmitted directly through the main sources of Islamic law, the *Qur'an* and *Sunnah*. There are a number of ancillary sources of Islamic law derived from scholarly investigation of Islamic rule when a particular situation/issue is not explicitly stated in the *Qur'an* or *Sunnah*.

Generally speaking, Islamic law is divided into two main categories: *Ibadat* and *Mo'amalat*. *Ibadat* addresses the relationship between the individual and God. It focuses primarily on religious matters such as acts of worship, mandatory religious practices and the spiritual aspect of Islam. *Mo'amalat* covers the non-religious transactions including the relationship between individuals, such as the law of contracts, family law, criminal law, and the relationship between individuals and the State. Since this chapter is not intended to cover the religious aspects of Islam, the discussion shall focus exclusively on *Mo'amalat*.

Islamic law should be distinguished from *Fiqh*. Linguistically, *Fiqh* is the understanding of the explicit meaning and implications of a notion such as a doctrine, concept, ideology, school of thought or even a body of laws. With respect to Islamic law, *Fiqh* is the understanding of the explicit and implicit commands of Islamic law.

Similarly, Islamic law ought to be distinguished from *Sharia'* and scholarly opinions. *Sharia'* is comprised of the Islamic law commands that are enumerated in the *Qur'an* and *Sunnah*. Scholarly opinions that are extracted from the *Qur'an* and *Sunnah* are not *Sharia'*; rather they are opinions based upon their authors' understanding of the *Qur'an* and *Sunnah*. Nowadays, Western scholars incorrectly use the terms *Fiqh* and *Sharia'* interchangeably to refer to Islamic law.

1.3   A Brief History of Islamic Jurisprudence

Recall that the basic sources of Islamic law, the *Qur'an* and *Sunnah*, are timeless fundamental sources of Islamic jurisprudence which are not subject to alteration from the moment of revelation till the end of days. The period of the revelation of the *Qur'an* and instituting the *Sunnah* constitutes the initial phase of Islamic law. The ancillary sources of Islamic law, apart from Prophet Muhammad's companions' opinions, have been subject to development and went through many phases after the death of Prophet Muhammad.

1.3.1   Revelation Phase

The revelation phase of the basic sources of Islamic law, namely the *Qur'an* and *Sunnah*, lasted 23 years from the commencement of the message of Islam when the Prophet Muhammad was forty years old until his death at age 63.[6] The Prophet Muhammad lived in a Bedouin society that was influenced by the harsh desert environment which is reflected in their laws and customs. Some customary practices were admirable such as the hospitality extended to guests and travellers and the pre-Islamic treaty of *Hilf al-Fudul* (Alliance of *al-Fudul*), which

---

[6] The Prophet Muhammad lived 63 lunar years (571 AD – 632 AD).

aimed to uphold justice and aid the oppressed. Islam upheld such practices in that the Prophet Muhammad spoke very highly of this alliance and expressed his agreement to join such an alliance if it had occurred after the revelation of the message of Islam. In contrast, other practices were reprehensible, such as the murder of young girls by their fathers out of fear of poverty, due to concern that women would not be capable of providing for themselves, and/or the possibility that women may bring shame to the family if they engage in non-permissible sexual intercourse. Here, Islam attempted to extinguish unfair laws and customs and replace them with its own jurisprudence by various means.

The *Qur'an* was revealed in Mecca and Medina. Islamic law in the Meccan period is notable for laying the foundation of the most general and imperative rules of law. In order to set the foundation of the emerging state not only were the vital rules of conduct entrenched into the new society but also the basic system of governance principles, such as the *Shura* doctrine (mutual consultation) in the decision-making process, were expounded in the *Qur'an* and in the Prophet Muhammad's practices. The interpretation of this concept has shaped the Islamic State and, indeed, has reflected dramatically on Muslim political life ranging from the death of the Prophet Muhammad to current times. The concept of *Shura* is critical in deciding two distinctive matters, the Muslim State ruler's succession process and the composition and rule of a Muslim State Parliament or *Shura* council. The Prophet Muhammad, the exemplary model for Muslims, exercised *Shura*, in war and in peace, by creating a *Shura* council with up to seventy members.

Remarkably, Qur'anic law in the Meccan period utilized various sociological and psychological methodologies to create an atmosphere of acceptance of the new rules of conduct. The *Qur'an* invited people to think about creation, meditate and challenge rooted ideologies. The *Qur'an* employed the fear of pain and the hope of pleasure as most effective tools, moving forces of nations, to pave the road to the individual's acceptance of the new faith: Islamic law. To create a good citizen of the Islamic State, the *Qur'an* in the Meccan period attempted to build a sense of self-monitoring of one's actions regardless of the State's justice system.

Later, after the general rules of conduct were in place and the new faith ideologies were well-rooted in Mecca, the Islamic State took its formal shape in Medina which reflected significantly on the mode of legislating. The portion of the *Qur'an* revealed in Medina had more detailed legislations to complete a uniform and comprehensive justice system. For example, exhaustive rules of family law including inheritance, bequests, marriage and custody were laid down in *Surah An-Nisa*. Several criminal law and evidence rules were expounded in *Surah An-Noor*. Constitutional principles, such as equality and privacy rights, were expounded in *Surah Al-Hujraat*.

Generally speaking, legislating in the revelation phase was marked by five common features:

    a. Only real issues, not hypothetical or future issues, were subject to legislating.

    b. The Prophet was the only authority that conveyed God's will in law-making whether in the *Qur'an* or *Sunnah*.

    c. There was ease of understanding of the laws, with no problems in application or interpretation of law of the *Qur'an* and *Sunnah*. Any possible ambiguity was swiftly resolved by the Prophet.

d. The foundation of Islamic law was completed before the death of the Prophet. What was left for Muslims with respect to resolving future social challenges has been an easy task limited to the creation of ancillary sources in light of the *Qur'an* and *Sunnah*.

e. Islam, the new faith, attempted to root its principles in a gradual process. For example, prohibition of alcohol, which was then commonly consumed in Arabia, took three gradual phases. At the start, the *Qur'an* stated that consumption of alcohol produces both benefits and harms, but the harm outweigh the benefit. Later, the *Qur'an* prohibited performing prayers while intoxicated. Finally, the *Qur'an* prohibited intoxicants totally. It is worthwhile and remarkable to note that total prohibition of alcohol was not recommended until the new Islamic society showed their unshakeable faith in Islam.

1.1.1   Expansion of Ijtihad Phase

After the death of the Prophet, the Islamic State was confronted with new legal questions and social challenges that were not expressly adjudicated in the *Qur'an* or *Sunnah*. Numerous circumstances contributed to the emergence of the *Ijtihad* phase, including the death of the Prophet, the legislative and judicial authority and the significant expansion of the Islamic State. Therefore, it was inescapable to engage in *Ijtihad* to resolve new legal questions. *Ijtihad* means exerting one's reasoning faculty in determining a point of law by independent interpretation of the Islamic legal sources, such as the *Qur'an* and *Sunnah*. The golden age of *Ijtihad* lasted for approximately three centuries beginning with the death of the

Prophet. Various methodologies were employed to conduct *Ijtihad*. The Prophets' companions typically consulted each other before making *Ijtihad*. The consultation process involved initially inquiring about any possible *Sunnah* practice or Prophetic Qur'anic interpretation that would resolve the legal question at hand. If not found, they conducted *Ijtihad*. If they unanimously agreed on *Ijtihad*, such *Ijtihad* was elevated to reach the degree of *Ijma* (consensus) which is binding to the Islamic State. If there is no *Ijma*, the Islamic State Leader's *Ijtihad*, as representative of the State, became the official interpretation of Islam and thereby binding to the State.

Many Islamic law ancillary source methodologies were not well developed in this era; Islamic law sources were typically limited to the *Qur'an*, *Sunnah*, *Ijma* and *Qiyas*.

Islamic law scholarship adopted two general approaches in *Ijtihad*. The first approach, exerting one's effort to reach a conclusion on a legal matter, occurs by investigating the natural meaning of the text, whether the *Qur'an* or *Sunnah*, and applying it to the issue in question. Some who follow this approach go even further to explore not only the natural meanings but also the rationales, critical analogies and the spirit of the legislation in the legal decision-making process. The second approach is *Zahiri* methodology or the literal approach which restricts itself to the apparent meaning of the *Qur'an* and *Sunnah* as an exclusive rule of interpretation. The follower of this approach makes no consideration to the legislative's rationales or *Qiyas* in the decision-making process.

Initially, during the expansion of the *Ijtihad* phase, the companions of the Prophet Muhammad and the next generation of scholars, *Tab'een*, never explored hypothetical legal issues.[7] Indeed, it has been reported that the second Muslim *Caliph*, Umar Ibn al-Khattab, condemned those who asked a question of law that has not materialized. Later, creating hypothetical legal questions and drawing conclusions became very common among scholars and paved the way for the creation of various Islamic schools of thought. 1.

1.1.2   The Rise of Islamic Scholarship - Schools of Thoughts Phase

Every scholar had a number of students that followed him in learning circles, writing his scholarship and discussing with others the knowledge he had received. This led to the emergence of many schools of thought, each creating their own methodological interpretation of the *Qur'an* and *Sunnah* and ranking the ancillary sources of Islamic law differently. Some of these schools of thought did not recognize ancillary sources.

Some schools of thought were products of a particular political stance such as *Zaidiyya*, *Kharijites* who developed the *Ibadiyah* School of thought, Shia' *Al-imamiyyah* that then branched into numerous schools of thought including Twelvers, *Ismaili*, and *Batnaya*. On the other hand, the vast majority of Muslims nowadays are Sunni Muslims that follow one of four Sunni schools of thought: *Hanafi*, *Shafi'i*, *Maliki* and *Hanbali*.

Islamic schools of thought spread geographically regardless of place of origin. The *Maliki* school of thought was founded in Medina and spread throughout the North African States, Qatar, Bahrain and

---

[7] Tab'een are those individuals who did not meet the Prophet Muhammad but met and followed the footsteps of the companions of the Prophet Muhammad.

Kuwait with some competition from the *Shafi'i* school of thought in Egypt. The *Shafi'i* school of thought emerged in Egypt and Iraq then spread to Lebanon, Syria, Yemen, parts of Saudi Arabia and parts of India. The *Hanafi* School of thought emerged in Iraq and spread to central Asia, including Afghanistan, parts of Iran and became the official religious sect of the Ottoman Empire. The *Hanbali* school of thought emerged in Baghdad and spread to Saudi Arabia and parts of Qatar and Bahrain. The *Twelvers Shia* school of thought emerged and spread in Iraq, parts of Saudi Arabia and Iran. Both the *Shia Ismaili* and *Batnaya* schools of thought emerged in North Africa including Egypt and were the official sect of the State. Now *Shia Ismaili* and *Batnaya* have nearly disappeared from Egypt as well as most of North Africa. There are still some followers in Syria, Lebanon, parts of India and South Africa.

1.1.3 *Taqlid* Phase

After a lengthy period of very active Islamic scholarship, a new era emerged, that of blind following of the earlier scholarship, the era of *Taqlid*. This occurred for a host of reasons including the declining social, political and economic state of affairs. Furthermore, many scholars declared the closing of the gates of *Ijtihad*, claiming that all questions had been answered, all issues settled and that any new scholarship shall be redundant. Perhaps those scholars intended to prevent scholarship from being produced in unhealthy environments such as scholarship formulated under foreign occupation or scholarship formulated under oppressive regimes. This tainted scholarship can, indeed, mislead the public and have long lasting effects. What is really interesting is that any scholar with comprehensive knowledge of Islam would undoubtedly know that the gates of *Ijtihad* have been open and will remain open from the dawn of Islam until the End of Days. This is because *Ijtihad* is the mechanism by which Islam deals with new questions and situations. Hypothetically speaking, even if every question has been answered at any given moment in time, circumstances shall change over time calling for new scholarship addressing the new circumstance.

In fact, during the *Taqlid* phase, characterized by abstinence from *Ijtihad*, outstanding *Ijtihad* did occur such as the *Ijtihad* of the renowned scholars Al-`Izz Ibn `Abd al-Salam (1182 AD – 1261 AD) and Taj al Din al-Subki (1327 AD – 1370 AD). The majority of scholars who were involved in *Taqlid* engaged in extensive comparative analysis of scholarship of the various schools of thought. Codification and re-arrangement of scholarship was a natural consequence to facilitate such comparative studies.

1.1.4   Calls for The Renewal of Islamic Law Scholarship

Islamic law is dynamic, capable of responding to new social needs and challenges. Accordingly, many scholars have called for a renaissance of Islamic scholarship. This includes both the codification of Islamic law principles to replace legislation not in compliance with Islamic law, and the creation of new *Ijtihad* to respond to new social challenges. The scholars who pioneered the renewal movement produced new scholarship methodologies. Sheikh *Mahmoud* Shaltut (1893 – 1963) endeavoured to show similarities between various schools of thought to create harmonious scholarship. Professor Muhammad Abu Zahra (1898 – 1974) explained the developmental phases of Islamic schools of thought and placed its methodology and *Ijtihad* in a historical, social and political contextual framework. Professor Abu Zahra also elucidated the biographies of the schools of thought founders, examined their approaches, innovative methodologies, objectives and their impact on Islamic law scholarship. Most recently, Professor Yusuf Al Qaradawi (1926-) has adopted a moderate approach that refuses to follow one school of thought methodology to answer all questions of law. Instead, he examines various sources of jurisprudence and utilizes the appropriate school of thought methodology suitable for the issue in question.

1.2   Sources of Islamic Law

1.2.1   Fundamental Sources

1.2.1.1 *The Qur'an*

The *Qur'an* is the holy book of Islam that contains the speech of God as revealed to the Prophet Muhammad in Arabic. Any translated text is not the *Qur'an* proper; rather, it is merely the translator's understanding of the meanings of the *Qur'an*. Truly, the general meanings of the *Qur'an* can be translated, but the metaphors, implied doctrines, the linguistic artistry and the like are impossible to be translated. For instance, the *Qur'an* (24:30) states: *Tell the believing men to lower their gaze, and protect their private parts. That is purer for them. Verily, Allah is All-Aware of what they do.* One of the linguistic characteristics of the *Qur'an* is politeness in addressing all matters. "Lowering the gaze" is a metaphor for avoidance of gazing upon forbidden things such as undressed members of the opposite sex who are not their spouses. "Protection of the private parts" is also a metaphor for prohibition of illegitimate sexual intercourse. Thus, a typical translation would read: Tell the believing men to lower their gaze (from looking at forbidden things), and protect their private parts (from illegal sexual acts). However, once the additional comments are made between the brackets, it is no longer the *Qur'an*. The politeness has vanished and the translator has added what he believes to be the intended meaning and the translated text is merely an approximation of the true *Qur'an*.

The *Qur'an* was revealed gradually over 23 years.[8] The *Qur'an* itself testifies that the gradual revelation was intended to root the meanings, commands and doctrines in the hearts and minds of the Prophet and the people. The *Qur'an*, indeed, was an intellectual revolution to the Arabs, the initial recipients of the *Qur'an*, commanding them to abandon a long list of activities such as consuming alcohol, fornication, adultery, female infanticide and unjust war. If the entire *Qur'an* had been revealed at once, it perhaps could have been very challenging for the people to follow its commands and abandon so many of their laws and customs. The gradual nature of the revelation allowed for incremental changes that were likely more easily incorporated into daily life.

Although the *Qur'an* was memorized and inscribed on bones, flat stones, wood and leather during the life of the Prophet Muhammad, it was not compiled as a text until the reign of the Third *Caliph* of the Islamic State, 'Uthman. This authentic compilation is still in use to this day. The *Qur'an* may very well be the only book that has maintained its authenticity, without change, for over fourteen centuries.

The *Qur'an* is the prime source for Islamic law. Any other source of Islamic law is compared to the *Qur'an*, and when apparent contradictions arise, the *Qur'an* is the supreme authority. However,

---

[8] The Qur'an was revealed over the course of 23 *Lunar* years.

Qur'anic commands must be read in the proper context with full consideration given to the generality or specificity of its scope. An example of a general application command follows here: *O you who believe! Fulfil (your) obligations.*[9] This command is one of general, sweeping application to all branches of law including contracts, marriage and international obligations arising from treaties, conventions, etc. An example of a law branch specific command follows: *And divorced women shall wait (as regards their marriage) for three menstrual periods.*[10] This command specifies the elapsed period for divorced women to be eligible to remarry, which is a family law issue.

The Qur'anic commands should not be applied in isolation, separate from the comprehensive jurisprudential scheme of Islamic law. It is imperative to invoke all relevant doctrines, rules and basics in determining a matter. For example, in criminal law, defenses and exculpatory rules of evidence must operate when the circumstances warrant. Muslim *Caliph* Umar Ibn al-Khattab had ordered a moratorium on the punishment of theft, a *hudud* offense, when famine struck Arabia. This can be viewed as a direct application of the Islamic evidentiary rule that "doubt precludes *hudud's* punishment". The 'general doubt' in this case including the need to satisfy the necessities of life when famine becomes a fact, which embraces the entire population. Accordingly, the punishment of theft ought to be put on hold until the excusing circumstances cease to exist. Similarly, the interpretation of the Qur'anic commands should not be too broad or unduly narrow; either extreme would prevent the achievement of its intended goal. For instance, the *Qur'an* prohibits Muslims'

---

[9] Qur'an 5:1.
[10] Qur'an 2:228.

production and/or consumption of intoxicants. This prohibition should not be extended to growing fruits, e.g. grapes, which might be used to produce the intoxicant, e.g. wine. This prohibition also should not be interpreted narrowly in order to allow the manufacturing of the equipment that is used solely for the production of intoxicants.

Islamic law rulings can be either definitive (*Qat'i*) or speculative (*Zanni*) with respect to authenticity and/or meaning. This basically divides Islamic rulings into:

1. Definitive meaning and authenticity,
2. Speculative meaning and authenticity,
3. Definitive meaning with speculative authenticity, or
4. Speculative meaning with definitive authenticity.

'Definitive textual meaning' conveys that the text is clear, specific and not subject to interpretation. An example of definitive meaning involves the elucidation of the husband's share of his deceased wife's estate: *In that which your wives leave, your share is a half if they have no child.*[11] An example of speculative meaning is the elapsed period for divorced women to be eligible to remarry. The *Qur'an* states: *And divorced women shall wait (as regards their marriage) for three menstrual periods.*[12] Because it is not clear whether the menstrual period is counted from the beginning or the end of menses, this text is speculative in meaning. The entire *Qur'an*, as explained earlier, is definitive with respect to its authenticity but its rulings can be either speculative or definitive with respect to meanings. On the other hand, *Sunnah* can be either speculative or definitive with respect to meanings and authenticity. An example of *Sunnah* speculative with

---

[11] Qur'an 4:12.
[12] Qur'an 2:228.

respect to authenticity is the *Sunnah* transmitted by a single narrator (*Akbar Ahad*).

In this context, Islamic law commands can be divided into mutable or immutable laws. Immutable commands are prefixed rulings that are suitable for application from the time of initial revelation until the end of time. All definitive commands of the *Qur'an* and *Sunnah* are immutable commands whether they apply to a particular branch of law or have general application to all branches of law. On the other hand, areas of speculative meaning of the *Qur'an* are mutable and subject to interpretation. Similarly, speculative *Sunnah*, either in meaning and/or authenticity, is mutable and subject to interpretation.

Lastly, the *Qur'an*, from a legal scholar's perspective, is not only a religious book; rather it is also the primary source of legislation and proper authoritative weight must be given to every word, story and statement in the *Qur'an*. For example, the story of the Prophet Moses aiding two women in watering their flocks as he was departing Egypt was articulated in the *Qur'an* as follows:

> *Then there came to him one of the two women, walking shyly. She said: "Verily, my father calls you that he may reward you for having watered (our flocks) for us." So, when he came to him and narrated the story, he said: "Fear you not. You have escaped from the people who are Zalimun (polytheists, disbelievers, and wrong-doers)." And said one of them (the two women): "O my father! Hire him! Verily, the best of men for you to hire is the strong, the trustworthy."* [13]

In this story, the women concluded that two character traits of the Prophet Moses rendered him qualified for hire, strength and

---

[13] Qur'an 28: 25-6.

trustworthiness. This story has inspired Islamic law scholars, throughout the centuries, to require strength and trustworthiness as chief, indispensable qualities for all public officials including the head of the Islamic State.

Similarly, the *Qur'an* is filled with jurisprudential policies that enlighten legislators' law-making. For example, the *Qur'an* explains that punishment is personal and that the lack of knowledge of the prohibition precludes that punishment. The pertinent verse declares: *No one laden with burdens can bear another's burden. And We never punish until We have sent a Messenger (to give warning).*[14] A direct application of this policy would have significant outcomes on all branches of law. For example, under Islamic criminal law, the category of negligent offenses would vanish. This is because negligence offences, in non-Islamic law systems, assume that the actor is not aware that he is violating the prohibitory norm, nevertheless the legislature requires such awareness. In contrast, under the Islamic system, when awareness is lacking, there is neither crime nor punishment.

The dependence of Islamic State legislature on the *Qur'an*, as the prime source of legislation, requires familiarity with the Qur'anic sciences to help in the interpretation and application of the *Qur'an*. Examples of these sciences include knowledge of the surrounding circumstances and context of Qur'anic revelation and rules of interpretation including knowledge of *Nasekh* (abrogated verses).

While most Qur'anic verses were revealed without any incident to trigger their revelation, knowledge of the circumstances and the reasons for those verses that *were* revealed for a reason, is

---

[14] Qur'an 17:15.

indispensable to comprehend a verse's complete meaning. For instance, verse (2:281) reads:

> And be afraid of the day when you shall be brought back to Allah. Then every person shall be paid what he earned, and they shall not be dealt with unjustly.

This verse was the last verse revealed in the *Qur'an*. This draws our attention to its meaning. It summarizes the entire message of Islamic law: a warning that bad deeds will be punished and good deeds will be rewarded – justice is destiny. This circumstance emphasizes the importance of the principles and suggests that the Islamic State must implement justice to the minute degree in all its affairs, notwithstanding any domestic or foreign influence. While this principle seems logical and typical in any state, its application in the Islamic State is indeed profound, in comparison to current state of affairs in the typical Muslim majority state. For example, the Islamic State cannot give up its land, or any part of it under any circumstances. Similarly, the Islamic State cannot give preferred treatment to foreigners, such as so-called royal families, or any group of individuals. All people are the same. For example, nowadays in the oil rich Gulf Muslim States, individuals are paid according to their nationality and clan relationship. Perhaps the highest paid for the same job is the citizen of that state while Westerners fall into the second category with less pay. Other workers, including other Arab State nationals, fall into third and fourth tiers of pay for equal jobs. This discriminatory policy would evaporate under proper application of Islamic law in a proper Islamic State.

Similarly, the Islamic Legislature ought to be familiar with rules of interpretation and knowledge of *Nasekh* (abrogated verses) to realize the limitations and applicability of verses that pertain to Islamic law.[15] In so doing the legislature may rely on authentic scholarly interpretation of the *Qur'an* and invoke the science of *Usul Al-Fiqh* (Principles of Jurisprudence) when needed. To illustrate the importance of such knowledge, consider the following. The *Qur'an* reads:

> *And those who launch a charge against chaste women, and produce not four witnesses, (to support their allegations), flog them with eighty stripes; and reject their evidence ever after: for such men are wicked transgressors. Unless they repent there-after and mend (their conduct): for Allah is Oft-Forgiving, Most Merciful.*[16]

These verses suggest that the punishment for false accusation of unchasteness is flogging with eighty stripes. The language of the verse is so broad that it can apply to husbands who accuse their wives of unchasteness. However, a more specific verse indicates a different standard for spouses. The *Qur'an* (24:6-9) reads:

> *And for those who launch a charge against their spouses, and have (in support) no evidence but their own, — their solitary evidence (can be received) if — they bear witness four times (with an oath) by Allah that they are solemnly telling the Truth. And the fifth (oath) (should be) that they solemnly invoke the curse of Allah on themselves if they tell a lie. But it would avert the punishment from the wife, if she bears witness four times (with an oath) by Allah, that (her husband) is telling a lie; And*

---

[15] Scholars disagree about whether some verses in the Qur'an abrogate others. Some scholars suggest that abrogation never happened. Others suggest a large or small number of verses are abrogated by another verse in the Qur'an or Sunnah.

[16] Qur'an 24:4-5.

> *the fifth (oath) should be that she solemnly invokes the wrath of Allah on her-self if (her accuser) is telling the Truth.*

These verses exempt a husband from the punishment if he makes an oath five times testifying to the truth of the matter. Some scholars might label the husband exception stated in verses 6-9 an abrogation to the resolution stated in verses 4 and 5. Others, who understand the language of the *Qur'an*, know that verse 4 was elaborated in general terms to deal with every issue unless there is an exception to the rule, which actually occurred in the later verses. Lack of knowledge of the *Qur'an*, the applicability of verses, and their limitations cripples a legislature's ability to analyze and understand the *Qur'an*.

Finally, since the application of the legal rule stated in a particular verse is always dependent upon its classification, the legislature ought to be acquainted with various jurisprudential verse classifications. *Qur'an* verses might be *'aam* (general), *khas* (specific), *mutlaq* (absolute), *muqayyad* (restricted), *mujmal* (comprehensive), or *mubayyan/mofsar* (explicit). Perhaps the most important classification is that *Qur'an* verses are either *Mohkamat* or *Mutashabihat*. *Mohkamat* verses are hard facts. They are the foundations of the *Qur'an*. They are plain, easy to understand, and not subject to interpretation. In contrast, *Mutashabihat* verses are open to interpretation by qualified scholars/legislature and may not be easy to understand.[17]

---

[17] See, Qur'an (3:7-8) "He it is Who has sent down to thee the Book; in it are verses basic or fundamental [of established meaning]; they are the foundation of the Book: others are not of well-established meaning. But those in whose hearts is perversity follow the part thereof that is not of well-established meaning. Seeking discord and searching for its hidden meanings...". The Prophet Muhammad warned those who seek Mutashabihat verses to reach a desired conclusion. See Tafsir Ibn Kathir, Sura Al-i-'Imran 3:7: "The Messenger of Allah [the Prophet

1.4.1.2 Sunnah

Linguistically, *Sunnah* refers to a law, lifestyle, continuity or method. Normatively, *Sunnah* comprises the Prophet Muhammad's sayings, his tacit or explicit approval and his practices. *Sunnah* was recorded by the companions of the Prophet and transmitted on his authority over the years. *Hadith* consists only of the *sayings* of the Prophet Muhammad. Therefore, *Sunnah* and *Hadith* are different; nevertheless, they are typically used interchangeably in Western literature. For the purpose of Islamic law study, *Sunnah* must be understood in the normative sense.

Authenticated *Sunnah* is the second source of Islamic law. It is as important as the *Qur'an* as a source of jurisprudence because both share the same origin, God. While the wording of the *Qur'an* was *revealed* by God, *Sunnah* was *inspired* by God and the wording is that of the Prophet Muhammad. The *Qur'an* testifies that following *Sunnah*, as a source of law, is mandatory.

Unlike the *Qur'an*, which is unquestionably protected from alteration or even suspicion of alteration, *Sunnah* after the death of the Prophet Muhammad required authentication. Scholars over the centuries utilized various strict methodologies to authenticate *Sunnah*. Sunni Islam, the predominant Islamic branch comprising about 90% of the world's Muslims, recognizes a number of authenticated *Sunnah* collections that include *Sahih al-Bukhari, Sahih Muslim, Muwatta al-Imam Malik, Sunnan Abu Dawud, Sahih*

Muhammad] recited, 'It is He Who has sent down to you the Book. In it are verses that are entirely clear, they are the foundations of the Book; and others not entirely clear,' until, Men of understanding and he said, 'When you see those who argue in it [using the Mutashabihat], then they are those whom Allah meant. Therefore, beware of them.".

al-Tirmithi, Sahih an-Nisa'i, Sunan Ibn Majah and *Musnad of Abu Dawud*. Sunni Muslims consider Al-Bukhari's collection the most reliable source and *Sahih* Muslim's collection as the second most reliable. Shia Islam has utilized different authentication methodologies and accordingly have created different authenticated *Sunnah* collections. The most predominant Shia Islam *Sunnah* book is *al-Kafi fi 'Ilm al-Din*.

Sunni Islamic scholars have invented complex techniques to authenticate and classify *Sunnah*. This necessitated the creation of the sciences of *Hadith*. These sciences served important functions including measuring the reliability ranking of a hadith, e.g. sound (*Sahih*), good (*Hasan*), weak (*Da'if*) or fabricated (*Maudu'*), studying the history and reliability of reporters of Hadith (Rijal al-Hadith) and the number of reporters involved in each stage of Hadith transmission, e.g. consecutive, (*mutawatir*), or isolated (*ahad*). These sciences are important not only to authenticate Sunnah but also to invoke the reliability scale in forming legislative opinion. For example, the reliability classification, whether hadith is sound (*Sahih*), good (*Hasan*), weak (*Da'if*), or fabricated (*Maudu'*), is a cornerstone of invoking a *Hadith* as a basis for legislation. Fabricated *Hadith* is never a good source of legislation, while weak *Hadith* might be considered in collaboration with other sources of legislation. Notably, these examples of the sciences of *Hadith* are not an exhaustive list; rather they demonstrate the depth of the subject-matter and the heavy burden upon the legislature that is engaged in Islamic law-making.

1.4.2   Ancillary Sources

Beyond the *Qur'an* and *Sunnah* there are a number of ancillary sources of Islamic law that have been recognized by Muslims. The rank and importance of these sources vary among schools of thought. The following is a brief explanation of these sources.

1.4.2.1   *Ijma* (Consensus)

Ijma is the consensus of Islamic scholars' opinions on any Islamic principle, at a specific moment. Islamic scholars throughout the centuries have unanimously agreed that consensus is ranked as the third most important source of Islamic law. *Ijma* may take different forms. It can be universal when all Islamic law scholars agree upon a particular issue at a specific moment.[18] *Ijma* may also take a more limited form when scholars in a given community or state agree on a particular issue at a specific moment.[19] Universal *Ijma* is binding to all Muslims worldwide, while limited *Ijma* is binding only to the community where it has occurred unless other communities adopt it. The application of the concept of Universal Ijma nowadays is, indeed, problematic given the current state of affairs of Muslims. Enormous populations of Muslims are distributed in many states worldwide speaking a variety of languages without effective, uniform methods of communication between scholars. Indeed, numerous adjudications and opinions, which typically have been represented as consensus, were actually subject to interpretation.[20] In fact, some scholars deny

---

[18] S. Abul A'al, Maududi, *The Islamic Law and Constitution*, (Khurshid Ahmad Trans. &ed.) (12th ed.), (Lahore, Islamic Publications 1997), 67-68.

[19] Id.

[20] Yusuf al-Qaradawi, *Al-Ijtihad fi al-Shari'ah al-Islamiyyah*, 3rd ed. (Kuwait, Dar al-Qalam 1999), 45.

the existence of *Ijma* altogether, suggesting that doubt will remain as to whether the scholars unanimously agreed on particular issues.[21] In contrast, in the early Islamic State during the course of the lives of the close companions of the Prophet Muhammad, the limited numbers of Muslims all speaking one language made Universal *Ijma* an achievable reality.

Logically, *Ijma* would never occur if it required the agreement of every Muslim. Certainly, some Muslims may disagree especially if they do not have sufficient knowledge of Islamic law. Therefore, the concept of *Ijma* permits only qualified individuals, who have been recognized by the Islamic nation as qualified scholars, to vote given their skillful integration of proper understanding, investigation and analysis to achieve sound opinions. Notably, Islam does not require formal qualification to be a scholar. Rather the general recognition of an individual's scholarship by the public suffices. The process of recognition of one's knowledge of Islam and one's ability to perform Islamic legal reasoning is both democratic and informal. Every Muslim vote is counted in the recognition of one's scholarship. However, there is no formal procedure for such recognition; rather, the free Islamic society bestows the title of scholar upon whom it wishes after demonstration of appropriate knowledge of Islam and of the current circumstances relevant to the issues at stake and in consideration of the piety of the scholar. When *Ijma* occurs, a challenge by questionable scholarship shall not undermine the value of *Ijma*. For instance, Muhammad Sa'id al-'Ashmawi, an Egyptian judge, promoted a number of controversial interpretations of Islam including the permissibility of consumption of alcoholic beverages for Muslims. He suggested that the *Qur'an* does not prohibit alcohol;

---

[21] Id.

rather, it only recommends avoidance of alcohol.[22] This interpretation is contrary to *Ijma* that occurred at the time of the Prophet Muhammad and held until now that alcohol is strictly prohibited for Muslims. al-'Ashmawi's proposal was insufficient to blemish the validity of *Ijma* regarding the prohibition of alcohol given that the vast majority of Muslims do not recognize him as a scholar of Islam and the weight of Islamic law authorities is against his proposal.

Ijma serves a very important function in Islamic society. It promotes uniformity of the application of the legal rules, erodes confusion arising from conflicting opinions and eases the application of law. In this context, before reaching a resolution, the Islamic legislature in the law-making process must acquaint itself with the legal opinions that were subject to *Ijma* in order to refrain from proposing an opinion that is in conflict with the *Ijma*. However, a knowledgeable legislature may reach an opinion contrary to *Ijma* only when the *Ijma* was based on a set of facts that have changed with time. This possibility is denied by numerous scholars who have insisted that consensus cannot be abrogated.

Notably, *Ijma* can be also be abrogated if new *Ijma* on the same issue occurs. This occurs when the collective legal opinion that gathered consensus was based on particular circumstances, interest or customs that have eroded with time. At that point, the legal opinion should also be changed accordingly.

If *Ijma* has not occurred with respect to a particular issue, the majority opinion is the correct choice for the Islamic legislature for two good reasons. First, the *Shura* principle mandates the majority opinion prevail providing it is not contrary to the *Qur'an* or *Sunnah*.

---

[22]   See Qur'an 5:90.

Second, the Prophet Muhammad advised that, in troubled times, when the truth is unclear, every Muslim must join the main body of Muslims – the majority.[23]

1.4.2.2   Prophet Muhammad Companions' Opinions

The majority of Islamic scholars have suggested that the Prophet Muhammad's companions' opinions are a valid source of Islamic jurisprudence. The *Qur'an* (9:100) and the Prophet Muhammad have spoken very highly of them.[24] Furthermore, they lived very closely with the Prophet which provided them with a golden opportunity to learn and understand the *Qur'an* and *Sunnah* better than others. If ambiguity arose, they had the chance to clarify it with the Prophet. It is also possible that what was transmitted to later generations of

---

[23]   See Sahih Muslim, Bk. 20, No. 4553: "Hudhaifah bin Al-Yaman said: People used to ask the Messenger of Allah (may peace be upon him) about the good times, but I used to ask him about the bad times fearing lest they overtake me. I said: Messenger of Allah, we were in the midst of ignorance and evil, and then Allah brought us this good (time through Islam). Is there any bad time after this good one? He said: Yes. I asked: Will there be a good time again after that bad time? He said: Yes, but therein will be a hidden evil. I asked: What will be the evil hidden therein? He said: (That time will witness the rise of) people who will adopt ways other than mine and seek guidance other than mine. You will know good points as well as bad points. I asked: Will there be a bad time after this good one? He said: Yes. (A time will come) when there will be people standing and inviting at the gates of Hell. Who so responds to their call they will throw into the fire. I said: Messenger of Allah, describe them for us. He said: All right. They will be a people having the same complexion as ours and speaking our language. I said: Messenger of Allah, what do you suggest if I happen to live in that time? He said: You should stick to the main body of the Muslims and their leader. I said: If they have no (such thing as the) main body and have no leader? He said: Separate yourself from all these factions, even if you have to eat the roots of trees (in a jungle) until death comes to you and you are in this state."

[24]   Qur'an 9:100.

Muslims as companions' opinions was in fact part of *Sunnah* but slipped through the *Sunnah* authentication process. For all these reasons, the vast majority of *Sunni* Islamic scholars, in contrast to *Shia* Islamic scholars, have followed the Prophet's companions' opinions in their scholarship.

1.4.2.3   *Qiyas* (Analogical Deduction)

Qiyas utilizes an analogical approach in reaching Islamic legal opinion when the *Qur'an* and/or *Sunnah* does not explicitly provide a resolution to an issue. It reaches a conclusion by showing similarities between an explicit ruling found in the *Qur'an* or *Sunnah* and an unresolved Issue. *Imam* al-Shafi', a prominent Islamic scholar, had suggested that the *Qur'an* and *Sunnah* encompass explicit or implicit rulings for every issue. If a ruling is not explicit, a scholar must investigate the *Qur'an* and/or *Sunnah* textual meanings and objectives to find similarities that lead to a ruling.

Qiyas is not a creation of Islamic scholars. Indeed, the *Qur'an* utilizes analogical and counter analogical reasoning in numerous places. The Prophet also used *Qiyas* frequently either in adjudication or to explain matters to people. In a cited incident, a woman went to the Prophet and said: Messenger of Allah, my mother has died and there is due from her a vow of fasting; should I fast on her behalf? Thereupon he said: You see that if your mother had died in debt, would it not have been paid on her behalf? She said: Yes. He (the Prophet) said: Then observe fast on behalf of your mother. This incident provides an example of how to determine a ruling; it also teaches the Islamic nation the analogical deduction methodology utilized to reach adjudication when a ruling is not explicit.

There are four elements of *Qiyas*:

i.   *Al-Asl* (the original case, explicitly decided matter). The original case is the source of the legal rule. The original case surely can be found in either the *Qur'an* or *Sunnah*. The majority of Islamic scholars also suggest that the original case could have been a case decided under *Ijma*. For example, there is *Ijma* that women, upon reaching the age of majority, have full financial independence that entitle them to enjoy full capacity to enter into contracts, make bequests and the like. Accordingly, under *Qiyas*, the majority of Islamic scholars have suggested that women cannot be forced to marry. However, the original case cannot be a case decided under *Qiyas*.

ii. *Al-Fara'* (secondary case, undecided matter). The secondary case must fulfil two conditions to be eligible for resolution. First, no explicit resolution to the matter should be found in the *Qur'an, Sunnah* or *Ijma*. Historically, some scholars had fallen into error by conducting *Qiyas* on a matter already decided. This tendency was rejected by the vast majority of Muslims. Second, the secondary case must share with the original case *'Illa* (effective cause or *ratio legis*). Any variation, even minor, of the common denominator in *Al-Asl* and *Al-Fara'* precludes *Qiyas*. An example of proper *Qiyas* with a common denominator is the prohibition of alcohol. The *Qur'an* explicitly prohibits alcohol because of its intoxicant effect on the human brain. Any beverage, food or otherwise that causes intoxication is also prohibited under *Qiyas* because the original case, the prohibition of alcohol, and the secondary case, other intoxicants, share one common denominator: the intoxication. Accordingly, under *Qiyas*, an intoxicating drug is also prohibited.

iii. *Al-Hukum* (rule). This is the rule of law that has been established in the *Qur'an, Sunnah* or *Ijma*. Four conditions in *Al-Hukm* ought to be found to render it eligible for the *Qiyas* process. First, *Al-Hukum* must have a practical implication when applied to a real secondary case. Imaginary secondary cases based upon impractical hypotheses are not subject to *Qiyas*. Second, *Al-Hukum* must be comprehensible from all its aspects especially its reasons, rationales and aims. For example, prohibition of alcohol, gambling, homicide and adultery are comprehensible given that the rationale for prohibition is obvious. Each of these acts causes harm and accordingly, any act leading to that harm can also be prohibited. For example, since the prohibition of homicide is intended to protect human life, any act endangering human life unjustifiably is also prohibited. In contrast, sometimes *Al-Hukum* may not be very clear such as in the ritual manner of praying Muslims were ordered to perform. It is not entirely comprehensible for a number of reasons including lack of knowledge of the rationale of praying only in one particular manner. Accordingly, the ritual manner of praying ought not to be employed as *Al-Hukum*. Third, *Al-Hukum* should not be an exception to a rule. Exceptions are not rules in themselves. Therefore, they are not subject to *Qiyas*. Fourth, *Al-Hukum* should not be designated to a particular unique single case that is inappropriate to extend to other cases. For example, the Prophet once gave double weight to the testimony of a particular Muslim in a particular incident. The exceptional nature of this incident included being decided by the Prophet to address a unique case, and the exceptional circumstances prevent it from being considered a rule.

iv. *'Illa* (effective cause, *ratio legis*). *'Illa* is the reason, cause or rationale of the legal rule. As explained earlier, *'Illa* for the prohibition of alcohol is intoxication. Thus, all intoxicants are prohibited in Islam under *Qiyas*. *'Illa* is either explicitly stated in the *Qur'an* or *Sunnah*, based on scholarly consensus (*Ijma*) or implicit in the *Qur'an* or *Sunnah* such that scholars may deduce it. An example of an obvious *'Illa* can be found in this Qur'anic verse: *O you who believe! Approach not the prayer when you are in a drunken state until you know (the meaning) of what you utter...* Al-Hukum, the rule, in this verse is not the prohibition of praying while intoxicated. *'Illa*, the effective cause, is the state of intoxication that may prevent one from understanding what one is uttering. An example of *'Illa* based on *Ijma* is the case of grandfather guardianship. *Ijma* had concluded that a father can have guardianship of his children. *'Illa* here is that the fatherhood relationship justifies such action. Under *Qiyas*, the same *'Illa* can be found in the case of the grandfather that the grandfather- fatherhood relationship justifies that he can be a guardian for his children and the children of his children. An example of implicit *'Illa* for prohibitions, in general, can be found in the following Qur'anic verse (7:157): *Those who follow the Messenger, the Prophet who can neither read nor write (i.e. Muhammad) whom they find written with them in the Taurat (Torah) and the Injeel (Gospel) , - he commands them for Al-Ma'ruf (i.e. Islamic Monotheism and all that Islam has ordained); and forbids them from Al-Munkar (i.e. disbelief, polytheism of all kinds, and all that Islam has forbidden); he allows them as lawful At-Tayyibat (i.e. all good and lawful), and prohibits them as unlawful Al-Khaba'ith (i.e. all evil, harmful and unlawful).* In this verse the *'Illa,* the effective cause for all prohibitions, is their evil and harmful nature (*Al-Khaba'ith*). Accordingly, numerous scholars have concluded that all acts that share the same *'Illa,* being harmful and evil, are also prohibited. Smoking cigarettes, for example, is said to be prohibited by several scholars because it is harmful in nature. In sum, to extend the ruling of the original case correctly to a secondary case, a scholar must find a clear rule on the original case and both the original and secondary case must share a common denominator/*ratio legis.*

1.4.2.4 *Istihsan* (Juristic Preference)

Perhaps the most acceptable definition of *Istihsan,* suggested by a Hanafi jurist, Abul Hasan al Karkhi, is that *Istihsan* is the departure from an established precedent in favour of a different ruling for a stronger reason. In other terms, *Istihsan* occurs when a Jurist refuses to follow a general jurisprudential rule in forming a scholarly opinion, as it had been applicable to similar matters, for a good reason that renders the non-application of the general rule in this instance in harmony with *Sharia.* So *Istihsan* is an exceptional ruling contrary to a general rule. For example, looking at the private body parts by medical personal is permissible for medical treatment contrary to the general prohibition. The most common use of *Istihsan* occurs when an employment of strict *Qiyas* (analogy) shall result in awkward findings. *Istihsan* here is utilized not only to avoid awkwardness but also to reach a conclusion in harmony with *Sharia.*

The Hanafi School of jurisprudence has divided *Istihsan* into two broad categories. The first is *Istihsan* in *Qiyas*. This category deals with conflicts between two analogies (*Qiyas*) that reach different conclusions. One of these analogies is the recognizable, explicit and direct application of *Qiyas* that reaches a repugnant conclusion. The other analogy is obscure and implicit, but reaches a fairer conclusion. *Istihsan*, the juristic preference, is utilized here to favor the obscure and implicit analogy for its fairer conclusion. The second category of *Istihsan* occurs when there is conflict between a conclusion that arises from *Qiyas* and *Ijma*, *Sunnah* or a necessity. *Istihsan*, at this point, favors the conclusion arising from following *Sunnah*, *Ijma* or a necessity at the expense of direct application of *Qiyas*.

The Maliki and Hanafi schools of jurisprudence employ *Istihsan* in reaching juristic opinions, whilst several other scholars have criticized *Istihsan*. The renowned Islamic scholar, al-Shafi' concluded that use of *Istihsan* is improper methodology for a number of reasons. First, *Sharia* is perfectly explained explicitly in the *Qur'an* and *Sunnah*, or implicitly by using *Qiyas* to the *Qur'an* and *Sunnah*. Therefore, there is no need for *Istihsan*. Second, the Prophet Muhammad never used *Istihsan* in his decision-making process, nor approved it for his companions. Third, there is nothing in the *Qur'an* or *Sunnah* to support the notion of *Istihsan*. Fourth, there are no clear guidelines or acceptable methodology for *Istihsan* which may encourage scholars to use it unjustifiably to reach a desired conclusion.

1.4.2.5 'Urf (Custom)

'Urf consists of well-known unwritten rules of conduct that a community of people has agreed upon in every day transactions and are practiced repeatedly by individuals and communities. Islam did not repudiate all sorts of customs that existed prior to its emergence. Rather, Islam rejected only those customs that conflicted with its rules. Accordingly, Islamic law scholars divide a custom into two categories: first, the conflicting custom(s) that have been unequivocally rejected by the *Qur'an* and/or *Sunnah*, such as extra-marital sexual acts and manufacturing or consuming intoxications and second, the non-conflicting custom(s), those that do not conflict with the *Qur'an* and/or *Sunnah* explicitly or implicitly. This sort of custom can be general or specific. A general custom is one that was adopted by the entire Islamic nation, and is thereby, applicable in all Muslim states. A specific custom is one which is adopted only by a particular community(s), and accordingly, is applicable only to that community(s). Due to the evolving nature of custom, customarily binding rules of conduct, whether specific or general, are subject to change to meet social changes, provided that they do not violate the primary sources of Islamic law: *Qur'an* and *Sunnah*.

1.4.2.6   Maslahah Mursalah (Public Interest)

Islamic law scholars differ on the applicability and scope of public interest as a source of Islamic jurisprudence. The *Zahiri* School of thought, based on a strictly literal methodology of interpretation, completely rejected the notion of public interest asserting that all interests have been considered in the original sources of Islamic jurisprudence; the *Qur'an* and *Sunnah*. On the other hand, the vast majority of scholars have accepted public interest as a source of Islamic jurisprudence. However, these scholars have suggested a different public interest scope. Some scholars argued that the only public interest worthy of consideration is the interest specified in the original sources, the *Qur'an* and *Sunnah*. They maintain that the rationales and goals of these interests are clear with no possibility of error given its righteous origin. They assert that following this guideline prevents infusing Islamic legislature with opinions based upon whims presented under the guise of public interest. Alternatively, numerous other scholars contend that the scope of public interest ought to be broad enough to include any meaningful interests such as protection of life, progeny, intellect, wealth and religion.

The founder of the *Maliki* school of thought, *Imam* Malik, had advocated public interest as a source of jurisprudence. He concluded that three requirements must be met to deem interest worthy of consideration. Initially, the interest ought to be compatible with the principles delineated in the *Qur'an* and *Sunnah*. Any conflict in goals, rationales and doctrines of the *Qur'an* and *Sunnah* prevents an interest from consideration. Secondly, the interest must be intelligible and receive wide public acceptance. Lastly, a general public need for the interest must exist such that ignoring this interest would likely result in a gap in law or disorder.

1.4.2.7 *Sadd Al-Zara'i* (Blocking the Means to Wrongdoing)

Islamic law scholars realized that blocking the means to prohibitory norms violation is a valid source of Islamic jurisprudence. The rationale for this source of law is straightforward. Law is made to avoid harm and/or gain benefit. All means that facilitate benefit are permissible and should be encouraged and all means that facilitate the commission of harm should be discouraged and prohibited. Thus, to prohibit a conduct under the *Sadd al-Zara'i* doctrine, one needs to examine the outcomes of such conduct. If a rule, conduct or means facilitates the commission of a crime, such a conduct would be deemed unlawful. In this context, an actor's intention is irrelevant to blocking the means to the prohibitory norm. What is surely relevant is the relationship between ends and means. If the ends are prohibited, then the means should also be prohibited.

With respect to the relationship between the means and the ends, the renowned scholar *Imam* al-Shatibi has divided *Sadd al-Zara'i* into four general categories. The first category deals with ends that are completely harmful with no benefit whatsoever. A consensus of Islamic law scholars has been reached that such means are prohibited. The second category looks at circumstances where the benefits of means are certain and the harm generated by the means is speculative and possibly rare. For instance, growing, buying and selling grapes are definitely beneficial for the society while the possibility of harm still exists but is speculative and rare. For example, the buyer may make wine from grapes thus producing prohibited goods from lawful activity. Here also a vast majority of Islamic law scholars suggest that that the means, growing grapes in this case, is lawful. The third category of means occurs when the likelihood of harmful ends is high but does not reach the realm of certainty such as selling weapons at the time of social unrest or selling grapes to wine makers. Numerous renowned Islamic law scholars including *Imam* Ahmed and *Imam* Malik have suggested that such means remain lawful because of lack of certainty of harmful ends. The last category is almost identical to the third category but the probability of causing harm by the means are very high but still not certain. The schools of thought sharply disagreed on the permissibility of the means in this case. *Imam* Abu Hanifa and *Imam* al-Shafi'i suggested that the means remain lawful because the harmful ends are uncertain. On the contrary, *Imam*

Ahmed and *Imam* Malik suggested that the means ought to be unlawful because of the high possibility of resultant harmful ends.

The Prophet Muhammad on several occasion endorsed the 'blocking the means' doctrine. He had forbidden monopolies because of the negative social impact of a monopoly including possible resultant inflation and the scarcity of goods. He had forbidden the creditor from taking gifts from the debtor because the gifts can be considered, in fact, fixed interest, prohibited in *riba* (usury) but labelled as gifts to avoid the prohibition of *riba*.

As a final point, blocking the means of violating the prohibitory norms, as a source of Islamic law, ought to be employed with utmost prudence. Virtuous activities might ultimately be prohibited, under the guise of blocking the means, if the legislature adopts over-sweeping application of that source. For instance, unduly restraining women's activities could be justified with the aim of protecting women from violence. To avoid this problem, the legislature must engage in a harm/benefit analysis. First, the harm and benefit that arise from an activity must be identified. Second, if both are present, the legislature ought to inquire whether these harms and benefits are real, verified or merely speculative. If the harm or the benefit is speculative or the likelihood of occurrence is very remote, then the Islamic doctrine that doubt does not trump certainty might be employed to exclude any speculative harm or benefit from the equation. Third, the Islamic doctrine that avoidance of harm is more important than gaining benefit prevails. In this context, the free movement of women is surely beneficial to women and to society at large. However, it may expose women to harm. The harm here is speculative, at best. Accordingly, society shall enjoy the real benefit manifest in women's free movement and discard the speculative harm that may occur from exposing women to violence while they practice free movement.

1.4.2.8 *Istishab* (Presumption of Continuity)

Istishab denotes the presumption of existence or non-existence of a fact or rule of law until rebutted by a new fact or new rule of law. This presumption is both logical and essential in daily activities. A living person is assumed to bear the liabilities and enjoy the rights like other individuals until a new fact is affirmed, i.e. his death. Every activity is presumed to be lawful until the law prohibits it. The ownership of a property is presumed to continue until conclusive evidence shows otherwise. al-Khwarizmi had concluded that *Istishab* is the last resort in the decision-making process. He suggested that when a scholar is asked to make an Islamic ruling, a *fatwa*, he ought to look at the Qur'an, then *Sunnah*, then *Ijma*, then *Qiyas*, in that order, to discover a resolution. If he does not find one, he must utilize the *Istishab* doctrine to presume the existence or non-existence of a fact or rule of law.

Istishab is divided into four general categories:

i.   Presumption of non-liability/non-existence. This presumption establishes that non-liability or non-existence of a fact continues until otherwise proven. Numerous legal and factual presumptions branch out of this presumption such as presumption of innocence in criminal trials, presumption of non-liability in civil trials, presumption of non-legal liability for individuals under the age of discretion or mentally handicapped individuals, and lack of matrimonial obligations until proof of the marriage contract.

ii. Presumption of liability/existence. This presumption is the same as the previous category but in positive terms. Thus, it establishes that the existence of liability or existence of a fact continues until otherwise proven. For example, a husband is required to fulfil his matrimonial financial duties until he proves its fulfilment. The buyer is presumed to have not paid the price until he proves that he did.

iii. Presumption of continuity of rule of law. This presumption establishes that any rule of law, whether related to permissibility, prohibition or otherwise, continues to exist until rebutted. For instance, all consumed articles are presumed lawful to trade, consume, possess or own until a new rule of law, scholarly finding, or judicial decision rebuts the presumption of lawfulness. Consuming and trading in tobacco, as a relatively new issue to Islamic jurisprudence, bearing in mind it was unknown at the time of the Prophet Muhammad, has been subject to review among Islamic law scholars. Numerous scholars have concluded that the presumption of continuity has been rebutted and declared tobacco Islamically unlawful given the indisputably negative impact of smoking.

iv. Presumption of the continuity of the attribute. This presumption denotes that all things continue on in certain state until the contrary is established. For example, missing persons are presumed to be alive until indisputable evidence suggests otherwise. Similarly, the debtor is presumed to owe the debt to creditor until indisputable evidence indicates full or partial payment. Islamic law scholars have differed upon the scope of this presumption. The *Shafi'i* and *Hanbali* schools of thought have adopted a broad scope that allowed the presumption to operate as a rule of evidence to presume the continuity of an attribute and to establish a legal right based on that presumption. For example, the missing person presumed to be alive would be eligible for inheritance because he is presumed alive. On the contrary, in the *Hanafi* and *Maliki* schools of thought, scholars have limited the scope of the presumption as a rule of evidence that establishes the continuity of the attribute but does not establish any legal rights based on that presumption. In this context, the missing person is presumed to be alive but is not eligible for inheritance until demonstrating that he is really alive.

This discussion of *Istishab* leads to three significant conclusions:

a) *Istishab* is not a source of Islamic jurisprudence in itself; rather, it is a rule of evidence that proves or negates the state of affairs.
b) *Istishab* is utilized only when there is no other evidence that proves or negates a particular state of affairs.
c) The doctrine of *Istishab* roots a very important rule, with broad application in Islamic jurisprudence, that doubt does not vitiate a fact.

1.4.2.9 Pre-Islamic Divine Laws

Islamic scholars recognize that pre-Islamic laws, such as the laws elucidated in Judaism and Christianity, might be a source of Islamic jurisprudence unless abrogated explicitly in Islam. The rationale for accepting pre-Islamic divine laws as a source of Islamic jurisprudence is based on the logic that all Islamically recognized divine laws originated from one legislature: God. It is imperative to note that what Christian and Jewish people believe to be their laws is not binding to

Muslims; rather, what Muslims believe to be the *true* laws and teachings of Judaism and Christianity is determinative. In other words, only Islamic references are acceptable to determine pre-Islamic divine laws.

Islamic scholars differ on the applicability of Islamically recognized pre-Islam laws to Muslims. A school of thought affirms the applicability of these laws if Islam did not overrule these rules explicitly or impliedly. For instance, the *Qur'an* states:

> Verily, We did send down the Taurat (Torah) [to Musa (Moses)], therein was guidance and light, by which the Prophets, who submitted themselves to Allah's Will, judged for the Jews. And the rabbis and the priests [too judged for the Jews by the Taurat (Torah) after those Prophets], for to them was entrusted the protection of Allah's Book, and they were witnesses thereto. ....And We ordained therein for them: "Life for life, eye for eye, nose for nose, ear for ear, tooth for tooth, and wounds equal for equal." But if anyone remits the retaliation by way of charity, it shall be for him an expiation... And in their footsteps, We sent 'Isa (Jesus), son of Maryam (Mary), confirming the Taurat (Torah) that had come before him, and We gave him the Injeel (Gospel), in which was guidance and light and confirmation of the Taurat (Torah) that had come before it, a guidance and an admonition for Al-Muttaqun (the pious).[25]

These verses not only testify as to the laws of the Jewish and Christian people, but also continue to be applicable to Muslims from the moment of its revelation until the end of time. Moreover, the *Qur'an* attests that Muslims also should follow the footsteps of the other Prophets.

---

[25] Qur'an 5: 44-46.

In contrast, other schools of thought concluded that pre-Islamic divine laws are not applicable to Muslims given that all Prophets, except Muhammad, were sent to specific nations. This leads to an inescapable conclusion that these laws are nation-specific and not applicable to Muslims.

1.5   Islamic Law in Contemporary Legal Systems

Many Muslim-majority states adopt some form of Islamic law in their legislations.[26]   And yet in several non-Muslim-majority states an Islamic law presence is noticeable either in contemporary practice or as a historical source of law. Lord Philips, Lord Chief Justice in England and Wales, had concluded that Muslims can apply Islamic family law in the UK.[27] The Archbishop of Canterbury welcomed the UK's top judge's suggestion. Eventually, the law in the UK allowed Muslims to choose Islamic family law to settle their family disputes and enforce Islamic inheritance rules. However, for various political and religious reasons, the application of Islamic law in a number of non-Muslim-majority states has troubled some who see Islam in general and Islamic law in particular in competition with their political, religious beliefs and ideologies. For example, in Canada, the

---

[26] There are at least 57 Muslim majority states in the world currently. These states are members of the Organization of Islamic Cooperation. This organization is an international organization founded in 1969 that can be viewed as the collective voice of the Muslim world.

[27] Lord Philips reached this conclusion in a public speech on the issue of equality before the law delivered at the East London Muslim Centre on July 3rd, 2008. In this speech, Lord Philips made a lengthy review of the history of discrimination against women and religious minorities in the UK before reaching his conclusion.

Muslim Community in Ontario proposed applying Islamic family law in arbitrations given that other permitted religious family arbitration had succeeded in Ontario for years. The Ontario provincial government rejected the proposal.

To be sure, Islamic law is not a distinctive, alien creature to other contemporary legal systems. Islamic law has influenced various legal systems in non-Muslim-majority states.[28] Professor Makdisi concluded that common law's remarkable development in the twelfth century was likely due to importing many legal concepts from other legal systems, including Islamic law.[29] Common law in that era was primitive in comparison to other legal systems. The motive to develop common law and the opportunity to learn from other legal systems existed in the twelfth century. Many points of interaction between Islamic law and common law exist, such as in Sicily, where the opportunity of borrowing legal concepts may have been utilized. Concepts such as trial by jury, the action of debt and the assize of

---

[28] Naturally, not all aspects of Islamic law have counterparts in other legal systems. Many comparative law professors have discussed the distinctive features of Islamic law that render it remarkably different from the civil or common law systems. See, e.g., N. J. Coulson, "A Comparison of the Law of Succession in Islamic and British Legal Systems", (1978) 26 *American Journal of Comparative Law*, 227. Others utterly deny any possibility of Islamic law concepts borrowing from Roman or Jewish law, concluding that those who proposed that Islamic law borrowed from Roman or Jewish law failed to provide any evidence to support their conclusion short of basic similarities that could be a product of human intuition. See, e.g., S. G. Vesey-Fitzgerald, "The Alleged Debt of Islamic to Roman Law", 67 (1951) *Law Quarterly Review* 81; Gamal Moursi Badr, "Islamic Law: Its Relation to Other Legal Systems", (1978) 26 *American Journal of Comparative Law*, 187.

[29] J. A. Makdisi, "The Islamic Origins of the Common Law", (1999) 77 (5) *North Carolina Law Review*, 1635.

novel disseisin[30] introduced into the common law in the twelfth century existed only in Islamic law at that time.[31]

Following the same line of analysis, many scholars explored similarities between Islamic law and the common law. In this context, a number of scholars have discussed the resemblance between the Islamic law of *Waqf* (charitable trust) and the English law of trust.[32] Monica Gaudiosi conducted a case study of the establishment of Merton College, Oxford, in the thirteenth century.[33] Merton College was an unincorporated charitable trust that pioneered the law of trust in England. Gaudiosi concluded that the striking similarities between the Islamic law of *Waqf* and the English law of trust was indicative of the strong influence of the former on the latter. She observed that the English law of trust is more similar to the Islamic law of *Waqf* than to Roman and Germanic law, as a number of Western legal scholars had proposed.[34] She noted a number of reasons that led to her conclusion, including the cultural contacts between Islam and England in the medieval period. Under both legal instruments the property is reserved and inalienable while its usufruct is appropriated for a

---

[30] An action to recover lands of which the plaintiff had been disseized, or dispossessed.

[31] Professor Makdisi discussed in detail a number of legal concepts and attributed their introduction into common law to Islamic law. See id. at 1640-1696.

[32] See, e.g., H. Cattan, "The Law of Waqf", (1955) 1 *Law in the Middle East*, 212; Ann Van Wynen Thomas, "Note on the Origin of Uses and Trusts-Waqfs", *Southwestern Law Journal*, 162.

[33] M. M. Gaudiosi, "The Influence of the Islamic Law of Waqf on the Development of the Trust in England: The Case of Merton College", (1988) 136 (4) *University of Pennsylvania Law Review*, 1231.

[34] See, e.g., W. Holdsworth, *A History of English Law*, 3rd ed. (Merthuen and Co., Sweet and Maxwell, London 1945), 410-417

charitable purpose or for the benefit of individual(s) and the trust is secure by the successive appointment of trustees.[35]

Interestingly, Gaudiosi in her conclusion called upon the comparative law scholars to re-examine the true roots of the English law of trust. This process may indeed benefit modern common law of trust by learning how Islamic law dealt with trust law problems. Yet the need for non-Muslim-majority states to learn Islamic law far exceeds the area of the law of trust. Islamic law applications in the global economy are remarkable. Islamic law-compliant assets' global worth is about one trillion U.S. dollars and Islamic financial products are estimated at four trillion U.S. dollars.[36] The reach of the Islamic economy today necessitated the establishment of an Islamic finance dispute resolution mechanism to deal with disputes concerning the enforcement of contracts and build legal expectations for potential contractual parties in Islamic and/or mixed Islamic and non-Islamic markets. The expansion of multinational corporations that hold Muslim and non-Muslim majority state(s) nationalities, contracts between Muslim-majority states and non-Muslim states and foreign operations in Muslim majority state(s) have also created the need for lawyers to become familiar with Islamic Law principles. Such developments also gave rise to the need to codify Islamic law's financial principles to gain official recognition not only by Muslim-majority states but also at a global level. In Shamil Bank of Bahrain EC v. Beximco Pharm. Ltd., the parties entered into an agreement where they made the choice of law as follows: ""[s]ubject to the

---

[35] M. M. Gaudiosi, "The Influence of the Islamic Law of Waqf on the Development of the Trust in England: The Case of Merton College", (1988) 136 (4) *University of Pennsylvania Law Review*, 1231 at 1246.

[36] J. C. Colon, "Choice of Law and Islamic Finance", (2011) 46 *Texas International Law Journal*, 412.

principles of the Glorious *Sharia'a* (Islamic Law), this agreement shall be governed by and construed in accordance with the laws of England."[37] The court rejected the choice of law clause concluding that basic rules of Islamic Law are not sufficiently identified.[38] The court found that if the parties intended to apply Islamic law to the contract they should have identified a foreign law or code. Given that the Islamic economy is, indeed, large in size and important for international cooperation, there is a global need for universally recognized Islamic finance law. Notably, the need to learn Islamic law is not limited to the corporate law sphere. Common and civil law courts from time to time are required to interpret Islamic law.[39]

The question of reconciliating Islamic law with other legal systems, e.g. common and/or civil law, has emerged in various discourses. Initially, one ought to realize that Islamic law is, as Muslims believe, a divine law. This entails the supremacy of Islamic law over other laws in Muslim-majority states. Any law in conflict with Islamic law is deemed of no force or effect in Muslim-majority states, provided the decision-makers in these states uphold Islamic law basic principles. However, that does not mean that Muslim-majority states cannot cooperate with non-Muslim-majority states for the general welfare of humanity, and for their own benefit. Muslim-majority states may incorporate foreign law rules providing that such rules do not contradict Islamic law fundamentals. As previously explained, the Prophet Muhammad spoke very highly of *Hilf al-Fudul* (Alliance of al-Fudul), which aimed to uphold justice and aid the

---

[37] Shamil Bank of Bahrain EC v. Beximco Pharm. Ltd., [2004] EWCA (Civ) 19, [1], [2004] 1 W.L.R. 1784, 1787.

[38] Id. at [52], 1 W.L.R. at 1800.

[39] Consider on this matter D. F. Forte, "Islamic Law in American Courts", (1983) 7 *Suffolk Transnational Law Journal* 1, 1-2.

oppressed, even though this alliance was formed by non-Muslims in the pre-Islamic era. This alliance was not only in conformity with Islamic principles but also propagated the Islamic philosophy of justice for all, including the helpless and powerless who face oppression and tyranny. In this context, one ought to realize that Muslim-majority states have already joined numerous international treaties that promulgate rules aimed to advance mankind's prosperity and enhance international cooperation.

On the domestic front, most of the Muslim-majority states have merged Islamic law with foreign laws in their modern codes. Nevertheless, merging different legal systems in one code can be difficult given that not only may the rules of the systems differ significantly but also the underlying legal philosophy of the systems may not coincide. To muddy the waters further, merging Islamic law, a divine law, with other laws triggers many problems including the reluctance of non-Muslims in a Muslim majority state to accept the rival religion's law, the common state of ignorance of true Islamic law worldwide, the secular movement in Muslim-majority states that detest any laws based on a religion, not to mention external political powers that openly fight Islamic law because it contradicts their beliefs or interests.

The difficulty of merging Islamic law with other laws is best exemplified in the great legal scholar Abd el-Razzak el-Sanhuri's work. El-Sanhuri, an Egyptian with strong Islamic tendencies who received a large portion of his legal education in France, had been entrusted with drafting many Muslim-majority states modern codes. He drafted civil codes for Egypt, Syria, Iraq and Libya as well as the constitutions of Kuwait, Sudan and United Arab Emirates. Indeed, his influential scholarly work extends far beyond these states to almost every Arab state. Nevertheless, El-Sanhuri's struggle to merge Islamic law with French civil code rules is apparent from his own testimonies. El-Sanhuri presented the Egyptian civil code that he drafted as a victory for Islamic law.[40] Later he expressed dissatisfaction with the Egyptian civil code, because it included fewer Islamic law rules.[41] It has been suggested that El-Sanhuri had engaged in a comparative law analysis in an attempt to modernize Islamic law and failed.[42] This failure was attributed to the Muslim-majority states' attempt to modernize their legal systems without sacrificing their authenticity/ traditions/ Islamic law.[43] This line of argument oversimplifies the issue of merging more than one tradition/legal system into one code. Apart from the problems listed earlier relating to merging more than one legal system into one code, one ought to understand the law-making process from a historical perspective. Sanhuri was a devoted Muslim. His writing indicates that he believed deeply in Islamic law as a solution for social problems. In the meantime, he was entrusted to draft legislations and constitutions of numerous Muslim-majority states. These states were at the time, perhaps, at their historically lowest point in terms of economic, educational and literary development. Scientific and cultural advancements were lacking. The states were struggling for political and cultural independence from colonial powers. The political and intellectual sphere was not appropriate to produce codes fully compatible with Islamic law,

---

[40] Amr Shalakany, "Between Identity and Redistribution: Sanhuri, Genealogy and the will to Islamize", (2001) 8 *Islamic Law and Society Journal*, 201.

[41] Id.

[42] Amr Shalakany, "Sanhuri and the Historical Origins of Comparative Law in the Arab World", in Annelise Riles (ed.) *Rethinking the Masters of Comparative Law* (Oxford, Hart Publishing, 2001), 152

[43] Id.

reflecting the people's traditions, culture and beliefs. Perhaps the will existed to have a more Islamic law compliant legislation in the Islamic majority states, but political challenges and oppressive regimes precluded the will of the people from becoming fact. Once these adverse circumstances disappear, Islamic modern codes shall be born.

CHAPTER 2

The Modernity of Islamic Law: Human Rights and Codification[44]

⟿ ᦲᦲ ⟻

2.1   Introduction

Orientalists claim that Islamic law cannot be modernized for two main reasons. First, they allege that Islam's human rights standards are not in compliance with modern standards.[45] Second, they maintain that Islamic law cannot be codified because of lack of political will and that substantive Islamic law is incapable of

---

[44] I have presented parts of this chapter at a comparative law conference at Anatolia, Turkey (2015).

[45] Wael A.B. Hallaq "Can the Shari'a be restored?", in Yvonne Y. Haddad and Barbara F. Stowasser (ed.), *Islamic Law and the Challenges of Modernity* (AltaMira Press 2004), 22.

codification as modern legislation[46]. In fact, the issues of codification and human rights overlap and are closely intertwined.

Indeed, there is no political will in many Muslim majority state to create comprehensive codification of Islamic law. Moreover, several Muslim-majority states legal systems are unreceptive to the notion of expanding the scope of Islamic law via codification or otherwise. This is expected given that authoritarian regimes in Muslim-majority states fear broad Islamic law introduction through codification. Codification would open the door to implementation of Islamic human rights and an Islamic system of governance in the new code, which in turn, would pose a serious threat to the existence of the authoritarian regimes themselves. Islamic human rights would ensure essential safeguards to regime critics. The Islamic system of governance is anti-authoritarian. Indeed, codifying Islamic law would result in loss of power by the authoritarians.

Unfortunately, both the Islamic system of governance and Islamic human rights are commonly misunderstood by the West and misapplied in Muslim-majority states. These misconceptions and misapplications will be examined in detail in the following chapters. This will lead to a discussion of Islamic human rights and the feasibility of codifying Islamic law.

2.2   On Islamic Human Rights

The scope of human rights in Islam is vast, possibly broader than any known human rights code currently in existence. Three factual principles form a central umbrella under which all rights and

---

[46] For example, see, Jan Michiel Otto, Sharia and National Law in Muslim Countries: Tensions and Opportunities for Dutch and EU Foreign Policy (Amsterdam University Press, 2008).

freedoms are included: humanity's unity of origin, human diversity promotes knowledge, not superiority and the unalienable, inextinguishable trait of human dignity. The *Qur'an* affirms that all people, from different backgrounds, color, traditions, languages and social norms share one origin.[47] These facts lead to a unique outlook on human rights, i.e. that fairness, equality, and justice are natural rights because it is inconceivable to treat like as unalike. There is no "other" that can be discriminated against or treated unjustly. In contrast, apart from Islamic teachings, individuals throughout history have attempted to associate themselves with particular groups, e.g., racial, religious or even social classes, to the exclusion of others. Such artificial divisions have created inhumane treatment of the "other." The inhumane treatment has been mistakenly labeled "human rights violations". To be sure, inhumane is a distinct concept from human rights violations. Human rights violation terminology presupposes that individuals are naturally different and that the human rights code attempts to create equality and fairness among humans. In contrast, the unity of humanity concept presupposes that humanity is one thing. Therefore, enforcing equality and fairness among individuals is not aimed at achieving compliance with the human-made human rights code; rather, it complies with the natural law of humanity.

The second central principle is closely related to the first. The *Qur'an* teaches that human diversity is to promote knowledge, not

---

[47] O mankind! reverence your Guardian-Lord, who created you from a single Person, created, of like nature, his mate, and from them twain scattered (like seeds) countless men and women. Qur'an 4:1. Remarkably, the majority of world population also believes on unity of mankind: Followers of the Abrahamic religions, Islam, Judaism and Christianity, believes that all mankind are descendent of Adam and Eve.

superiority.[48] Humanity shares the origin, and the offspring developed into many nations with different habits, cultures, languages, and colors that they may know and learn from each other.[49] No individual or group should claim superiority over others because of natural or acquired characteristics that are not self-made, e.g. wealth, race, kinship or citizenship. Rather, superiority is achieved by righteousness.

The third central principle in Islam is the unalienable right of human dignity. In the *Qur'an*, God declared, "We have honored/dignified the sons (and daughters) of Adam."[50] The interpretation of this verse, according to Muslim belief, is significant. God has honored every human being. Consequently, no one can take away this honor from any human, anytime, anywhere. This rule is far-reaching, guaranteeing a dignified treatment to the disfavored "other," e.g., prisoners of war, detainees, and the destitute.

Under these principles, numerous human rights, many of which are unique, have flourished. These rights include: - The right to life.[51], - The right to live with dignity and be free from degrading

---

[48] (O mankind! We created you from a single (pair) of a male and a female, and made you into nations and tribes, that ye may know each other (not that ye may despise each other). Verily the most honored of you in the sight of Allah is (he who is) the most righteous of you. And Allah has full Knowledge and is well-acquainted (with all things). Qur'an 49:13.

[49] Notably, the majority of the world population also believes in the unity of mankind: Followers of the Abrahamic religions, Islam, Judaism and Christianity, believe that all mankind are descendants of Adam and Eve.

[50] Qur'an 17:70.

[51] Because of that, We decreed upon the Children of Israel that whoever kills a soul unless for a soul or for corruption [done] in the land - it is as if he had slain mankind entirely. And whoever saves one - it is as if he had saved mankind entirely. Qur'an 5:32.

treatment.[52], - The right to basic necessities of Life.[53], - The right to justice.[54], - The right to privacy.[55], - The right to be free from oppression.[56], -The right to protest against tyranny.[57], - The right to be free from unendurable burdens.[58],- The right to be safe.[59], - The

---

[52] O ye who believe! let not some men among you laugh at others: it may be that the (latter) are better than the (former): nor let some women laugh at others: it may be that the (latter) are better than the (former): nor defame nor be sarcastic to each other, nor call each other by (offensive) nicknames: ill-seeming is a name connoting wickedness, (to be used of one) after he has believed: and those who do not desist are (indeed) doing wrong. Qur'an 49:11.

[53] And in their wealth there is acknowledged right for the needy and the destitute. Qur'an 51:19.

[54] O ye who believe! stand out firmly for Allah, as witnesses to fair dealing, and let not the hatred of others to you make you swerve to wrong and depart from justice. Be just: that is next to Piety: and fear Allah. For Allah is well-acquainted with all that ye do) Qur'an 5:8.

[55] O ye who believe! Enter not houses other than your own, until ye have asked permission and saluted those in them: that is best for you, in order that ye may heed (what is seemly). If ye find none in the house, enter not until permission is given to you: if ye are asked to go back, go back: that makes for greater purity for yourselves: and Allah knows well all that ye do. Qur'an 24:27-8 O you who have believed, avoid much [negative] assumption. Indeed, some assumption is sin. And do not spy or backbite each other. Would one of you like to eat the flesh of his brother when dead? You would detest it. And fear Allah; indeed, Allah is accepting of repentance and Merciful. Qur'an 49:12.

[56] And fight them on until there is no more tumult or oppression, and there prevail justice and faith in Allah; but if they cease, let there be no hostility (and aggression) except to those who practice oppression. Qur'an 2:193.

[57] God does not love evil talk in public unless it is by someone who has been injured thereby. Qur'an 4:148.

[58] On no soul dos Allah place a burden greater than it can bear. It gets every good that it earns, and it suffers every ill that it earns. Qur'an 2:286.

[59] And remember We took your covenant (to this effect): Shed no blood amongst you, nor turn out your own people from your homes: and this ye solemnly ratified, and to this ye can bear witness. After this it is ye, the same

right to choose a religion or no religion/ freedom of belief.[60], - The right of habitation.[61],- The right to elect the government.[62], - The right to rule of law as the supreme law of the land.[63],

---

people, who slay among yourselves, and banish a party of you from their homes; assist (Their enemies) against them, in guilt and rancor. Qur'an 2:84-5.

[60] Let there be no compulsion in religion: Truth stands out clear from Error. Qur'an 2:256. If it had been thy Lord's will, they would all have believed, - all who are on earth! wilt thou then compel mankind, against their will, to believe! Qur'an 109:99.

[61] "O Adam! Dwell thou and thy wife in the Garden; and eat of the bountiful things therein as (where and when) ye will; but approach not this tree, or ye run into harm and transgression." Then did Satan make them slip from the (Garden), and get them out of the state (of felicity) in which they had been. We said: "Get ye down, all (ye people), with enmity between yourselves. On earth will be your dwelling place and your means of livelihood for a time. Qur'an 2:35-6.

[62] I shall discuss citizen's political rights in later chapters in detail.

[63] Centuries before the Magana Carta, the basic sources of Islamic law, i.e. Qur'an and Hadith, affirmed the rule of law at the doctrinal level and in application. Because the rule of law doctrine is exceptionally fundamental in Islamic jurisprudence it is monitored, and enforced not only by governmental organizations but also by the people under the right of Hosbah. No one is above the law. When the Caliph Umar Ibn al-Khaṭṭāb wore a long robe, a sign of spending a moderate amount of money on clothing, the people questioned him about the source of his earnings. See also Hadith "prophetic tradition" (Narrated 'Aisha: The Quraish people became very worried about the Makhzumiya lady who had committed theft. They said, "Nobody can speak (in favor of the lady) to Allah's Apostle and nobody dares do that except Usama who is the favorite of Allah's Apostle." When Usama spoke to Allah's Apostle about that matter, Allah's Apostle said, "Do you intercede (with me) to violate one of the legal punishment of Allah?" Then he got up and addressed the people, saying, "O people! The nations before you went astray because if a noble person committed theft, they used to leave him, but if a weak person among them committed theft, they used to inflict the legal punishment on him. By Allah, if Fatima, the daughter of Muhammad committed theft, Muhammad will cut off her hand!) Sahih Bukhari, Book of Al-Hudud, Hadith # 779. The Qur'an commands: O ye who believe! Be steadfast witnesses for Allah in equity, and let not hatred of any people seduce you

These are some of the Islamic human rights that have been recognized for more than 1400 years. As clarified earlier, Islamic scholars and Muslim-majority states have drafted an extensive list of Islamic human rights in declarations including, The Cairo Declaration of Human Rights in Islam (1990) and the Universal Islamic Declaration of Human Rights (1981).

Notably, Islamic human rights ought to be construed broadly and purposely. For example, the right to be free from unendurable burdens encompasses the right to be free from unbearable taxation. It follows that, for instance, the state cannot forcibly order citizens to join the military without providing financial and emotional support to their families. An employer in the Islamic state cannot burden employees with tasks beyond their capacity, and a student cannot be asked to pay tuition that she cannot afford.

It should be noted that many Islamic human rights overlap in various circumstances. The destitute citizen may invoke his rights against the state to improve his status. These overlapping rights include the right of habitation, the right to life, the right to live with dignity and the right to the necessities of life. Under these rights, the destitute can ask the state to provide shelter, medical care if needed, and basic income and employment rehabilitation to assist him to join the productive workforce if so feasible.

It cannot be over emphasized that the scope, understanding and limitations of Islamic human rights are very different from the Western model of human rights. Islamic Human Rights are a tool to

---

that ye deal not justly. Deal justly, that is nearer to your duty. Observe your duty to Allah. Lo! Allah is Informed of what ye do. Qur'an 5:8. See a study on the Rule of Law and the Doctrine of Stare Decisis in Islamic law, Ali Iyad Yakub, The Islamic Roots of Democracy, 12 *U. Miami Int'l & Comp. L. Rev.* 269, 294.

safeguard human dignity and to confront oppression from individual and government actions alike. It is never to be used to overpower, control or disparage the weakest segments in the society. For example, the Islamic human right of freedom of expression is designed to confront oppression. It does not protect speech that promotes hatred or ridicule, or that offends individuals, groups, cultures or religions. With rights comes responsibilities including the responsibility to live in harmony and respect towards different others. Under Islamic Human Rights freedom of speech/expression, one can criticize the government freely.[64] However, when Muslims are the majority in a state and Islamic law is constitutionally the religion of the state, Muslims are banned from insulting others' religions.[65] In contrast, freedom of speech, as understood by numerous Western nations, may permit offending others, including the weakest in society. For example, French President Macron in October 2020 defended the "right" to depict the Prophet Muhammed in offensive caricatures.

2.3 Islamic Human Rights: Politics and Islamophobia.

While most Muslim-majority states have a form of human rights laws, its application is contingent on a ruling regime's practices. The

---

[64] For example, Umar Ibn Khaṭṭāb, the head of the Islamic state was criticized when he attempted to limit dowry. (it has been narrated that Umar Ibn al-Khattab, said, "Do not be excessive in the dowry of women." A woman said, "It is not so, O Umar, for Allah said: You gave one of them a great amount," (Qur'an 4:20). Umar said, "Indeed, a woman has disputed Umar and she has defeated him."). Clearly Umar not only allowed criticism but also was not reluctant to admit he was wrong when reminded of Islamic law rule.

[65] And insult not those whom they (disbelievers) worship besides Allah. Qur'an 6:108.

correlation between dictatorship and Islamic human rights in Muslim-majority states is noticeable: the more oppressive and dictatorial the regime, the less Islamic human rights are recognized and maintained. On the other hand, Islamophobics associate Islam with abhorrent actions of a dictatorial regime. Muslims perceive such unfair associations as offensive. They are oblivious to the fact that fundamental Islamic human rights were recognized centuries before the Magna Carta, in a world when the notion of human rights was a philosophical concept with limited application in the ancient Greek and Roman Empires. Best practice occurred during the life of the Prophet Muhammad and the initial four *Caliphs*, known as the rightly guided *Caliphs*.

Muslims believe that, as the renowned Islamic scholar, *Imam* Muhammad Al Ghazali, framed it: we (Muslims) exported human rights principles to the whole world for centuries, and now the West is re-exporting to Muslims the same principles as a new human discovery as if we are not aware.[66]

The subject matter of Islamic human rights is very controversial in many ways:

First, there is enormous misapplication of Islamic human rights due to ill practices in many Muslim-majority states. This issue shall be discussed in detail in subsequent chapters.

Second, some Orientalists spared no effort to learn Arabic and Islamic jurisprudence which qualify them to analyze, criticize or even

---

[66] See, Muḥammad al- Gazālī, *Ḥuqūq al-insān baina ta'alīm al-islām wa-I'lān al-Umam al-Muttaḥida* (Human Rights between Islamic Teaching and United Nations Universal Declaration of Human Rights). (Alexandria, Egypt, Dār ad-Da'wa 1999)

explain Islamic law. However, Muslims doubt that many Orientalists have mastered the essential elements of Islamic law. These elements include professional proficiency of Arabic language, knowledge of the basic tools of Islamic jurisprudence such as *Usul Al-Fiqh* (principles of Islamic jurisprudence) and knowledge of Islamic schools of thought methodology and jurisprudence. One cannot overcome the hurdle of lack of essential knowledge by merely reading translations and work in languages other than Arabic. As Muslims believe: the *Qur'an* cannot be translated. There is only a translation of the meanings of the *Qur'an* that is never accurate or sufficient to deduce jurisprudence from the *Qur'an*. Furthermore, the work of Islamic law scholars over the past fourteen centuries was mainly written in Arabic. Without a doubt, language is not the only barrier to learning Islamic law. There is no institution in the western world that would qualify a person to be an Islamic jurist. Accordingly, lack of essential tools to learn Islamic law will certainly produce misinformed publications on Islamic law.[67]

Muslims believe that Orientalists address the issue of human rights in Islam in a manner that is offensive and unreasonable. Orientalists demand that Muslim-majority states' law conforms to their (the Orientalist's) standard of human rights. At times Orientalists have claimed that the standard is the "international standard" citing international instruments. Occasionally they have cited no particular authority to their claims of human rights. Either way, it does not seem reasonable to denounce someone's acts just because you do not like those acts. Muslims comprise at least 1.9

---

[67] Several misconceptions of Islamic law shall be clarified in the following chapters bearing in mind that due to size limitation, this volume cannot address every controversial issue.

billion persons, about one quarter of the world's population, including 57 Muslim-majority states. When 1.9 billion people voice an opinion concerning rights and freedoms, their collective voice has to heard and respected. When 57 sovereign nations agree upon a Human Rights standard, their judgement must be respected and acknowledged in the international arena. At this point, it is important to make it clear that I am not advocating for or against a specific right, but rather explaining why Muslims are angered by those who attempt to impose their standards onto Muslims. It is equally important to note that Muslims are willing to cooperate with other nations in advancing rights for human prosperity. The *Qur'an* commands Muslims to, 'Help you one another in virtue, righteousness, and piety; but do not help one another in sin and transgression.'[68] The Prophet Muhammad spoke very highly of the role of *Hilf al-Fudul* (League of the Virtuous) to uphold justice and support the beleaguered. In modern times, Muslim-majority states have joined many international treaties that promote human well-being.[69] To finish, when the Islamic world disagrees with the Western world regarding a "right", peaceful communication between nations is the ideal practice.

---

[68] Qur'an 5:2.

[69] For example, Muslim majority states had ratified International instruments that promulgate equality for women, such as the United Nations Convention on the Elimination of all forms of Discrimination Against Women (CEDAW). Recently some human rights declarations have been issued by private Islamic entities and by Muslim Majority States alike to articulate fundamental rights such as the Universal Islamic Declaration of Human Rights, UIDHR (1981) and the Cairo Declaration on Human Rights in Islam, CDHRI (1990). These rights include the sanctity of life (Art.2), women's rights (Art 6), freedom from slavery (Art11), freedom of movement (Art. 12), social welfare rights (Art.17), privacy & securities rights (Art18), presumption of innocence & equality rights (Art.19), freedom of expression (Art.22) and fundamentals of Islamic democracy (Art.23) of CDHRI.

Orientalists who demonize Muslims because they do not follow a specific standard or even call for forcible Islamic law reform are simply "other" hate-igniters.

2.4 Islamic Law Codification

Orientalists claim that Muslim-majority states, with respect to Islamic law codification, adopted three models: a secular model in which Islamic law has no role in law making, a "classical *Sharia* system" in which Islamic law is mostly uncodified and finally, a system modelled after European and Indian codes, which form the basis of the codified Islamic law of most of the Muslim-majority states.[70] The truth of the matter is that codifying Islamic law is a political issue. If Muslim-majority states were truly democratic and the people were properly represented, Islamic law codification would have a different standing now. The secular model mentioned above rejected Islamic law in its entirety. In "classical *sharia* systems", the regimes lack the political will to codify Islamic law. Muslim-majority states that codified Islamic law using a European template were under the direct influence of European Imperialism and unable to exercise free will. When European Imperialism collapsed in the twentieth century, the subsequent government did not show real interest in codifying Islamic law.

Certainly, Islamic law can be codified without the need to resemble European codes if the political will exists. Many attempts have been made in the past to codify Islamic law with limited success. As early as the eighth century, the *Caliph* Abū Jaʿfar al-Manṣūr (95-

---

[70] Jan Michiel Otto, Sharia and National Law in Muslim Countries: Tensions and Opportunities for Dutch and EU Foreign Policy (Amsterdam University Press, 2008).

158AH/713-775CE) had requested that the renowned Islamic scholar *Imam* Malik codify Islamic law, marking the first attempt.[71] In modern history, the Ottoman regime created an Islamic civil code, *Majallah al-Ahkam al-`Adliyyah*, to be applied uniformly in the Muslim world. In the twentieth century, several Muslim-majority states incorporated various Islamic law rules into their legislation. However, a comprehensive, refined and erudite Islamic law code has yet to be developed despite the combined efforts of various Islamic law scholars throughout the past fourteen centuries, to create rules of jurisprudence in light of the *Qur'an* and *Sunnah*.

The following discussion, although far from perfect, shall briefly highlight the fundamentals of the *Ta'zir* offenses category. Although only criminal law jurists will appreciate the forthcoming analysis, it is essential to prove that Islamic law rules are amenable to codification if the political will exists and that European code models are not needed as a springboard for such codification.

2.5 Category of Ta'zir Offenses.[72]

Islamic Criminal Law divides offenses into three categories, *Hudud*, *Qisas*, and *Ta'zir*.[73] *Ta'zir* is the broadest category of offenses,

---

[71] *See* Najmaldeen Zanki, "Codification of Islamic Law Premises of History and Debates of Contemporary Muslim Scholars", (2014) 4(9) *International Journal of Humanities and Social Science*,1.

[72] *See also*, Hisham M. Ramadan, "Larceny Offenses in Islamic Law", *2006 Mich. St. L. Rev*, 1.

[73] Hudud means a specific punishment prescribed by God for crimes that transgress upon God/social rights. Hudud crimes are: slander, zena (fornication or adultery), apostasy, baghee (unlawful rebellious acts), voluntary intoxication, hiraba (major crimes against public order and safety typically exemplified by armed highway robbery), and theft. The existence of the crime of apostasy is

encompassing all possible violations of the prohibitory norm that are not enumerated under *Hudud* and *Qisas* offenses and in which there are no prefixed punishments of *kaffarah/*expiation for violating the prohibitory norms.[74]   In *Ta'zir*, the Islamic parliament sets the punishment for offenses subject to jurisprudential guidelines in the *Qur'an* and *Sunnah*. Violation of the prohibitory norm in *Ta'zir* offenses may arise from either violating *Haq-Allah*, right of Allah/God- violating the Islamic prohibitory norm though no individual is harmed-, or *Haq-an-nas/ Haqqul ibad*, rights of people - violating the Islamic prohibitory norm leading to harm to an individual(s) - or both.[75]   The *Ta'zir* offense can be defined as a crime committed by commission or omission where the actor intentionally or recklessly caused unjustifiable harm, and there is no Islamic prefixed punishment for the harm caused.[76]

Although there is no explicit category of *Ta'zir* offenses in the *Qur'an*, several verses in the *Qur'an* indicate the necessity of creating the category of *Ta'zir* offenses. The *Qur'an* elucidates that wrongdoing ought to be punished unless the victim pardons the

---

debatable. *Qisas* means just and proportionate retribution. *Qisas* crimes encompass homicide and bodily injury offenses. *Hudud* offenses, that are frequently misunderstood and misrepresented in the west will be discussed in the following chapters.

[74] Notably, scholars presented various definitions of Ta'zir offenses, however, the essence of all definitions revolves around the above noted definition.

[75] The distinction between Haq-Allah, and haq-an-nas is significant in Islamic criminal law. An example of the violation of haq-an-nas, the right of people, is a debtor's refusal to pay back the creditor while refusal to pay Zakah is a violation of Haq-Allah.

[76] According to the majority view, general intention suffices to convict. There is no need for specific intention unless the Islamic legislature states otherwise.

offender.[77] Similarly, *Sunnah* indicates the necessity of creation of the *Ta'zir* category of offenses. Under *Ta'zir*, the Prophet Muhammad dispensed punishments under various circumstances including punishment of the solvent debtor who refuses to pay the creditor, the consumption of intoxicants and for Non-*Hudud* theft offenses.[78] If there is no prefixed punishment in the *Qur'an* or *Sunnah* for a particular offense, it is the responsibility of the Islamic State to create a system of punishment that ensures that violators will be punished to deter them from reoffending and deter others from following the path of the wrongdoers. Given the importance of *Ta'zir*, it is imperative to explain the Fundamentals of *Ta'zir* offenses.

2.6   The Elements of *Ta'zir* Offenses.

2.6.1   The Mental Element

The mental element in crime may take various forms depending on a number of factors including knowledge of the prohibition, knowledge of the nature of the actor's act(s), knowledge of the consequences of

---

[77] The recompense for an evil is an evil like thereof; but whoever forgives and makes reconciliation, his reward is with Allah. Verily, He likes not the unjust. Qur'an 42:40.

[78] For example, Non-Hudud -Ta'zir punishment for theft was mentioned in the following Hadith. "It was narrated from Amr bin Shuaib, from his father, from his grandfather Abdullah bin Amr that Allah's Messenger (PBUH) was asked about fruit on tree. He said, "Whatever a needy person takes without putting any in his pocket, there is no penalty on him. But whoever takes anything away, he must pay a penalty twice its value and be punished. Whoever steals something after it has been stored properly, and its value is equal to that of a shield, his hand must be cut off. Whoever steals something less than that, he must pay a penalty of twice its value and be punished." Hadith No. 4961, Book of Cutting Off the Hand of the Thief, Sunan An-Nasa'i.

the prohibited act, voluntariness of the conduct and the desire to harm or to achieve particular consequences.

2.6.1.1 Knowledge Is a Vital Factor in The Mental Element in *Ta'zir* Offenses.

Prior to explaining the culpable state of mind theories, it is imperative to discuss knowledge in detail, a crucial element of criminal liability. Several verses in the *Qur'an* repeatedly emphasize the necessity of knowledge as a prerequisite to punishment.[79] This proposition necessitates exclusion of ignorance as a state of mind. For that reason, the punishment is justified and warranted under Islamic law only if the actor is aware not only of his conduct, but also of the prohibition that has been violated, the consequences of his conduct in certain offenses, and has knowledge of the circumstances.[80] The *Qur'an* has asserted that no punishment is permitted without fair warning.[81] However, the application of such a general rule, that lack of knowledge averts punishment may, on occasion, lead to undesirable consequences. Offenders may deceptively claim that they did not have sufficient knowledge of the prohibition or the possible consequences of the conduct. Also, ignorance might be blameworthy in itself. Individuals are required to obtain knowledge of the rules of conduct that govern the society. For Muslims, they are required to obtain knowledge of the prohibitory norms that are expressed or implied in the *Qur'an* and *Sunnah*. Non-Muslims who reside in the Islamic State

---

[79] Whoever goes right, then he goes right only for the benefit of his own self. And whoever goes astray, then he goes astray to his own loss. No one laden with burdens can bear another's burden. And We never punish until We have sent a Messenger (to give warning). Quran 17:15, *See also*, 4:165, 35:24 &28:59 Qur'an.

[80] *See* Qur'an 17: 15, 26: 208 & 28: 59.

[81] Quran 17:15.

under *Dhimmah* Contract, the social contract between non-Muslims and the Islamic State, are also under legal obligation to know their legal duties, including knowledge of the Islamic State's prohibitory norms.[82] A non-Muslim temporary visitor, *Mosta'men/Mo'ahed,* to the Islamic State may enter under the Safety/*Aman* contract. The Safety contract necessitates that the visitor acquaint himself with Islamic State laws and obey them.[83]

Scholars had to accommodate the above considerations: The *Qur'an's* directive that no punishment is permitted without fair warning, and an individual's duty to acquire knowledge. Accordingly, Islamic law scholars have distinguished between four sets of circumstances in which lack of knowledge/ignorance might be excusable.

i. *The first type of ignorance is unjustified ignorance.* In this type, the actor may not be excused for ignorance when the crime committed is well-known to be prohibited such as killing, larceny or defamation. Abu Hanifa, contrary to the majority of scholars' views, suggested that a non-Muslim might be excused if the crime 's circumstances are permissible under his religious law. This proposal is based upon the freedom to exercise religion doctrine. Examples of these excused crimes are adultery, intoxication, and incest.[84] The judge who hears

---

[82] *See* Ibn Qayyim al-Jawziyyah, 2 *Ahkam Ahl adh-Dhimah* (Dhimmi's adjudications), (Cairo, Dar al-Hadith 2005).

[83] *See* Ibn Qudamah,10 *Al-Mughni wa'l-Sharh al-Kabir,* (Beirut: Dar Al-Fikr),72.

[84] During the reign of the Muslim *Caliph* Umar Ibn Abd Al Aziz, Umar asked the renowned scholar Al-Hassan Al-Basri for a fatwa regarding permitting non-Muslims, residing in the Islamic State, to marry their daughters, sisters and mothers. Al-Hassan replied: You have only to follow what your predecessors did.

claims related to these crimes is bound to apply the religious law of the non-Muslims that may excuse the actor from the punishment. For instance, in the past, in the Zoroastrian religion, fathers were permitted to marry their daughters. A judge hearing a matrimonial case where the husband is the father of the wife may adjudicate concerning inheritance, affinity, wife and child support or any other relevant issue without invalidating or nullifying the marriage as Islamic law would require. The judge, according to this view, should not impose any penalty for incest. However, support for Abu Hanifa's view by substantial jurisprudential evidence might be troublesome in the application. How far is the Islamic State willing to allow non-Muslims to practice their religious beliefs notwithstanding the Islamic prohibitory norm? If every group of individuals was to create their own religion and rules, many groups in the Islamic State would in effect be creating states within the Islamic State. What if the non-Islamic laws contradict the Islamic State's interests? Should the non-Muslims 'laws prevail over the Islamic State laws? If the Islamic state officially adopts the *Hanafi* madhab, then all these questions must be answered by the Islamic Legislature and guided by Islamic jurisprudence and relevant circumstances.

ii. *The second type of ignorance occurs when the prohibitory norm(s) is vague or subject to interpretation.*[85] In this type,

---

You are not to innovate (by imposing Islamic laws on non-Muslims). Al-Hassan advice to the *Caliph* clearly allowed non-Muslims to practice their family law although it's repulsive in nature to Muslims and violates the prohibitory norm.

[85] The prohibitory norm is the prohibitions enumerated in Qur'an, Sunnah or any other prohibition(s) made by the Islamic legislature.

ignorance may arise from either a lack of understanding or an erroneous understanding of the prohibition. This may occur when one follows a less favorable and unsound interpretation. As a result, if an actor, driven by his ignorance, follows a false interpretation or did not understand the prohibition and thereby violates the prohibitory norm, he might be excused providing that the Islamic State did not formally adopt another interpretation. Some scholars have suggested that the actor might be punished under the *Ta'zir* category only, since *Qisas* or *Hudud* punishments are not warranted because *Qisas* and *Hudud* require untainted knowledge of the prohibition, providing that the actor is not informed of the proper interpretation prior to the commission of the crime. Here the purpose of the *Ta'zir* punishment is not to penalize the ignorant actor for his poor interpretation but rather to punish him for misleading the public by purposely promoting a false interpretation if he did so.

iii. *The third type of ignorance is excusable ignorance.* This is divided into two subcategories:

A. The first subcategory is excusable ignorance where knowledge of the prohibitory norm(s) is inaccessible, and the actor did not intentionally contribute to the inaccessibility of the means of knowledge.

B. The second subcategory is ignorance of the prohibition in *Hudud* offenses since any doubt in *Hudud* precludes the punishment. [86]

---

[86] It should be noted that Islamic law scholars unanimously agree that any doubt precludes punishment in *Hudud* offenses. This rule is based on a number of hadith, most of which are weak hadith, but collectively uphold the meaning that

iv. The fourth type of ignorance occurs when a Muslim violates Islamic law in the non-Islamic State because of lack of knowledge of Islamic law. Some scholars have suggested that lack of knowledge in this case, not only precludes the punishment but also negates the criminality of the actor's conduct. Other scholars have affirmed that the actor's conduct remains unlawful, but the punishment is unwarranted because lack of jurisdiction.

2.6.1.2 Intention as a Basis for Liability

Having explained the knowledge factor in the mental element in crime, now we turn to the classification of states of mind as described by Islamic law scholars. Generally speaking, Islamic law scholars divide offenses into two main categories: intentional and unintentional offenses.[87] Intentional offenses require that the actor voluntarily desired the commission of the prohibited act and was aware of the prohibition. Intentional offenses are further divided into two subtypes: general and specific intention offenses. General intention offenses require that the actor intended the act **and** intended violating the prohibitory norm irrespective of the consequences of the act. In specific intent offenses, the actor not only knowingly violated the prohibitory norm but also desired the particular consequences of his conduct, e.g., shooting to kill. Concerning the *Ta'zir* category of offenses, both general intention

---

any doubt precludes punishment. Many scholars expanded the scope of this rule to also include *Qisas* offenses.

[87] Many Islamic law scholars have proposed a third category of equivalent to intentional conduct in homicide and body harm offenses. The proposition is that the actor only intended the conduct but did not intend the particular consequences.

and specific intention offenses are culpable mental elements in crime as long as the actor intended the violation of the prohibitory norm and the knowledge factor is satisfied to convict, as explained earlier, including the actor's awareness of the prohibition.

Unintentional offenses occur when the actor did not desire to violate the prohibitory norm. Three forms of unintentional offenses occur:

1. Mistake in desire: The actor intended the act but did not desire the consequences of his act(s). For example, the actor killed a human by misaiming at a valid target, e.g., shooting at a deer but missing and killing a person.
2. Mistake in the act: The actor intended an act but did not intend the commission of an offense. For example, the actor killed a human mistakenly believing that the human was a valid target, e.g., a deer.
3. Absence of volition: The actor lacked volition when committing the offense. For example, the actor killed a human under the influence of automatism.[88]

As a general rule, any harm caused unintentionally by mistake is not criminally culpable unless recklessness caused the harm.[89] This

---

[88] Islamic law scholars label this type of offense as equivalent to mistake in action. Scholars utilized many examples to explain the concept of equivalent to mistake in action including, falling on a child while asleep causing the child's death.

[89] On the authority of Ibn Abbas (RA), that the Messenger of Allah said: Verily Allah has pardoned [or been lenient with] for me my ummah: their mistakes, their forgetfulness, and that which they have been forced to do under duress. Hadith Hasan related by Ibn Majah, and al-Bayhaqee and others. It should be noted that Qur'an has mandated that mistake is culpable in certain instances. See [It is not for a believer to kill a believer except (that it be) by mistake; and

leads us to exclude negligence as a mental element of the crime. Inculpable negligence occurs when the actor inadvertently takes an unjustified risk. The actor evidently intended to do the act but was unaware that the act was prohibited and/or was unaware of the possible harmful consequences of his act; nevertheless, harm occurred because of the actor's conduct.[90]

Accordingly, the possible mental element required for conviction in *Ta'zir* offenses are either:

1. Specific intention: the actor intended the prohibited conduct and desired particular consequences. e.g., shoot to kill
2. General intention: the actor intended the prohibited conduct with or without intent to harm. e.g., shooting at a person not intending to kill or to cause harm.
3. Recklessness: the actor knowingly took an unjustified risk. The actor was aware of the prohibition and aware of the nature of his actions, and the harm was foreseeable; nevertheless, the actor proceeded with committing the prohibited conduct.

2.6.2 The Physical Element in *Ta'zir* Offenses

2.6.2.1 Act of Commission or Omission

Crimes can be committed by a commission - an overt physical act that causes harm, such as shooting to kill. Alternatively, crimes can be committed by omission - failure to act when the actor is under a duty

---

whosoever kills a believer by mistake, (it is ordained that) he must set free a believing slave and a compensation (blood-money, i.e. Diya)] Qur'an 4: 92.

[90] Notably the actor who causes harm by negligence might be liable civilly. See hadith "On the authority of Saad bin Malik al-Khudari, that the messenger of Allah said: "There should be neither harming nor reciprocating harm." hadith Hasan related by Ibn Majah, Al-Daraqutni and others.

to act, and the omission caused harm. For example, an actor may fail to provide necessities of life to an individual who is likely to die because of the actor's omission. If the actor is under a duty to act, the majority of Islamic law scholars have concluded that the actor is liable for his action(s) regardless of whether the crime was committed by omission or commission providing that all other elements of the offense are present.[91] A fraction of those who support this approach do not attribute criminal responsibility to offenders who cause harm by omission when the legal duty to act is disputable.[92] These rare scholars have concluded that the actor who refrains from saving a person from a blazing house or drowning is not guilty of an offense.

Contrary to the majority opinion, some *Hanafi* school of thought scholars have concluded that crimes cannot be committed by omission.[93] Thus depriving a person of necessitates of life such as food and water until he dies is not a crime because the act of deprivation is not a commission. In contrast, digging a trench into which a person falls then dies satisfies the requirement of committing a crime by commission.

2.6.2.2 Preparatory Acts, Attempt, and Impossible Crime

A crime passes through a number of stages before its commission. The initial stage is the consideration to commit a crime that might evolve into a desire to do a prohibited act or refrain from fulfilling a

---

[91] *See* Mansur al-Buhuti, 3 *Kashshāf al-Qinā' 'an Matn al-Iqnā'* (Beirut, Dar Al Kotob Al-Ilmiyah 1997), 36. Ibn Qudamah,10 *Al-Mughni wa'l-Sharh al-Kabir* (Beirut: Dar Al-Fikr),327.

[92] Ibn Qudamah,10 *Al-Mughni wa'l-Sharh al-Kabir* (Beirut: Dar Al-Fikr), 581-3.

[93] Ibn Nujaym, 9 *Al-Bahr ar-Raiq Sharh Kanz ad-Daqaiq,* (Beirut, Dar Al Kotob Al-Ilmiyah 1997), 15-8.

duty that would cause harm. In this primary stage, the actor is not culpable so long as he does not act upon his thoughts.[94] Once the actor, by an overt act, manifests his intention and initiates the commission of the offense and in doing so makes preparatory acts that might constitute a crime(s) in itself, the actor is culpable for whatever crimes he commits. A burglar who breaks and enters a dwelling intending to steal property, but is arrested before the completion of the crime, is liable for breaking and entering. In cases in which the preparatory acts are not crimes in and of themselves, Islamic jurists have adopted two distinct approaches. Scholars from the *Maliki* and *Hanbali* schools of thought attach criminal liability for any preparatory act(s) committed for the purpose of completion of an offense albeit such acts are not themselves prohibited.[95] Nevertheless, the punishment for these acts must be less than the punishment for the completed offense.

In contrast, scholars of the *Hanafi* and *Shafi'i* schools of thought have concluded that if the preparatory act(s) are not themselves prohibited, no criminal liability is attached. They have suggested that such preparatory acts fall under 'malevolent thoughts' and are not punishable under Islamic law. According to this view, to punish an actor for the non-prohibited preparatory act(s) is to punish individuals according to unascertainable desires which are contrary

---

[94] It is narrated on the authority of Abu Huraira that the Messenger of Allah (may peace be upon him) observed: Verily Allah forgave my people the evil promptings which arise within their hearts as long as they did not speak about them or did not act upon them. Sahih Muslim.

[95] See Ibn Qayyim, 3 *I'laam ul Muwaqqi'een 'an Rabibnb il 'Aalameen* (Beirut, Dar Al Kotob Al-Ilmiyah 1991), 177. See also 2 Abu Ishaq al-Shatibi, *Al-Muwafaqat fi Usul al-Sharia* (Dar Ibn Afan 1997),203.

to Islamic principles of forbidding second-guessing an individual's intentions.[96]

What if the actor proceeded in his criminal endeavor beyond the preparatory act and initiated the final step to commit the crime but failed to complete the crime for reasons beyond his control? In this case, the offender should be punished under the *Ta'zir* category only since the punishment for the completed offense, whether *Hudud* or *Qisas*, is not warranted until the offense is actually completed.[97] However, an offender may be punished by *Hudud* or *Qisas* as well as *Ta'zir* if the failed act resulted in crime in itself. For example, if an actor shot a victim intending to kill him but only injured the victim, the offender is liable for the injury caused under the *Qisas* category as well as liable under the *Ta'zir* category for attempted murder.

Attempted crime ought to be distinguished from the abandonment of the crime after its initiation. The actor may abandon the crime either because of reasons beyond his control, for example, a burglar who is arrested before breaking and entering a dwelling house, or by voluntarily refusing to commit the crime without any intervening circumstances precluding the crime completion. The majority of Islamic law scholars have suggested that any crime

---

[96] See [O ye who believe! Avoid suspicion as much (as possible): for suspicion in some cases is a sin: And spy not on each other behind their backs. Would any of you like to eat the flesh of his dead brother? Nay, ye would abhor it...But fear Allah: For Allah is Oft-Returning, Most Merciful.] Quran 49:12.

[97] ...And whosoever transgresses the set limits of Allah, then indeed he has wronged himself.... Qur'an 65:1. See also, Jamal al-Deen Abdullah bin Yusuf al-Zayla'I, *Nasb al-Rayah Takhrij Ahadith al-Hidaya* (Beirut, Dar Al Kotob Al-Ilmiyah 2010), 172-5. See also (Whoever punish with the punishment of a Hudd without the commission of a Hudd is a transgressor.) (Hadith narrated in Sunan al-Bayhaqi; many scholars had concluded that this Hadith is weak.)

involving *Haq-an-nas/ Haqqul ibad*, the rights of the people, is punishment-worthy even if the actor repented and abandoned the completion of the crime.[98] This rule suggests that when an actor refused to complete the crime without any intervening circumstances, the actor might be punished only for crimes committed in preparation for his intended crime. For example, in the case of burglary, the actor might be punished for breaking and entry only if he did not actually commit further offenses. Repentance does not preclude the punishment of any criminal acts performed in preparation for the actor's intended crime. If the *Ta'zir* crime involves violation of *Haq-Allah*, rights of Allah/God, scholars have disagreed on the effect of abandoning the crime.[99] Plausibly, when an actor is arrested prior to the completion of an offense but did not voluntarily abandon the crime, he remains liable for the attempt, as explained earlier, and for any other crime committed in the process of committing the intended crime.

Many scholars have concluded that an actor's criminal conduct is punishment-worthy even if the objective of the actor's conduct was impossible to achieve because of circumstances unknown to the actor. [100] This case is contemporarily known as the impossible crime. For example, an actor shoots to kill an already deceased person believing the person is alive; or an actor engaged in sexual intercourse with a woman believing that she is not his wife but she actually is. The rationale for the punishment in the case of impossible crime is that the actor not only intended the violation of the prohibitory norm but

---

[98] See Ibn Qayyim, 2 *I'laam ul Muwaqqi'een 'an Rabibnb il 'Aalameen* (Beirut, Dar Al Kotob Al-Ilmiyah 1991),116.

[99] Perhaps scholars had agreed that abandoning the crime precludes the punishment only in the case of Hudud of haraba. See Qur'an 5: 33-4.

[100] Ibn Ḥazm, 4 *Al-Ihkam fi Usul al-Ahkam* (Beirut, Dar Al Fikr 1997), 117.

also took all necessary steps to complete the crime. This is punishment-worthy, according to the majority of Islamic law scholars, since criminal intention manifest by an overt act triggers the punishment.

2.6.3 The Scope of Ta'zir Offenses

Ta'zir punishment is warranted under two set of circumstances: when *Qisas* or *Hudud* offense requirements are not satisfied, because the *Hudud* standard of proof of beyond all doubt is not satisfied but the actor's conduct remains culpable or when the Islamic legislature creates *Ta'zir* offenses under the general Islamic jurisprudence guidelines.

2.6.3.1 Application of Ta'zir When Qisas or Hudud Requirements Are Not Satisfied.

Generally, the majority of Islamic law scholars have acknowledged the permissibility of combining *Ta'zir* punishment with *Hudud* or *Qisas* punishment under various circumstances.[101] However, Islamic law scholars have debated the applicability of *Ta'zir* when the mental element required for conviction of *Qisas* offenses is not satisfied. This question is vital given that *Ta'zir* offenses are the *reserve* offenses category that is triggered when the prefixed Islamic punishment(s) requirements in *Hudud* and *Qisas* are not justified. Scholars adhering to the *Maliki* and *Zahiri/Dhahiri* schools of thought have suggested that in *Qisas* offenses, the actor is liable for the consequences of his action(s) and shall be punished so long as he had intended the commission of the prohibited act. In other words, only general

---

[101] Al-Ramli, 8 *Nihayah al-Muhtaj ila Syarh al-Minhaj*, (Beirut, Dar Al Fikr 2002), 18.

intention suffices for conviction in the *Qisas* offenses. It seems that *Maliki* and *Zahiri/Dhahiri* scholars assume that individuals regularly intended the consequences of their actions. This approach leads to the conclusion that the *Ta'zir* category is inoperative in the *Qisas* offenses, since general intention, meaning only intention to act, suffices to convict in *Qisas* offenses unless the Islamic state creates an offense based upon an alternative state of mind, i.e., recklessness.

In contrast, the majority of Islamic law scholars, comprising other schools of thought, have suggested that the actor is liable for his action(s) under the *Qisas* offenses if he intended the foreseeable consequences of his action, e.g., shooting to kill. In other words, the *Qisas* offenses are specific intent offenses.[102] These scholars have suggested that the intention to cause particular consequences can be inferred from actor's action(s). If the prohibited result is a natural consequence of the actor's action, then the consequence is objectively foreseeable, and the actor is liable under the *Qisas* category. This approach suggests that the *Ta'zir* category is operative in the *Qisas* offenses when the mental element requirement is not satisfied, (e.g., the specific intent to cause a particular harm was not proven, the harm was not foreseeable, or the harm was not a natural consequences of the act), and there is no prefixed Islamic penalty such as *Diya*.[103]

---

[102] See (The Prophet said: If anyone is killed blindly or, when people are throwing stones, by a stone or a whip, his blood-wit is the blood-wit for an accidental murder. But if anyone is killed intentionally, retaliation is due. If anyone tries to prevent it, the curse of Allah, of angels, and of all the people will rest on him.) Sunan Abi Dawud. *See Also,* Ibn Qudamah,10 *Al-Mughni wa'l-Sharh al-Kabir,* (Beirut, Dar Al-Fikr), 322-334.

[103] *Diya* is blood money, the financial compensation to the victim or the victim's heirs.

Similar to the *Qisas* crimes, if the definition of *Hudud* offense is not satisfied because of the absence of an essential element, *Ta'zir* punishment might be triggered depending on the Islamic legislature's will to enforce a specific rule of conduct in the society and subject to general Islamic jurisprudence.[104] For example, finding a man and a woman in an indecent position that does not satisfy the requirement of *Zina* conviction may trigger *Ta'zir* punishment for the actors.

Typically, two main factors reduce the punishment of *Hudud* offenses; lacking any form of knowledge and the existence of any kind of doubt with respect to an essential element of an offense.[105] For example, in *Zina* offense, the mental element required for conviction is to knowingly violate the prohibitory norm, i.e., intention to perform the act of penetration outside marriage. The actor must be aware of the nature and quality of his conduct and aware of the prohibition.[106] Here, a distinction must be made between lack of knowledge of the prohibition and erroneous knowledge that leads to violating the prohibitory norm. Those who are unaware that *Zina* is prohibited, such as newly converted Muslims, might be excused from the punishment entirely. However, those who know that *Zina* is prohibited and commit *Zina* believing it to be lawful in their

---

[104] See Mansur al-Buhuti, 6 *Kashshāf al-Qinā' 'an Matn al-Iqnā'* (Beirut, Dar Al Kotob Al-Ilmiyah 1997), 154.

[105] See the Hadith "doubt preclude applying Hudud punishments" (weak Hadith) see also Hadith "avoid inflicting the fixed punishment of Hadd on Muslims as much as you can; for it is better for the judge to make a mistake in releasing 'an offender' rather than committing a mistake 'in convicting an innocent.'" Sunan AL-Tirmidhi Book of Al Hudud; see also Ibn Majah "avoid inflecting the punishments of Hudud if you can find justification for such avoidance" Book of Hudud.

[106] See Ibn Qudamah,10 *Al-Mughni wa'l-Sharh al-Kabir*, (Beirut, Dar Al-Fikr), 116-118.

circumstances might be excused from the *Hudud* punishment of *Zina* but liable under *Ta'zir* category of offenses.[107]

Another example is demonstrated by theft offense. The mental element of theft requires the following: the actor should know the nature and quality of his conduct, that his act constitutes a crime, that the property was owned by another, that he was not permitted to acquire the property and that the actor intends to deprive the owner of the property and intends to own the property.[108] If any form of knowledge required for conviction in a theft offense is lacking, the punishment of theft under *Hudud* category is not warranted. However, the Islamic legislature may impose the *Ta'zir* punishment subject to the Islamic jurisprudence guidelines.

Finally, Islamic jurists almost unanimously concluded a jurisprudential rule that the presence of any doubt in the existence of an essential element of an offense precludes the punishment of *Hudud*. When doubt exists, the Islamic State may impose the *Ta'zir* punishment subject to general Islamic jurisprudence guidelines. Scholars have advanced many examples to explain this rule application. In the *Qazf* (defamation) offense, if an actor told an individual that he was acting as the people of the Prophet Lot, which

---

[107] It has been reported in Malik's Muwatta that Tulayha al–Asadiya was the wife of Rushayd ath–Thaqafi. He divorced her, and she got married in her idda–period. Umar Ibn al–Khattab beat her and her husband with a stick several times, and separated them. Then Umar Ibn al–Khattab said, "If a woman marries in her idda–period, and the new husband has not consummated the marriage, then separate them, and when she has completed the idda of her first husband, the other becomes a suitor. Clearly Umar Ibn al–Khattab did not apply Zina punishment under Hudud because there was a doubt.

[108] See Ahmed Fathy Bahnasi, *Al-Syasah-Al-Ganaeyah Fe Al Sharia Al-Islamiah* [The Penal Policy in Islamic Law], (Cairo, Dar Al-Sharouq 1988),357, See also Ibn Hazm, 12 *Al-Mohala Ba-Al-Athar* (Beirut, Dar Al-Fikr 2001), 107.

suggests the commission of the act of sodomy, some scholars concluded that the *Hudud* punishment of *Qazf* should not apply. They have concluded that the actor's statement carries more than one meaning and that at least one meaning is virtuous, that the allegedly defamed person was doing the acceptable acts of the Prophet Lot's people, not sodomy.[109] However, the Islamic state may impose the *Ta'zir* punishment to eliminate societal harm generated by ambiguous statements that may carry an offensive connotation.

2.6.3.2   The Application of *Ta'zir* Under the General Islamic Jurisprudence Guidelines

Some scholars have suggested that the judiciary should play a legislative as well as judiciary role in the *Ta'zir* offenses.[110] A judge would define the acts that constitute a crime and then impose the appropriate punishment. The alternative view, which is worth supporting, is that the Islamic legislature should draft the *Ta'zir* criminal code to include all violations of the prohibitory norms guided by Islamic jurisprudence. This approach does not eliminate the judge's role in imposing appropriate sentences from the range of alternative punishments set forth by the legislature. However, it eradicates the judge's unbridled discretion to set the crime and the punishment and limits his judicial function to the imposition of criminal sanctions only when the Islamic prohibitory norm is violated. A judge would continue to have the power to impose the appropriate punishment according to various factors including the defendant's character, his criminal history, the impact of a particular

---

[109] Ibn Qudamah,10 *Al-Mughni wa'l-Sharh al-Kabir*, (Beirut, Dar Al-Fikr), 219-20.

[110] *See,* Ibn al-Humam, 4 *Sharh Fath al-Qadir*, (Beirut, Dar Sadir), 212.

punishment on the offender, the impact of the crime on the community and recidivism. In this context, the judge's power to impose the appropriate sentence aims to rehabilitate the offender, support the general and specific deterrence rationales of the *Ta'zir* punishment and empower the judge to remedy social problems.[111]

In the end, the Islamic jurisprudential guiding principles that govern the creation of the *Ta'zir* offenses can be summarized as follows:

A. *Hudud* and *Qisas* offense categories provide clear guidance for lesser offenses. This guidance gives the legislature indication as to the punishable conducts, and the appropriate punishment for lesser offenses is included in the offense of *Ta'zir*. For example, murder is a *Qisas* offense which indicates that the lesser included offense of attempted murder should be punishable under *Ta'zir* category. The punishment for attempted murder must be less than the punishment for murder as a direct application of the jurisprudential rule that punishment of *Hudud* is warranted only for the complete offense of *Hudud*.[112] Similarly, the *Hudud* offense of *Zina* suggests guidelines that all sexual acts that do not qualify as *Zina* are punishment-worthy providing that punishment for the sexual acts must be less than the punishment for *Zina*. More generally, new crimes continuously emerge in an ever-

---

[111] It should be noted that *Ta'zir* in Arabic Language denotes *Ta'deeb* "make someone behave properly". This obviously indicates that the prime rationale for the punishment for *Ta'zir* offenses are rehabilitation and deterrence.

[112] See (Whoever punish with the punishment of a Hudd without the commission of a Hudd is a transgressor.) This Hadith narrated in Sunan al-Bayhaqi, while considered by many scholars to be weak, is generally accepted a directive on a jurisprudential basis.

changing society, and there is a social need to respond to such challenges by creating new *Ta'zir* offenses. Here, the rationales underlying the prohibition in *Hudud* and *Qisas* offenses can be utilized to create new *Ta'zir* offenses capable of responding to new social challenges. For example, the prohibition of homicide under *Qisas* indicates that any act(s) that threatens human lives can be criminally prohibited under the *Ta'zir* category of offenses.

B. The *Qur'an* and *Sunnah* are filled with jurisprudential doctrines that ought to be followed when creating offenses under the *Ta'zir* category. An example of these doctrines is the *Qur'an's* directive that an act is not punishable until fair warning is given to the individuals.[113] This doctrine is contemporarily known as the prohibition against retroactive laws.[114]

C. When codifying *Ta'zir* offenses, the Islamic legislature may utilize extensive Islamic jurisprudential theories that have

---

[113] See Qur'an 17: 15, 26: 208, 28: 59.

[114] It should be noted that this rule tolerates some exceptions such as the permissibility of retroactively imposing penal law when the laws under which the accused is charged were replaced by a more favorable law for the accused. A historic ruling explains the exception. In the pre-Islamic era, the monetary compensation and retribution for homicide and battery varied according to the social status of the victim. The compensation for wrongful death of a Jewish person from Banu Nadir tribe was double of that received if the victim was a Jewish person from Banu Qurayza. If the victim was a noble person and the offender was not, the tribe of the victim may choose to kill a noble person(s) from the tribe of the offender in retaliation notwithstanding his innocence. When Islamic law preempted these laws and implemented equitable laws, the accused persons immediately benefited from the change. Obviously in modern times, if the Islamic legislature repealed Ta'zir crime or reduced the punishment, a defendant would not receive any possible benefit from amendment.

been presented over the past fourteen centuries. For example, the renowned Islamic scholar 'Izz al-Din 'Abd al-'Aziz Ibn 'Abd al-Salam had suggested numerous jurisprudential rules that might be considered when drafting legislation. One examples of these rules is that eliminating harm is preferred over gaining a benefit. When the legislature must choose between harms, one ought to choose the lesser harm and necessity may excuse committing prohibitions.[115] Likewise, *Imam* al-Shatibi has identified five higher objectives of Islamic law, namely, the protection of religion, life, intellect, procreation, and property.[116] Any threat to these objectives is a threat to society at large that may trigger enacting *Ta'zir* offenses to protect society.

---

[115] 'Izz al-Din 'Abd al-'Aziz Ibn 'Abd al-Salam, *Qawa'id al-Ahkam fi Masalih al-Anam* (Beirut, Dar al-Jil 1980).

[116] Abu Ishaq al-Shatibi, *Al-Muwafaqat fi Usul al-Sharia* (Dar Ibn Afan 1997).

CHAPTER 3

The Call to Abandon Islamic Law: Toxic Politics, Media, Academia and Dictatorship.

3.1 Introduction

Perhaps one the most controversial issues in Western literature currently is Islam. Maxime Rodinson concluded that views on Islam vary "from seeing Muhammad, the prophet of Islam, as a sheer satanic imposter to religious genius".[117] Islamic law is at the centre of the controversy. Islamic law has been viewed negatively, to a significant degree, for various reasons including Muslims' failure to properly portray Islam to non-Muslims, demonizing Muslim-majority states for political gain and competing with other faiths. Islamic law has

---

[117] Maxime Rodinson, *Maxime Europe and the Mystique of Islam* (I.B. Tauris 2002), 78.

been branded as archaic and nonoperational in modern societies, incapable of codification like modern codes, and inhumane contrary to modern human rights standards. Invitations to Muslim-majority states to abandon Islamic law have become louder in recent years. Some authoritarian regimes in Muslim-majority states have succumbed to the influence of western powers and have gradually abandoned Islamic law principles that have been enshrined in their societies for centuries. The people of these Muslim-majority states have not accepted these changes in their laws. They whisper, out of fear of retaliation by their regimes, that their regime has changed the laws to mollify western powers at the expense of their faith, traditions, and customs. Indeed, when foreign powers exert political force to change the laws of Muslim-majority states, they are sowing the seeds of political instability in these Muslim-majority states. Furthermore, armed opposition and terrorist entities may rationalize their heinous acts by claiming that puppet regimes have undermined the sovereignty of the Muslim-majority states as they acquiesce to the foreign powers.

Plausibly, foreign influence on Muslim-majority states to abandon Islamic law stems from lack of understanding of Islamic law driven by ill practices that are unfairly branded as Islamic law or by simple disrespect and intolerance to "others" who differ from western people, although the "others" are their counterparts in humanity. Dealing with intolerance to the "other" is far beyond the scope of this volume because it should involve an extensive sociological, psychological and historical analysis of the relationship between Islam and the West. While misunderstanding and misapplication of Islamic law will be clarified in the following chapters, this chapter will focus on the toxic environment in which misunderstanding and misapplication of Islamic law thrive.

3.2   Demonizing Islam: Academia, Media and Politicians.

Muslims are bombarded day and night with negative propaganda of Islam and Muslims. The propaganda employs many outlets including academia, politics and mass media. In academia, those who are unhappy with Islam, seemingly, initiate an organized campaign to demonize and spread fear of Islam, eventually calling for the complete reform of Islam including reformation of Islamic law scholarship. Amitai Etzioni claimed that Islam is a threat to America.[118] Brigitte Gabriel linked Islam with racism, bigotry, and intolerance.[119] Nazila Chanea called for a new "emancipatory" interpretation of Islam.[120] Donna Erzt demanded abrogation of *Ijtihad* altogether.[121] The call for Islamic "reform" coincided with the intentional misrepresentation of any favourable Islamic concepts.   For instance, Professor Ann Elizabeth Mayer concluded that the Cairo Declaration on Human

---

[118] Amitai Etzioni, *Security First* (Yale University Press 2007). He concluded (our conflict, in this view, is not with one interpretation of Islam, nor with radical Islamists, not even simply with a contemporary and particularly virulent manifestation of Islam –but simply with "Islam".) Id. at 88.

[119] She concluded (Yet, the all-pervasive racism, bigotry and intolerance of Islam clearly reveal itself in the hypersensitivity of its leaders and their followers ....), Brigitte Gabriel, *They Must be Stopped* (St. Martin's Griffin 2010), 190.

[120] Nazila Chanea, "Human Rights of Religious Minorities and Women in the Middle-East", 26 *Hum. Rts. Q.*705, 728.

[121] See Donna E. Erzt, "Religious Human rights in Muslim States of the Middle East and North Africa", 110 *Emory Int'l L. Rev.* 139. She concluded (Ijtihad, or creative interpretation, is a classic Muslim methodology for adopting archaic or obsolete doctrines, including those derived from divine revelation) Id. at 160.

Rights in Islam offered no guarantee of equal protection of the law.[122] In fact, article 19(a) of The Cairo Declaration on Human Rights in Islam expressly states that all individuals are equal before the law, without distinction between the ruler and the ruled.

To be sure, most of academia in the U.S., Canada and Europe is controlled by anti-Islamic or Islamophobic groups. It is noticeable that most of the academic writing on Islam in the West has adopted negative and misinformed views. This has provoked me intellectually to enter the sphere of Islamic law although it was not my primary interest. I have attended conferences where I have found many papers presented lacking the methodology or knowledge requisite in conducting Islamic law research. Accordingly, I published an article to outline the prerequisite knowledge required to conduct research on Islamic law.[123] Apart from atypical circumstances that permitted this publication to see the light, publishing an objective or positive view on Islam in the U.S., Europe or Canada is an uphill battle. If I cite original writings in Arabic or show a bright side to Islamic law, publishers and reviewers are not happy. If I criticise Orientalist writing because it misinforms the public, they are not happy. Academia in the U.S., Canada and Europe largely exists in the realm of demonizing Islam and Islamic law. Freedom of speech is only a slogan reflecting the implied fact: you are free to say whatever I allow you to say! Here I forward two examples to show this unfortunate state of affairs.

---

[122] Ann Elizabeth Mayer, *Islam and Human Rights: Traditions and Politics* (Westview Press 2006), 89

[123] Hisham Ramadan, "Toward Honest and Principled Islamic Law Scholarship" 2006 *2006 Mich. St. L. Rev*, 1573.

Example one: I was invited by a prominent journal on Islamic studies to review a book published by Cambridge University Press entitled "Crime and Punishment in Islamic law: Theory and Practice from sixteenth to the twenty-first century" , authored by Rudolph Peters.[124] I was critical of the book because I believe it misinforms, reflects white superiority and is very offensive to Muslims. The following is the book review I submitted:

"Crime and punishment in Islamic law" by Rudolph Peters falls under the category of Islamophobic publications that feed the religious intolerance propaganda machine. The author in chapter two touches upon some aspects, but did not provide a sufficient summary, of substantive and procedural Islamic criminal law in less than 62 pages. Chapter three briefly offers an overview of criminal law procedures during the Ottoman Empire. In chapter four, the author gives some examples of abolition of Islamic law in a number of states due to colonial regimes. In chapter five the author provides some examples of applied Islamic law in a number of countries including Saudi Arabia, Iran, and Sudan.

The shortcomings of the book can be divided into two broad categories: a) confusing the reader by unjustifiably labelling some ill practices of Muslim States' governments as Islamic, (a feature commonly associated with bias against Islamic law), and b) inadequate and erroneous descriptions of Islamic law. In an example of deliberate confusion, the author on page 9, relying upon al-Mawardi's description of the then current practices in the eleventh century in a Muslim state, emphasized that beating an accused during interrogation as a way of physical pressure is allowed. Similarly, on

---

[124] The book was published by Cambridge University Press (2005), *Themes in Islamic Law Series*.

page 10, the author concluded that "simple suspicion was sufficient for establishing guilt". Undeniably, such practices are never Islamic by the virtue of the *Qur'an* and *Sunnah*; nevertheless, the author portrayed the ill treatment of an accused as the model of Islamic law application. The author should be aware of the *Hadith*: *Hudud* punishments should be averted by the slightest doubts or ambiguities. In other words, the burden of proof is that: guilt must be established beyond *all* doubt. This is higher standard of proof than the common law standard of beyond reasonable doubt.

The erroneous description of Islamic law is exemplified in countless instances in the book. The author on page 6 incorrectly concludes that jurists attempt to assign a hierarchy of authority within one school of Islamic jurisprudence, to manage the diversity of opinions. To be sure, no scholar could or should do so. The weight of a scholar's opinion has always been measured by the entire Islamic nation that credits or disagrees with a legal opinion according to a number of factors including, the known knowledge of a *scholar*, his piety and the foundation of such an opinion. The Prophet Mohammed customarily approved each scholarly opinion that reached various conclusions, if it was based on different understanding. If this is the case, scholars have no authority, whatsoever, to rank legal opinions. Again on pages 39-40, he mangles the concept of compensatory damages (*diya*), which is closely tied to the victim's capability of earning money, awarded to the victim's family in case of homicide, with the application of the capital punishment in an attempt to label Islamic law as an unfair and primitive law. He states

> *"the yardstick for determining equivalence is a person's status, to which a monetary value is attached. This status, as we shall*

see is determined by sex, religion, and by whether a person is a slave or free. The principle of equivalence prescribes that a person may not be sentenced to death for killing a person of lower monetary value".

Accordingly, a man cannot be killed for killing a woman or a child. In fact, the explicit meaning of a number of *Hadith* and its application refute the author allegations.

Although on page 7, the author classifies both theft and unlawful sexual intercourse as *Hudud* offenses with mandatory fixed punishments, on pages 55 and 59 he describes them as torts not as crimes. Without a doubt, both theft and Zina (unlawful sexual intercourse) are *Hudud* offenses.

Interestingly, the author in his conclusion draws an inappropriate analogy between Islamic law and Western Europe in the Middle Ages that shows a lack of understanding of Islamic law and European criminal law. For instance, on page 186 he states that homicide prosecution is private "to the extent that prosecution depends entirely on the will of the victim or his heirs". He further stated that a similar system was adopted in Western Europe in the Middle-Ages "where the state was absent or weak and the accepted reaction to manslaughter was revenge on the killer's tribe, taken by the next of kin". First, in medieval Europe, next of kin's power to prosecute was not granted as a right exclusive to the next of kin, rather it was a rule of evidence that was created when Europeans were primitive societies struggling with ignorance. This paragraph extracted from a medieval manuscript would explain that: "there are two kinds of homicide, the first is called murder …no one is allowed to make an accusation of this kind unless he is a blood relative of the deceased, and within this limit of proof of the accusation is awarded to him … there is another kind of homicide is called simple homicide. In this no one is allowed to prove an accusation unless he is a blood relative of the deceased or bound to him by homage or lordship, and can speak about the death from what he has seen himself" obviously, there is no match in the author's analogy. Therefore, the only possible reason for this analogy, and many others in the book, is to stigmatize Islamic law by comparing it to primitive laws.

Finally, the motive of the author to deliberately confuse the issues and misstate Islamic law is manifest in many parts in the book. On pages 103-4, the author attempts to justify religious intolerance and ignorance of Islamic law by the imperialistic powers of the nineteenth century. Among other reasons he stated to justify abolishing Islamic law by imperialistic powers was that the law must be enforced impartially, without regard to persons. All subjects should be treated with equal footing before the law. To be sure, when the Europeans arrived in the colonies, they gave themselves preferred treatment in the courts in the sense that they were literally above the law. The establishment of so-called mixed courts in Egypt where the Europeans received preferred treatment is an example. Ultimately, the author's statement is self-revealing, echoing the imperialistic mentality that degrades the native laws of the land, such as Islamic law, and elevates their own laws which represent their culture.

Unsurprisingly, the Islamic studies journal that invited me to write a review refused to publish my review.

Example two: The typical process of publishing a book involves sending the proposed manuscript to at least two reviewers. If only one reviewer is a critical of the book, the publisher will refuse publication. In the current state of affairs, if a book proposal shows a positive view on Islam, most likely it will not be published because most reviewers, who are academic faculty, bluntly hate Islam. For instance, I have written a manuscript showing the proper model of the Islamic state to differentiate between the Islamic state in theory and the contemporary models of Muslim-majority states. When submitted to publishers, many reviewers, the *de facto* decision makers, did not like showing a positive view of Islam. Indeed, when it comes to Islam, the reviewers' biases are so obvious. A reviewer criticized my manuscript stating that the author[myself] "takes for granted the argument that Islam is a *perfect* religion". So I forwarded these questions to the publishers as a part of my response with no response from the publisher: Is it unusual or unexpected that a Muslim would view his religion positively? Is a book that does not criticise Islam worthy of publication? The reviewer continues his line of thought concluding that "Even there are no citations from the Islamic scholars and philosophers who criticized Islam such as Zakaria al Razi who died in 925 A.D or Ibn al-Rawandi." I responded to the publisher contending that the topic of my book does not seek to address authors who criticise Islam. The book is about the proper model for the Islamic state. Also the work of Ibn al-Rawandi that the reviewer suggested I should discuss has not survived. I am aware that there is a book on the market which is purported to be authored by Ibn al-Rawandi but this book cannot be authentic. All that scholars of Islam have received are some hearsay statements about Ibn al-Rawandi. The reviewer stated "There are clear verses in *Qur'an* that encourage violence and killing of *qafirs* and *mushriqeen* (non-Muslims) (Qu'ran,9:5) but the author then ignores these verses as it does not fit with his view about Islam." Any true scholar of Islam knows that this verse never justifies violence against non-Muslims. Rather, it permits Muslims to fight back in case of aggression against them. Without this verse, Muslims would not have the right of self-defense. In any event, this verse was not discussed because it is outside the topic of my book but the reviewer criticizes me for not mentioning it because, clearly, he was unhappy with my positive views of Islam. The reviewer criticizes my manuscript because "He[myself] clearly hates Ataturk and his revolutions in Turkey." Is this a valid reviewer comment? Does the reviewer not believe in free speech and that I can criticize any political leader? Does my criticism of a political leader render my manuscript less worthy? The reviewer ultimately concluded that I have to publish my manuscript with an Islamic publisher seemingly suggesting that Muslims' thoughts should be confined between Muslims! It is difficult to see any validity to the reviewer's comments and certainly no constructive reasonable criticism can be garnered from his review. But journal editors and book reviewers control publications and accordingly shape Western consciousness towards Islam. Islam is a hot political issue. There are two schools of competing thought nowadays. One is driven by Islamophobia and will undermine any book that shows the positive side of Islam, a religion of 1.9 billion persons. The other, minority view of Islam attempts to show that Islam can live in harmony and peace with the rest of world. The minority view is normally suppressed in the U.S., Canadian and European academia. Islamophobic academics' lack of satisfaction with substantive Islamic law is multi-faceted. It stems from the notion that Western law represents modernity, civility and righteousness. Non-compliance with Western law systematically engenders criticism and demonization.[125] Secondly, the reader is confused by the unjustifiable labeling of some ill practices of Muslim States'

---

[125] Wael A.B. Hallaq "Can the Shari'a be restored?", in Yvonne Y. Haddad and Barbara F. Stowasser (ed.), *Islamic Law and the Challenges of Modernity* (AltaMira Press, 2004) 2004), 22.

governments as Islamic.[126] Finally, inadequate and erroneous descriptions of Islamic law abound.[127]

The dominant Islamophobic or anti-Islam speech carries serious consequences. The influence of the negative views of Islam on political decision-making is sometimes apparent and sometimes can be inferred from the circumstances. Muslims' fear that Western politicians are prisoners of their ignorance of Muslims as the "other" is real. The fear is that Western politicians' decisions, regarding Muslims who reside in the Western world or in Muslim-majority states, are crippled by ingrained biases against the "other", the Muslim, who is different in color, religion, and culture. So long as the "other" does not comply with so-called Western norms, they shall be treated differently. It cannot be over-emphasized that such an attitude is very destructive to Muslims and to Western national interests alike because the decision-making process is undermined by erroneous facts.

For example, in his book *Inside Sudan*, Donald Petterson, former US ambassador to Sudan, Somalia, and Tanzania, asserted that the US suspended aid to Sudan when the former Sudanese President An-Nimeiry became more dictatorial after he became a "born-again Muslim."[128] To be sure, "born-again Muslim" has no meaning; "born again" is a Christian concept. Petterson likely meant that An-Nimeiry became a more devout Muslim. If so, why would Petterson associate Islam with dictatorship? Why would Petterson utilize a Christian

---

[126] Rudolph Peters, *Crime and punishment in Islamic law* (Themes in Islamic Law Series), (Cambridge University Press 2005).

[127] Id.

[128] Don Petterson, Inside Sudan: Political Islam, Conflict, And Catastrophe, (Westview Press 2003), 12.

derived term such as "born-again Muslim" to justify branding a regime as dictatorialship? The answer might be that any deviation from a Western religion is considered wrong and triggers a negative response. Also, the answer might be that a strong association with Islam parallels an association with terrorism and thereby justifies punishment.

While the An-Nimeiry regime was never virtuous, the regime's later inclination towards Islamic movements did not automatically make it evil. Donald Petterson's view is only one example of how decision-makers think and demonstrates the mentality of those who make serious decisions. Furthermore, it illustrates how think tanks and ambassadors prejudicially frame vital information before sending it to Washington D.C.

Indeed, it seems that bias towards Islam is deep-seated and shapes Western states' policies. Petterson emphasized that one of the significant factors that shaped US policy in the late 1990s was that American Christians believed that the Sudanese government engaged in Islamic jihad (or holy war) against the southern Sudanese Christians.[129] Former US President George W. Bush's core constituents, who were religious Christians, demanded harsher sanctions on Sudan. The unmistakable message conveyed to the Muslim world was that US Christians not only care about other Christians but also have the power to shape secular US policies in the Muslim world.

Moreover, some Christian missionaries have caused serious political instability within Muslim-majority states through various means, including by directly influencing politicians, promoting

---

[129] Id at 16.

hatred against Islam, and inciting violence. For example, Reverend Michael Howard, who founded bible colleges in southern Sudan and Malawi, describes his views of Islam as follows:

> *It is the aim of Muslims to overturn Africa and rename it the Islamic continent. Once having achieved this objective, they will commandeer all the rich resources of the continent together with her unassailable strategic position; Africa is to become the launching pad for international Jihad and in particular, the destruction of the great Satan, America... International Islam is international terrorism... Islam is going into the entire world to breach their hearsay.* [130]

Missionaries admit their goals openly and show their pride in achieving it. Reverend Howard further concedes that

> *...one day the entire world would say thank you to the nation of New Sudan for making them aware of the evils of Islam... History teaches that the best form of defense is to attack. It is the time for the Christians to start going on the offensive... It is time for Christians in the West to literally bombard their prospective media and MPs and congressional representatives with the truth and ensure they are doing something about it.* [131]

In the course of achieving these missionary goals, Reverend Howard did not object to the violation of fundamental human rights. He approved of extrajudicial killing by firing squad for the mere accusation of a crime such as theft. [132]

Repeatedly, hatred of Islam or Islamophobia has become mainstream political speech. Numerous politicians use the tone of

---

[130] Michael Howard, *To Save a Nation: The Battle to Stop Islam in Sudan,* (Out of Africa publishers 2004), 90-91.

[131] Id at 289.

[132] Id at 178.

religious intolerance towards Muslims in their speeches as this resonates with their followers. For example, in response to the 2016 terrorist attack in Brussels committed by Muslims, the front-running United States' Republican presidential candidate, Ted Cruz, now a US senator, concluded: "We need to empower law enforcement to patrol and secure Muslim neighborhoods before they become radicalized."[133] Thus, in Cruz's view commission of a crime by a few justifies "sequestering" an entire group. Similarly, the former US President, Donald Trump, during the presidential campaign in 2016, called for a ban on Muslims entering the United States and then attempted to enforce it through executive order as president.[134] He claimed that Islam hates America.[135] Likewise, former Canadian Prime Minister Stephen Harper declared his worst fear in these terms: "Islamism is the biggest threat to Canada."[136] When German Chancellor Angela Merkel addressed a congress of conservative Christian Democrats , Germany's current ruling party, with respect to Muslims as a religious minority, she concluded that "mosque cupolas" should not be higher than "church steeples". When the Swiss People's Party (SVP), Switzerland largest party, introduced a referendum on banning the building of minarets "mosque cupolas" in Switzerland because minarets are a sign of "Islamization", the referendum passed with a clear majority of 57.5 percent of voters. Giorgio Ghiringhelli, a right-wing activist who successfully

---

[133] http://www.bbc.com/news/election-us-2016-35867967. Retrieved on March 30, 2016.

[134] http://www.bbc.com/news/uk-politics-35037553. Retrieved on March 30, 2016.

[135] http://www.washingtontimes.com/news/2016/mar/10/donald-trump-doubles-down-islam-hates-america-clai/. Retrieved on March 30, 2016.

[136] http://www.cbc.ca/news/politics/harper-says-islamicism-biggest-threat-to-canada-1.1048280. Retrieved on March 30, 2016.

campaigned to ban burqas in Switzerland is now calling on authorities to outlaw Muslims from praying in public.[137] He warns of the "danger of the Islamization of our Western society" and that Muslim prayers are "anything but innocent".[138] Most recently French President Emmanuel Macron made it clear that his biases do not target some Muslims practices or even Muslims in general but is aimed at Islam as a religion itself. He stated that "Islam is a religion that is in crisis all over the world today, we are not just seeing this in our country,".[139] Macron's statement is not a mishap in France, rather it reflects a pattern of behavior that does not tolerate the "other" dissimilarities. A Court of Nanterre ordered a halal supermarket in Paris to close because it did not sell pork or wine. The Court ruled that the supermarket's license is as a "general food store". Refusal to sell pork or wine is inconsistent with being a "general food store".[140] Interestingly enough, there is no obligation upon "general food stores" to carry specialty religious or ethnic food. For example, there is no obligation to carry Halal, Kosher or vegan food, while it is mandatory to carry the typical French food such as wine and pork.

It is difficult to escape the conclusion that these politicians utilize fear of the other, in this case, fear of Muslims, to garner votes.[141] These

---

[137] https://www.independent.co.uk/news/world/europe/switzerland-muslim-prayer-ban-burqa-public-islam-religion-a8780896.html.

[138] Id.

[139] https://www.trtworld.com/magazine/what-explains-macron-s-obsession-with-islam-and-muslims-40297.   Retrieved on October 12, 2020.

[140] https://www.independent.co.uk/news/world/europe/paris-halal-supermakret-france-closed-not-sell-pork-wine-alcohol-islam-muslim-religion-good-price-colombes-a8092316.html. Retrieved on October 12, 2020.

[141] http://national.deseretnews.com/article/6455/canadian-prime-minister-uses-anti-muslim-comments-to-garner-votes.html. Retrieved on March 30, 2016. [LR Please use academic references to bolster this claim]

Islamophobic statements were well received by a considerable segment of the population as the election results indicate. The hostile language towards Muslims coincided with terrorist attacks *by* some Muslims as well as attacks *on* Muslims in the Western states.[142]

The media in Western states has inflamed pre-existing religious tensions between Muslims and the Christian West. When a terrorist act is committed by Muslims, the media employs the language of "Islamic terrorism," "Islamic terror," "radical Islam," "Islamic extremism" and the like. On the contrary, when a terrorist organization, such as Ku Klux Klan, which insists that it is a "Christian organization" aimed to protect Christians from others, commits violence, it is hardly reported in the media as "Christian terrorism." Similarly, when a Christian pastor, claiming to be a "Prophet of God" while attempting to use his gun, was shot at the US Capitol in March 2016, the media described only a "gunman at the U.S. Capitol." No suggestion was made by the media, in Western states or Muslim-majority states, that the gunman's act constituted "Christian terrorism."[143] Likewise, when Buddhist monks in Myanmar committed religious cleansing and killed at least tens of thousands of Muslims, the Western media rarely, if at all, used the

---

[142] For example, see Council on American-Islamic Relations Reports Unprecedented Backlash against American Muslims after Paris Attacks https://www.cair.com/press-center/press-releases/13277-cair-reports-unprecedented-backlash-against-american-muslims-after-paris-attacks.html. Retrieved March 31, 2016.

[143] See editorial "Alleged Capitol gunman charged in shooting incident" the Washington post, March 26, 2016. https://www.washingtonpost.com/local/public-safety/gunshots-reported-at-us-capitol-complex/2016/03/28/f1b961ba-f515-11e5-8b23-538270a1ca31_story.html?utm_term=.0f5e7d073499. Retrieved on November 7, 2018.

terminology "Buddhist terrorism."[144] And again, when tens of thousands of Muslims were killed, tortured and burned alive by Christians in the Central African Republic, Western media labeled the criminal groups as "Christian militias" not "Christian terrorists" as if the label terrorism is exclusively utilized to demonize Islam and Muslims only.[145]

A final example: Radovan Karadzic, a war criminal found guilty of genocide for the 1995 Srebrenica massacre and sentenced to 40 years in prison for his crimes, described his acts of systematically slaughtering Muslims and blowing up mosques as "just and holy" according to his Christian beliefs. The media utilized various words to report his actions, but the language of "Christian terrorism" or "white terrorism" was not among them. These examples of biased media reporting serve not only to shape the views of citizens of Western states towards Muslims and incite violence against Muslims in the West, but also distress Muslims worldwide.[146] Samuel Huntington's 1991 clash of civilizations prophecy is given credibility and, as a result, extremists groups, such as the Islamic State of Iraq and al-Sham "ISIS" and al-Qaeda, gain more recruits.

3.3 Muslim Fear

Very little attention is paid to the Muslim views of the non-Islamic world. From a Muslim standpoint, the worldviews are not that of one

[144] http://www.bbc.com/news/magazine-32929855. Retrieved on March 31, 2016.

[145] https://www.washingtonpost.com/world/africa/tens-of-thousands-of-muslims-flee-christian-militias-in-central-african-republic/2014/02/07/5a1adbb2-9032-11e3-84e1-27626c5ef5fb_story.html. Retrieved on March 31, 2016.

[146] Anya Cordell, Hate speech against Muslims incites violence, Washington post, October 3, 2011.

state or civilization. Rather, worldviews are shaped by numerous opinions and various observations of dubious facts as understood by different states, religions, groups, ideologies and socioeconomic markers. No one can or should claim to possess the ultimate truth in all matters. Truth is in the eye of the beholder. When addressing an issue concerning one group, it is indispensable to consider the views of that group. Therefore, when addressing issues related to Muslims, it is imperative to consider their opinions. Muslims believe that Islam delivers an independent ideology from the all other cultures, religions and social norms in the world. Islamic concepts are not dependent on other's views or desires. This ideological independence is often referred to in the prophetic Hadith: Islam prevails, and nothing supersedes Islam.[147] While such an approach may not be ideal for many who perceive Islam as competition to their religion or as a threat to their political or ideological agenda, it is a fact in the eyes of Muslims.

Muslim's fear of the West is real and can be understood in the context of historical and contemporary perspectives. Apart from Muslims' general admiration of Western technological advancements, Muslims view the history of their relationship with the "Christian West" hostilely. Purportedly carried out "to save the holy land [Jerusalem] from the infidels" (Muslims and Jews), the Crusades, in which millions of Muslims and Jews were killed, remains vivid in Muslims' collective consciousness. The brutal Spanish inquisition trials provide another example of the European cleansing of Muslims and Jews. Most recently, the Iraq War serves as a testimony to the deadly West's assault on Muslims, in which hundreds of thousands fell victim to an unjustified invasion. Currently, Muslims recognize

---

[147] The hadith is listed in Al-Bayhaqi, Al-Sunan al-Kubra.

unmistakable hatred toward Islam voiced by some world leaders as a sign of future conflict between West and Muslim-majority states. The highest authority in Sunni Islamic thought, The Grand *Imam* of al-Azhar, Sheikh Ahmed el-Tayeb expressed his resentment toward French President Macron's statement that "Islam is in crisis all over the world today" by saying:

> At a time when we seek to promote the values of citizenship and coexistence with the sages of the West, irresponsible statements are made, which take the attack on Islam as a cover to achieve pathetic political gains. This non-civilized behavior against religions establishes a culture of hatred and racism and breeds terrorism.[148]

The history of the West's conflicts with other civilizations magnifies Muslims' fear that Western states may do whatever it takes to achieve their goals irrespective of its merits. Tens of millions, mostly civilians, were killed in World War II. The United States targeted civilians when using atomic bombs to force Japan to surrender. Many Muslims believe that the West has built its civilization by stealing less developed states' natural resources, enslaving people or simply annihilating them. The former colonial powers, including France, the United Kingdom, the Netherlands, and Spain, absorbed the wealth of the colonies to augment their own. Natives of the Americas, Australia, and New Zealand were almost annihilated in order to expand the West's civilization.

Having conveyed Muslims' fears, Muslims are aware that Muslim-majority states' history is not totally virtuous. They are aware that numerous past and current regimes in Muslims majority states have

---

[148] https://mugtama.com/hot-files/item/112405-2020-10-05-12-04-56.html. Retrieved on October 12, 2020.

committed atrocious acts. They appreciate several Western values and do not blame the West entirely for their current unfortunate state of affairs in many places in the world. Truly, Muslims are aware that they bear their fair share of blame. However, Muslims believe that it is unfair to generalize wrongdoing, demonize Islam and attribute liability to Muslims worldwide.

3.4   Calls to "Reform" Islamic Law

When negative propaganda towards Islam stirs negative feelings and becomes the chief factor in political decision-making, one outcome is logical: Reform Islam. Islamophobic individuals cannot erase a religion with 1.9 billion followers but they may try to "reform" it, to erase Islamic identity to suit their agenda. The new breed of so-called "reform" scholars strive to spread *new* Islamic law and import jurisprudential doctrines that are at odds with the Islamic jurisprudence matrix. "Reformers" criticize the early Islamic jurisprudence that was elaborated by exceptional scholars and instead suggest that the new jurisprudence not be bound by the recognized rules of interpretation. Certainly, some Islamic scholarship is limited to a particular time and place and accordingly should be revisited to examine its applicability to our time. Yet, the aim of the "reformers" is not to revisit nonoperational Islamic jurisprudence rules due to irrelevancy to time and place; rather they either call for wholesale rejection of traditional jurisprudence in favor of new, "reformed" Islamic law that serves political, religious and economic goals that do not necessarily coincide with Islamic ones or they undo Islamic jurisprudence rules gradually without any recognizable Islamic limitation.[149]

To be sure the attempt to "reform" Islamic law is not new. In fact, it has deep roots, especially in academia. Many years ago, Ali Abdul Razik, a *Sharia* Court judge, drafted a "reformers" methodology blueprint in his book, *Al-Islam wa-usul Al-hukm* (Islam and the sources of political authority).[150] In his book, Ali Abdul Razik challenged the legitimacy of some matters that are considered by the vast majority of scholars and the Muslim public to be both fundamental and indisputable. He denied the existence of the *Caliphate* as an Islamic political institution, contending that those scholars who demanded the *Caliphate* never advanced any support to their claim from the *Qur'an*.[151] He also suggested that although the *Caliphate* was intended to be conferred by free election, history showed that the Islamic State government was established only by force, not a free election.[152] He contended that the first *Caliph*, Abu Bakr, was a king that took power by force and many close followers of the Prophet Muhammad had refused to elect Abu Bakr.[153] He concluded that the state established by the Prophet Muhammad had

---

[149] For example, see Abdullahi Ahmed An-Na'im, Toward an Islamic Reformation: Civil Liberties, Human Rights, and International Law, (Syracuse University Press 1996).

[150] Ali Abdul Razik, *Al-Islam Wa-Usul al-Hukm* (Cairo, Mat'ba Misr 1925), Recent translation of the book is "Islam and the Foundations of Political Power", Abdou Filali-Ansary (ed.), Maryam Loutfi (Trans.) (Edinburgh University Press 2012).

[151] Ali Abdul Razik, *Al-Islam Wa-Usul al-Hukm* (Cairo, Mat'ba Misr 1925), 22.

[152] Id at,35-37.

[153] Id at, 109-115.

nothing to do with Islam.[154] Instead; it was a necessity, for the sake of spreading the message of Islam.[155] He presented the following rationales: If the Prophet Muhammad had established a real functional Islamic state, then why did he not establish pillars of the state including branches of the government, i.e., appointing judges and provincial governors? Nor did the Prophet Muhammad explain the doctrine of *Shura* (consultation).[156] Accordingly, Ali Abdul Razik asserted, the Prophet Muhammad's message of Islam had nothing to do with forming an Islamic state.[157] Most interestingly, he denied the Islamic duty to establish an Islamic judiciary (*Sharia* courts) and Islamic law of transactions maintaining that the State and Islam must keep separate.[158] Remarkably, this proposition called for the elimination of Ali Abdul Razik 's post as *Sharia* Court judge.

To support his theory, he listed some verses from the *Qur'an* that he claimed ruled out the possibility of the Prophet Muhammad becoming the political head of state including:

> And We have not made you a watcher over them nor are you a Wakil (disposer of affairs, guardian, trustee) over them.[159]   &
>
> Your Lord knows you best; if He wills, He will have mercy on you, or if He wills, He will punish you. And We have not sent you (O Muhammad) as a guardian over them.[160]

Ali Abdul Razik's thesis triggered a storm of criticism, not only for its substance, but also because one of Egypt's intellectual elites had

---

[154] Id at, 68.
[155] Id at, 81.
[156] Id at, 70.
[157] Id at, 90-93.
[158] Id at, 121.
[159] Qur'an 6:107.
[160] Qur'an 17:54.

produced such unorthodox opinions. Ali Abdul Razik was not an average uneducated person. He was an appointed *Sharia* court judge in Al Mansoura, Egypt belonging to one of the wealthiest and most politically influential families in Egypt. He was a graduate of Al-Azhar, a prestigious Islamic university, and had received the official rank of a scholar. What Ali Abdul Razik proposed was appalling to the Al-Azhar community of scholars as no scholar of Al –Azhar had ever before endorsed such controversial opinions. The scholar's council of Al-Azhar University held a hearing to question him about the claims stated in the book. Ali Abdul Razik failed to defend his book. The council stripped him of his official rank as an Al-Azhar scholar terminating his association with Al-Azhar. Accordingly, Ali Abdul Razik's views shall not be considered representative of Al-Azhar's views. The renowned scholar Muhammad Rashid Rida described Ali Abdul Razik's opinions in Al-Manar Magazine as misleading and an echo of the imperialists' and enemies of Islam propaganda.

A brief analysis of this book easily explains why his opinions angered Islamic scholars. Firstly, Ali Abdul Razik attempts to rewrite history to promote his ideology. Ali Abdul Razik concluded that the first *Caliph*, Abu Bakr, took power by force and that many close followers of the Prophet Muhammad refused to elect him. This claim is utterly contrary to recorded history as Sunni Muslims know it. After the death of the Prophet Mohammed, the Prophet's companions held a meeting to elect a leader, and Abu Bakr was elected. Admittedly, in the initial process of the election, some people may not have voted for him. However, once Abu Bakr was elected, other contenders conceded to him. No use of force, whatsoever, took place in Abu Bakr's election. Furthermore, Ali Abdul Razik submitted that Prophet

Muhammad abstained from establishing the pillars of an Islamic state, such as the appointment of judges and provinces governors, and did not explain the doctrine of *Shura* (consultation). Again, Ali Abdul Razik attempted to re-write history. It is a well-known historical fact that the Prophet Muhammad appointed governors and judges as needed. For instance, he appointed Muaz Ibn Jabal as governor of Yemen. The Prophet Muhammad not only explained the Islamic doctrine of the executive branch of the government consultation before decision making but also practiced it. On numerous occasions related to Muslims affairs, the Prophet Muhammad convened his consultation council which was comprised of up to seventy members. Secondly, Ali Abdul Razik engaged in an erroneous interpretation of the *Qur'an* to promote his ideologies. He concluded that the verses (6:107) & (17:54), stated above, show that Prophet Muhammad's divine authorization is limited to teaching and the promotion of Islam and does not extend to establishing an Islamic state. In fact, the vast majority of Islamic scholars agree that those verses only affirm the doctrine of freedom of religion in Islam. These verses direct the Prophet Muhammad not to interfere with the non-believers' faith because the divine did not send him as a guardian over non-believers' actions in matters of belief. Finally, Ali Abdul Razik's denial of the Islamic duty to establish an Islamic judiciary (*sharia* courts) is puzzling given that he never relinquished his post as *Sharia's* court judge.

Ali's methodology is indeed the blueprint for contemporary "reformers": rewriting history, making an odd interpretation of Islamic texts that is neither acceptable to the vast majority of Muslims nor representative of what Muslims know about their religion.[161] Such interpretations of the *Qur'an* and Hadith either attempt to manipulate the ordinary meaning of words or take words out of context to achieve whatever they intend to prove.[162]

Nevertheless, Ali Abdul Razik's methodology of interpretation is, indeed, celebrated and promoted in most Western intellectual societies especially within academia. Islamic scholars in Western countries are branded according to their attitude towards Islam as a religion notwithstanding the quality, objectivity or originality of their work. The label "Islamist" is sufficient to negatively impact potential academic appointment or trigger a negative review of a book or a scholarly article. Classification and labeling of Islamic law scholars have become the benchmark for faculty hiring and have a broad impact on the content taught in universities that teach Islamic studies. This in turn shapes Western states' governmental and non-governmental policies so that certain favored materials are presented, and particular government policies are promoted. Criticizing Islamic law and promoting its "reform" has become the ticket to academic success as a Muslim Ph.D. student concedes:

> In American neo-Orientalism, the Orient can speak only when it has set out to upbraid itself and praise the west.[163]

The unspoken branding of Islamic scholars has now become mainstream. For example, Niaz Shah classifies Islamic scholars as

---

[161] For example, Ali Abdul Razik's interpretation of Qur'an verses 6:107 & 17:54 discussed earlier.

[162] Id.

[163] Purdue University, Purdue e-Pubs Open Access Dissertations Theses and Dissertations January 2015 Invisible Humans, Visible Terrorists: U.S. Neo-Orientalism Post 9/11 and Representations of the Muslim World Khalid Mosleh Alrasheed.

secular, non-compatible, reconciliatory and "proposed interpretive approach."[164] Apart from the eccentric secular approach to Islamic law interpretation, Shah claims that the non-compatible approach is supported by Muslim-majority states' governments and conservative secularists who emphasize the independence of Islamic law from other legal systems including the Western legal system. The reconciliatory approach suggests that Islamic law is compatible with the dominant "international standards" and that any Islamic incompatibility can be subject to reform to comply with "international standards." The interpretative approach suggests that Islamic law can be subject to re-interpretation in the light of the *Qur'an.*

To be sure, branding is not a healthy academic phenomenon. Ideas should be discussed, explained, criticized, refuted or developed. But branding authors and thereby casting out their ideas without appropriate refutation is simply a sign of academic weakness.

An example of ideas that can be discussed is the issue of compatibility of Islamic law with the "international standards" as raised by Niaz Shah. For Muslims, the issue of compatibility with "international standards" is not a question when interpreting Islam. As noted earlier, Muslims believe that their religion supersedes any other standard. Above and beyond all other consideration, the critical question arises: Given that Muslims are 1.9 billion within 57 Muslim majority nations in addition to Muslim minorities in non-Muslim States and given that their religious beliefs are reflected in Islamic law, if Islamic law is not part of the "international standard" then what is the "international standard"? Are international standards only

---

[164] Niaz A. Shah. "Women's Human Rights in the Koran: An Interpretive Approach", 28 *Hum. Rts. Q.* 868-903. (2006)

Western states standards? "International standards" that ignore the beliefs of Muslims who compromise of at least 20% of the world's population are not only unfair but also offensive to Muslims.

Even as minorities, shouldn't Muslims be able to enjoy their sovereignty by practicing their religion and applying their laws? Political doctrines such as "if you are not with me, you are against me" or "I and I alone is the criteria for right and wrong" are counterproductive. In the international arena, it shows utter contempt towards the international law principle of mutual respect and cooperation between Muslim and Non-Muslim States.

To be sure, Shah's and other's classification of Islamic law scholars has minimal if any impact, though it can serve to trigger discussions between Muslims. To speak of "reform" or *Tajdid*, as Muslims phrase it, one ought to consider the autonomy of Muslims as humans appreciate the number of Muslims worldwide and disfavor West/white superiority culture. Opinions of black African, Arab or Asian are not less worthy than American or European opinions.

One must understand Islamic law reform or *Tajdid* from a Muslim perspective to initiate a dialogue with Muslims and to reach a solution to whatever problems may arise between Muslim and Non-Muslim nations. Contemporary Islamic law scholarship distinguishes three trends of *Tajdid*:

First, there is the narrow constructions approach: the followers of this approach may strictly adopt a particular Madhab, illustrate a school of thought blindly or are literalists. Those who follow a particular Madhab strictly and blindly do not question Madhab methodology or the rationale for any matter in question. If an issue arises, they search in the established Madhab scholarship for an answer. If an answer is not found, they automatically prohibit it. Literalists, on the other hand, focus primarily on the literal interpretation of the *Qur'an* and *Sunnah.* They exclude other sources of Islamic law such as *Usul Al-Fiqh* (Principles of Jurisprudence), the objectives of Islamic law, the effective cause of adjudication or the need to change the *fatwa* (scholarly opinion) because of change of circumstances that had justified issuing that *fatwa.*

Second, there is the overly broad construction approach of interpretation: the followers of this approach sometimes place an interest, notwithstanding its legitimacy, in a preferred position over the prefixed Islamic textual adjudication listed in the *Qur'an* or *Sunnah,* even if there is an apparent conflict between the interest and the Islamic text. Some overly broad constructionists justify the status quo, notwithstanding its injustice or incompatibility with clear Islamic principles. The status quo is justified because it represents popular justice or is preferred by the government. Various labels might be used to justify the wrong. Thus, overly broad constructionists have labeled self-defense against foreign invasion as terrorism, and many "Islamic" scholars have spared no effort in justifying foreign invasion and prohibiting the universally recognized right of self-defense. Surely, overly broad constructionists are preferred in Muslim majority dictatorial regimes, empowering these regimens by providing moral grounds for their actions regardless of its fairness or compatibility with Islamic law.

Third, the intermediary approach: this approach respects and follows the prefixed adjudications enumerated in the *Qur'an* and *Sunnah* while taking into consideration public interest, the objectives of Islamic law and *Usul Al-Fiqh* methodologies and deductions. This approach follows strict guidelines including:

i. *Ijtihad* is permitted only after every effort is made in reviewing primary sources of Islamic law, the *Qur'an* and *Sunnah*, the established Islamic scholarship and utilizing the recognized rules of interpretation.

ii. No *Ijtihad* is needed in prefixed adjudications that are enumerated in the primary sources of Islamic law such as the prohibition of alcohol and usury.

iii. This approach places the proper weight to speculative and determined matters. While many scholars mistakenly claim that various matters are pre-determined and accordingly are not subject to *Ijtihad*, the followers of this approach avoid this mistake by examining the issues thoroughly before making such a claim. For example, they avoid some scholars' erroneous speculation that *Ijma* (consensus) had occurred, thus there is no place for *Ijtihad*, where in fact, *Ijma* has not occurred.

iv. The followers of this approach strike a balanced approach between *hadith* and *Fiqh* such that both are given proper weight in the issue at stake. This balanced approach avoids the common mistake among many scholars who favor either *hadith* or *Fiqh* at the expense of the other.

v. Given that *Ijtihad* is based upon both knowledge of Islamic law and knowledge of the concurrent circumstances, the follower of this approach deals with the concurrent circumstances fairly and objectively. He neither gives up Islamic fundamentals under political or social pressures nor does he reject new ideas just because they are new, especially if they are beneficial for the nation. The followers of this approach also realize that new scientific, social and economic development necessitates new corresponding *Fiqh* to deal with the new issues. *Fiqh* should be understood as a dynamic science that is subject to change when the circumstances require.

Remarkably, many scholarly followers of this approach have been unified of late in an attempt to move forward to a collective *Ijtihad* and establish an international union for Muslim scholars. While this union has had a positive impact on Islamic scholarship clustering numerous renowned Islamic scholars and eroding *fatwa* confusion, it has been subject to much criticism by some Muslim Majority State governments because of its bold opinions on contemporary political practices in Muslim-majority states.

These are categories of meaningful reform/*Ijtihad* under Islamic law's recognized principles. Calls for Islamic law reform by utilizing Western templates and values not only lack an Islamically recognized basis but is also offensive to Muslims.

3.5   An Overwhelming Sentiment of Hostility Toward Islam

Apart from Western political praise for distrustful calls for Islamic law reform explained earlier, many Muslims have very negative views of Western politics towards Islamic majority states. The role of the United Kingdom and France in the creation of nation-states, as opposed to one unified Islamic state, in the Middle East is well-known. Many believe that the United Kingdom assisted in the creation of Saudi Arabia at the expense of the collapsing Ottoman Empire, the last unified Islamic state. The Sykes–Picot Agreement in 1916 to divide the Middle Eastern Muslim-majority states into areas of British and French control is not remote history for Muslims. Muslims perceive this agreement as an imperialistic powers agreement to destroy the unity of their nation in order to steal their natural resources and eliminate Ottoman Empire rivalry.

This negative view and fear are ongoing as a product of Western politics. For example, the former Sudanese Prime Minister Sadiq al-Mahdi suggested that the 1989 Sudanese coup was orchestrated by the Americans.[165] He believed that the Americans convinced the Islamic movement to end the democratic process with the help of undercover agents. The Americans, according to Sadiq al-Mahdi, believed that the current structure and leadership of the Islamic movement in Sudan would fail miserably in running state affairs and, as a result, the public would come to dislike the Islamic movements.

Even Western values invoked selectively in Muslim-majority states serve political gains. Issues of Fundamental Human Rights are raised or ignored depending on Western interests or authoritarian governments' interest in Muslim-majority states. For example, colonial France suppressed free speech in Algeria by appointing *Imams* (Islamic preachers) who are aligned with the France. The alternative, which is consistent with the important value of free speech and would bring an undesirable result to France is free election of *Imams* who would likely advocate for independence by every means possible, including violence against the occupying French forces. After independence, consecutive Algerian governments took additional oppressive steps by forcing all *Imams* in Algeria to deliver a governmentally preapproved weekly speech that promoted governmental views. In 1980, Algerian President Bendjedid encouraged the Islamic movement to balance the political spectrum and confront other political movements, such as the socialists and the

---

[165] Sadiq al-Mahdi, "Mustaqbal al-Harakah al-Islāmīyah fī Doo' al-Motgherat al-Akheerah", in *Al-Sudan Bayn Aldeen wa al Siyasa* (Al-Mesbar Publishing 2014).

Berbers. He gave a free rein to *Imams'* speeches for political gain. Due to the presence of the Islamic movement, free speech has increased and became more challenging to the government's absolute authority over political life. In 1982, many Islamically prohibited commercial businesses, such as bars, were subject to violent attacks. It is unknown whether these attacks were a product of a mistaken understanding of Islam, a result of an unwarranted presumption by some individuals unjustifiably giving themselves the right to enforce Islamic public morality, or the covert involvement of the government attempting to suppress Islamic speech. In any case, it was an opportunity for the state to conduct a massive crackdown on *Imams*. Many were detained if their public addresses were not compliant with governmental interests. The outcome was over-reaching: Not only were those statements that incited violence suppressed, but the entire fundamental right of free speech was eliminated. The West, including France, who had taught oppressive regimes how to utilize free speech to achieve political gains showed little or no criticism of this breach of free speech. Here, it is worth noting that I am not defending violent acts, but rather, demonstrating the Muslim view that human rights in Muslim-majority states are criticized by the West only when their interests so require.

Similarly, fundamental Islamic beliefs, such as *jihad* against foreign invaders, are invoked and promoted when the West or Muslim-majority state governments need to achieve a political goal.[166] For example, when the Soviet Union invaded Afghanistan, many Muslim-majority states allowed volunteers to travel to Afghanistan to

---

[166] *Jihad* is the struggle for justice and truth. It could mean a personal struggle to do the right deeds. It could also mean engaging in an equitable war to uphold justice.

liberate it. The West not only expressed full support for this position but also happily supplied arms to those who were engaged in *jihad* against the "evil" Soviet Union.

In contrast, when the American-led coalition invaded Iraq, of course, western states did not employ the concept of *jihad* against themselves. When the *jihadists* fought the invading forces they were branded as Islamic terrorists. Likewise, Muslim-majority states that were close allies, or at least not open enemies of the United States, prohibited volunteers from their countries from joining the Iraqi resistance.

This contradictory position concerning the concept of *jihad* or the invocation of a human right is typical in politics worldwide, achieving particular goals by manipulating facts or turning a blind eye to human rights' violations. But the average Muslim receives an unmistakable message: when it comes to beliefs, values or human rights, do not trust Western powers, oppressive Muslim-majority state media or governments; they are hypocritical and attempt to deceive for ulterior motives. The outcome is nothing short of devastating. Some Muslims may succumb to hate speech against westerners and Muslim-majority states alike. These hate speeches justify all sorts of violent and criminal acts; sowing the seeds of terrorism. The irony here is that when Western states turn a blind eye to human rights violations, such as the oppression of free speech in Muslim-majority states, they are in fact extinguishing the best tool to fight terrorism: knowledgeable Islamic voices that are capable of refuting unjustifiable violence.

CHAPTER 4

Misapplication of Islamic Law

―――――――――― ౨⌒౨⌒ ――――――――――

4.1   Introduction

It is difficult to imagine that misapplying Islamic law in Muslim-
majority states is an accidental or innocent act keeping in mind its
significant harm to Muslims' lives. Authoritarian regimes twist
Islamic law applications to achieve outcomes that serve their own
interest. One can speculate on their various motives, from conceding
to the demands of Western powers that support their regimes, to
weakening political opposition parties that would benefit from the
proper application of Islamic law. In addition, the misapplication of
Islamic law can be a product of absurd, non-Islamic societal customs.
Without a doubt, misapplication of Islamic law not only harms a
Muslim society but also portrays Islam as an unfair religion which, in
turn, invites foreign political powers to intervene and incite the
authoritarian regimes to "reform" Islamic law. For example, when the
Taliban regime in Afghanistan denied women education, which is

contrary to Islamic teachings, not only did this tarnish the image of Islam but it also negatively impacted Afghani society in many ways. The Taliban regime's ill practices, such as denying women education, were presented as one of the justifications for the invasion of Afghanistan.

The misapplication of Islamic law may take place through one or more branches of the government. It may encompass various models. However, I will limit the discussion in this chapter to three models of Islamic law misapplication. Each model represents a branch of the government's **intentional** Islamic law misapplication. These models are: the executive branch's misapplication of Islamic law, exploitation of the judiciary to wrongly apply Islamic law, and finally legislative defiance towards the people's will through misapplication of Islamic law. These models are commonly utilized by authoritarian regimes to advance their agendas. These models are sufficient to demonstrate the root causes, depth and the impact of the issue.

4.2   Executive Branch of The Government Misapplication Of Islamic Law.

Applying Islamic law in Muslim-majority states has always been subject to the political will of the ruling regime. The regimes that misapply Islamic law are either secular or sham Islamic. Each should be discussed distinctly because of the dissimilarities of motives and their supporters.

4.2.1   Secular Leadership Supported by Western Powers Misapply Islamic Law Intentionally and Boldly: The Example of Tunisia

Secular leaders in Muslim-majority states, especially authoritarian regimes, tend to bend Islamic law's mandatory rules to advance their agendas. Intuitively, secular and anti-Islamic forces would support any proposition that minimizes the rule of Islam. This state of affairs generates the notion that there is an organized war against Islam. The following example explains these dynamics.

The law of succession is laid out in detail in *Muhkamat* – decisive-verses in the *Qur'an* that are not subject to interpretation or violation. Yet, the late President of Tunisia, Beji Caid Essebsi, proposed an amendment to the Tunisian law of succession to equate between men and women in inheritance. Such a proposal violates Islamic law wisdom that awards women less, equal or greater shares than men depending upon the circumstances.[167]. Beji Caid Essebsi was one of the political players who in pre-revolution, consecutive secular dictatorship regimes, was famous not only for being secular but also for attempting to restrict Islamic practices.[168] He had served as Minister of Foreign Affairs from 1981 to 1986. After the revolution, he was appointed as interim Prime Minister serving from February 2011 to December 2011. He was widely celebrated by the West especially by France, the former colonizer of Tunisia, who awarded him numerus prestigious French awards as well as an honorary degree

---

[167] The issue of women's inheritance shares shall be explained in the detail in the following chapters.

[168] Gall, Carlotta, "Tunisia's Secular Government Cracks Down on Mosques in Aftermath of Massacre." The New York Times, July 23, 2015.

from the world renowned Paris-Sorbonne University.[169] Plausibly, Beji Caid Essebsi's proposal that violates the Islamic law of succession in a Muslim majority state, can be viewed from a Muslim standpoint as a natural step for him given his association with the former dictatorship and the approval he garnered from non-Islamic Western powers. However, Essebsi's proposal deepened the division between the two ideologies that compete to control Tunisian politics: a large portion of the Tunisian population, represented by the Islamic Ennahdha Party, who publically rejected the proposal, and the secular, sometimes anti-Islamic, ideology that was supported by several Western powers including France. The current French President, Emmanuel Macron publically expressed his pleasure with such a proposal. Let us assume, hypothetically, giving Macron the benefit of the doubt that he truly intends to support what he believes to be praiseworthy equality. The fact that Essebsi's proposal sometimes equates between brothers and sisters in inheritance shares supports this hypothesis. But then again this hypothesis collapses under the weight of cumulative evidence. First, there is evidence of systemic bias against Muslims in France. French secular law that bans all religious attire in public schools and for public servants at their place of work is applied selectively. While the headscarf (*hijab*) is very similar to the Catholic habit, Muslim women are prohibited from wearing headscarves whereas the Catholic habit is welcomed. Second, President Macron, as a head of state ought to know that Islamic inheritance law is not discriminatory given that women in numerous

---

[169] For example, he had received the Grand Cross of the Order of the Legion of Honor in 2018 from France and Knight Grand Cross with Collar of Order of Merit of the Italian Republic in 2017.

inheritance occasions receive equal or greater shares than men with the same degree of affinity.

In October 2020, Macron revealed his hatred to the "other" concluding that "Islam is a religion that is in crisis all over the world". To be sure, when the political players, especially those who openly hate Islam, act in such a manner, it invites public speculation and conspiracy theorists to make conjectures that produce negative effects. The message conveyed to the general Muslim population is a negative one: the West supports any attempt to undermine Islamic tenets. Islam in Muslim-majority states is not only a religion but also a culture, lifestyle, moral standard and identity. As a result, when a Western nation supports a proposal that conflicts with Islam, it is viewed by Muslims as an attempt to erase their Islamic identity. This Muslim view is supported by ancillary factual evidence. In October 2020, French President Macron asserted the French people's right to freedom of expression in publishing caricatures that negatively portrayed the Prophet Muhammed, an act extremely offensive to Muslims. To be sure, freedom of expression claims are invariably applied to the detriment of the most vulnerable in society including Muslims. But groups with significant political or social patronage are always protected. If Macron had made an offensive statement about Judaism, he would be labeled anti-Semitic. If Macron had made an offensive statement about blacks, he would be labeled racist. If Macron had made an offensive statement about the LGBT community, he would be labeled homophobic. But when he made an offensive statement about Muslims and Islam, it is freedom of expression!

The media is also subtly disingenuous in reporting the news. In France, in October 2020, the tensions heightened after the publication of a caricature offensive to Muslims. Four unfortunate criminal events took place; two made by Muslims against non-Muslims and two made by Islamophobics against Muslims. Media coverage and the official response varied depending upon the identity of the victims and the offenders. When the violent offender was a Muslim, President Macron showed anger and spoke of an "Islamist terrorist attack". French and Western media repetitively aired the news of the "Islamist terrorist attack" day and night. On the other hand, when Muslims were the victims of a non-Muslim offender, the media covered the story only briefly and Macron totally ignored the incidents.[170] No reference was made to the religion of those attacking the Muslim victims as being Christian or Catholics. Muslims see this double standard dogma as an organized campaign against Islam and Western leaders who support majority state leaders as agents of such dogma. This is especially true when a Western leader, such as Macron, supports minimizing the role of Islamic law in a Muslim majority state.

4.2.2   Sham Islamic Regimes' Misapplication of Islamic Law

While many Muslim-majority states claim to be Islamic regimes or at least declare Islam as the state's official religion or a source of legislation, they tend to violate Islamic law with impunity. Islamic human rights violations are common within Muslim-majority states. Basic Islamic rights such as the right to human dignity that includes equality and the state's duty to ensure basic human necessities such as food, healthcare and shelter either do not exist or are applied

---

[170] https://www.france24.com/en/live-news/20201022-two-french-women-charged-over-racist-stabbing-of-veiled-muslim-women. Retrieved Oct. 30, 2020.

selectively.[171] For instance, foreign workers in the Persian Gulf region receive un-Islamic treatment. Wages paid to nationals are several times those paid to foreign workers.[172] Nationals are not obliged to work overtime while foreign workers are.[173] Social security benefits are an exclusive right of nationals.[174] Free public education is limited in some Gulf States to nationals even if the non-nationals have lived, paid taxes and contributed to the state for years. Moreover, in some Muslim-majority states, female migrant domestic workers are vulnerable to sexual and physical abuse by their employers.[175] Numerous deaths of domestic workers were investigated under suspicion that they had been killed or died in an attempt to escape inhumane work conditions.

The right of citizenship, as dictated by Islamic law, is a guaranteed right to every Muslim in the Islamic State. Non-Muslims should be treated fairly, with full dignity and are generally equal to Muslims. Muslim-majority states in the Persian Gulf that openly and boldly

---

[171] Islamic law called for equality and human dignity. *See .e.g.* (O mankind! We created you from a single (pair) of a male and a female, and made you into nations and tribes, that ye may know each other (not that ye may despise each other). Verily the most honored of you in the sight of Allah is (he who is) the most righteous of you. And Allah has full Knowledge and is well-acquainted (with all things). Qur'an 49 :13, (O mankind! reverence your Guardian-Lord, who created you from a single Person, created, of like nature, his mate, and from them twain scattered (like seeds) countless men and women) Qur'an 4:1. (We have honored the sons (and daughters) of Adam) Qur'an 17:70.

[172] See U.N. Agency report, International Labor Organization, Tripartite Meeting on Social and Labor Issues Concerning Migrant Workers in the Construction Industry, Geneva 103 (1995).

[173] Id.

[174] Id.

[175] See, Amnesty International's report on North Africa and the Middle-East (2009). http://thereport.amnesty.org/en/regions/middle-east-north-africa.

practice discrimination against foreigners rely on a distorted understanding of nationalism created by the imperialistic powers that had colonized these states in the past as well as by power-thirsty Arabian families who ascended to power in the twentieth century. Nationalism, in this context, is aimed at creating artificial borders dividing one state and repudiating fundamental Islamic human rights including equality rights. History testifies that British and French imperialism divided former colonies including the ailing Ottoman Empire into many States especially in the Middle-East. Those royal families in the Gulf who claimed absolute monarchy, with the help of imperialistic France and Britain, endorsed a false sense of nationalism to establish the sociocultural basis for the new state(s). Many Islamic law rules were deliberately ignored. All-encompassing, Islamic laws of citizenship and Islamic human rights were ignored in order to limit the number of citizens, define the geographical borders, and satisfy the new citizens' ambition for greater wealth especially in oil-rich states. Kuwait, the United Arab Emirates and Saudi Arabian citizens would enjoy the wealth of the oil to the exclusion of other eligible Muslims, who under Islamic citizenship law would have been entitled to share the oil wealth.

Selective application of Islamic law in many Muslim-majority states extends far beyond labor relations. For example, under Islamic law, there are two paths for women to gain divorce without the consent of the husband. First, if the husband harms his wife, she may seek a judicial divorce where she is entitled to full financial rights including alimony and retention of her dowry. Alternatively, a wife may forgo her financial benefits and seek a divorce without the husband's consent, without alleging harm, and without explaining any reason for divorce. In this case, the wife must return her dowry, and she will not receive alimony. This path is known as *Khula'*. Egypt, a Muslim majority state, has always claimed that its Personal Status Law for Muslims is based on Islamic law. For many years, the Egyptian Personal Status Law had omitted the second path for divorce, *Khula'*. Many Muslim Egyptian wives were prisoners of abusive marital relationships, unable to prove harm in courts or trapped in an unworkable relationship.[176] Eventually, in January 2000, the Egyptian Personal Status Law was amended to include *Khula'*.[177]

4.3 Exploiting the Judiciary to Sequester Islamic Law: The Case of Egypt

Authoritarian regimes in Muslim-majority states that fear proper Islamic law application utilize artifices to eliminate Islamic law provisions that pose a threat to the regimes' foundations. The judiciary is typically exploited for that purpose, keeping in mind the judiciary in authoritarian regimes is never independent. Egypt is a good example to explain how authoritarian regimes exploit the judiciary to limit Islamic law.

The modern constitutions of Egypt of 1971, 2012 and 2014 affirm that Islam is the official religion of the state and that the principles of Islamic law are the principal source of legislation. These constitutional directives mandate integration of the principles of

---

[176] *See* Qur'an directions to husbands (And when you have divorced women and they have fulfilled the term of their prescribed period, either take them back on reasonable basis or set them free on reasonable basis. But do not take them back to hurt them, and whoever does that, then he has wronged himself...) Qur'an 2:231.

[177] See Egyptian Law of Personal Status article 20 (2000).

Islamic law into legal, social and political life. However, these consecutive Egyptian constitutions have also expressly indicated that the people of Egypt are sovereign and that they are the source of all power in the state, including legislative power. These constitutional principles seem problematic at first glance because, at least theoretically, there is apparent confusion as to who holds the legislative authority. Who has the final word in legislating, Islam or the people? Is the application of Islamic law subject to the people's approval? Or is the people's sovereignty, the power to make legislation, constrained by Islamic law?

This answer affects not only the ultimate source of power in Egypt but also the social and economic fabric of Egyptian society. The supremacy of Islamic law, if it exists, shall limit government powers to a large extent. For example, Islamic law prohibits taxation except for *zakah* for Muslims and the equivalent *jizya* for non-Muslims, unless scholars of Islam issue a *fatwa* (religious opinion) to permit taxation for the socioeconomic needs of the state.[178] If the government does not follow Islamic law and invokes the broad sovereignty of the people, the parliament may impose taxation irrespective of Islamic restrictions.

Some argue that the recent Egyptian constitutions are clear in their assignation of authority. The constitutions have indicated that the principles of Islamic law are the primary source of legislation; accordingly, any exercise of the people's sovereignty shall be subject to Islamic law. In other words, while people are sovereign and autonomous, their power to create legislation is always limited by Islamic law. This understanding of the constitutional provision is

---

[178] See Imam Al-Dhahabi, Al-Kaba'ir (The Major Sins).

logical given that the Egyptian constitutions have maintained that Islam is the religion of the state and the source of all legislation. Concluding otherwise not only nullifies the express directive of the constitutions but is also absurd and illogical.

Nevertheless, modern Egyptian courts' practices under the recent constitutions shows a tendency to minimize, or totally ignore, Islamic law's role while maximizing people's unlimited sovereignty, irrespective of the constitutional directive mandating Islamic law as the source of legislation. The judicial role in limiting Islamic law application started shortly after the amendment of the Egyptian constitution in 1980 to include a constitutional provision affirming that the principles of Islamic law are the primary source of legislation. In light of this change, the rector of Al-Azhar, the well-reputed Islamic institution in Sunni Islam, challenged the constitutionality of Section 226 of the 1948 Civil Code, which permitted fixed interest on loans (*riba*), a prohibited transaction under Islamic law.[179] Although permitting *riba* is obviously in conflict with Islamic law, the Supreme Constitutional Court of Egypt denied the retroactive application of Section 2 of the constitution, denying the supremacy of Islamic law in this instance. The Court decided, without explanation, that the supremacy of Islamic law is applicable only to prospective legislation. Accordingly, all legislation passed before the enactment of Section 2 of the 1980 constitutional amendment affirming the supremacy of Islamic law remained valid notwithstanding its conflict with Section 2 of the constitution.

---

[179] *Riba* is roughly translated as usury. It is an unjustified increment in business transactions of borrowing, lending or sale of goods. Article 2 of 1980 constitution maintained: "Islam is the religion of the state and Arabic its official language. Islamic law principles are the source of legislation".

In 1996, the Supreme Constitutional Court adopted another approach to prevent Islamic law supremacy over legislations passed after the 1980 constitutional amendment.[180] The Court distinguished between Islamic law rulings that are certain or definitive with respect to their meaning or authenticity and those that are uncertain or speculative, and concluded that its supervisory power is limited to Islamic law rulings that are definitive. Speculative rulings, in meaning or authenticity, are subject to *ijtihad*, scholarly religious opinion, and fall exclusively within the government's power to interpret. This decision unleashed Egyptian legislative and executive branch powers to enact laws or create decrees notwithstanding the supremacy of Islamic law, so long as the issue in question is speculative in meaning or authenticity.

This decision drastically undermined the principle of Islamic law's supremacy. The primary sources of Islamic law are the *Qur'an* and *Sunnah*. All Qur'anic rulings are authentic; however, many rulings are speculative in meaning which provides an avenue for the Court to ignore whatever the Courts' believe to be speculative in meaning, even if it was in fact definitive. Similarly, because many rulings in *Sunnah* are subject to debate concerning their authenticity and/or meaning, the Court may ignore *Sunnah's* rulings alleging that such rulings are speculative. Moreover, in spite of being an unrecognized authority in Islamic law, Egypt's Supreme Constitutional Court gave itself the power to determine the issue of certainty in meaning and authenticity of *Sunnah* and *Qur'an*. As a result, the Court became free to ignore any Islamic law rulings under the guise of uncertainty or speculation in meaning or authenticity. Indeed, the Constitutional Court's self-empowerment to determine

---

[180] Case No. 8 of Judicial Year 17, decided on 18 May 1996.

the authenticity and the meaning of Islamic law texts is problematic. The Constitutional Court judges are not trained to perform this task. Furthermore, a non-Muslim Constitutional Court judge would then be allowed to pass judgements Islamic law matters — an act prohibited under Islamic law.

Such judicial inclination to reject Islamic law when desired by the government creates severe consequences. The successive governments of Egypt were and remain free to pass legislation without significant consideration to the limits imposed by Islamic law. Taxes and other financial burdens are imposed without consideration of Islamic law. Islamic human rights and rules of governance are ignored. Judges in the lower courts who have little to no expertise in Islamic law now can make decisions on Islamic law.

To further muddy the waters, over the past 30 years, an unprecedented number of peculiar *fatwas* have surfaced in Egypt to dispute the meaning of various Islamic law rulings on previously settled issues like *riba*.[181] Some contemporary Islamic law scholars have declared that fixed interest is not *riba* and accordingly does not contradict Islamic law. To justify discounting the explicit prohibition of *riba* found in the *Qur'an*, these scholars disputed the meaning of the *riba* prohibition. Some of these Islamic law scholars have an official role, such as the rector of *Al-Azhar*. Having a *fatwa* issued by the *Al-Azhar* rector allowed the Egyptian government to circumvent the Islamic law limitation mandated in the constitution, permitting fixed interest in banking. There was no need for Egypt's Constitutional Court to

---

[181] Relying on Islamic scholars in an official capacity to justify ignoring Islamic directives is not an uncommon strategy in oppressive regimes, as history can attest. Authoritarian regimes in the Middle-East always find scholars who falsely justify tyranny under Islamic law.

dispute a *riba* prohibition. This judgment could have triggered social unrest, but was unnecessary because the moral authority *Al-Azhar* rector *Fatwa* is undeniable.

Later, The Egyptian constitution of 2012 attempted to resolve this dilemma in Section 4 by requiring the state to consult the Committee of Senior Islamic Law Scholars from *Al Azhar* in all matters relating to Islamic law. Thus, all previous Egyptian Supreme Constitutional Court decisions related to Islamic law shall not be binding to the committee while the committee's interpretation and application of Islamic law in Egypt is binding to all Egyptian courts. Such a state of affairs allowed the committee to revisit all controversial Supreme Constitutional Court decisions related to Islamic law and to propose resolutions that shall reverse these peculiar Court's decisions.

In 2013, when the military coup d'état seized power in Egypt and ejected the democratically elected Islamist government, military generals appointed a committee to revise the 2012 constitution. The revision was approved in a referendum in 2014. The revised constitution omitted Section 4 of the 2012 constitution, leaving the interpretation and application of Islamic law once again in the hands of Constitutional Court judges. Once again, the distinction in meaning between definitive and speculative and the authenticity of Islamic law rulings licensed Egypt's government to ignore Islamic law's constitutional supremacy with impunity.

It is worth noting that *Al-Azhar*, the most prestigious authority in Sunni Islam, issued an Islamic constitution model in 1978. Although the constitution model was brief and fell short of listing numerous fundamental Islamic governance doctrines as well as Islamic human rights, it declared in Section 1 that Islamic law is the source of all legislation. Such a declaration is fundamentally different from the formula presented in Egypt's successive constitutions of 1971, 2012 and 2014, which maintained that the principles of Islamic law are the *primary* sources of legislation. The insertion of the qualifier "*principles*" before Islamic law in the modern Egyptian constitutions opens the door for various interpretations. On the other hand, the *Al-Azhar* formula of declaring Islamic law the source of all legislation, limits the legislative power in law-making to Islamic principles. This is true even when the Islamic rulings are speculative in authenticity and meaning. In effect, the *Al-Azhar* formula eliminates the Egyptian Constitutional Court's unbridled discretionary power to ignore Islamic law rulings under the guise that a ruling is speculative in meaning or authenticity.

4.4 Legislature's Intentional Defiance to The People's Will to Implement Islamic Law: Morocco as An Example of The Selective Application of Islamic Rules

Shortly after Morocco declared independence from France, it passed the Fundamental Law of Morocco in 1961. The Fundamental Law was intended to be the supreme law of the land until a constitution was made. Article 2 of the Fundamental Law declared that Islam is the official religion of the state. Morocco's first constitution, which was adopted in 1962, has since amended several provisions of the Fundamental Law including a new clause declaring *Islam as the religion of the state*, instead of the prior provision in the Fundamental Law which declared *Islam as the official state religion*. The difference is clear: Islam as the official state religion is much more demanding than Islam as the religion of the state. Islam as the official state religion implies that Islamic law is a constitutional requirement. In contrast,

Islam as the religion of the state only declares the fact that the vast majority of Moroccans are Muslim and has no legal consequences for the state. Subsequent Moroccan constitutions, including the most recent iteration in 2011, have retained the less meaningful wording of the 1962 drafting that Islam is the religion of the state. Ironically, since successive Moroccan constitutions of 1962, 1972, 1992 and 2011 have declared that the King of Morocco is the protector of the faith and the grantor of the free practice of religious affairs, the King is required to apply Islamic law properly in Morocco; this has never occurred in practice.

Under the consecutive constitutions which declared Islam the religion of the state, Islamic law was applied selectively. The constitution provides for a monarchical system of governance, which violates the *shura*, mutual consultation, principle in Islam. At minimum, the *shura* principle requires that the candidate who wins the majority of eligible votes is appointed as the ruler of the state. [182]In Islam, there can be neither monarchy, nor supremacy of any human over others on the basis of color, race, lineage, or ethnicity.[183] Nonetheless, the unelected ruler of Morocco, the king, who takes power in violation of Islamic law, enjoys enormous unchecked powers. He is the Prince/Leader of the Believers (Muslims) and heads the Supreme Scientific Council, which has the exclusive authority to issue *fatwas*.[184] The king is the sole grantor of the continuity of the

---

[182] Concept of Shura shall be discussed in detail later in this volume.

[183] The Prophet Muhammad said in his last sermon: "… you all share the same father. There is no preference for Arabs over non-Arabs, nor for non-Arabs over Arabs. Neither is their preference for white people over black people, nor for black people over white people. Preference is only through righteousness." Musnad Ahmad.

[184] Section 41 of 2011 constitution.

government and independence.[185] The king also heads the Supreme Council of the Judiciary.[186]

Paradoxically, Morocco has adopted Islamic *shura* in some aspects that do not conflict with the king's powers. For instance, the Moroccan constitution gives citizens the right to vote and to run for a seat in parliament.[187] The elected parliament consists of two houses, designated to legislate and supervise the government.[188]

Apart from the constitution, Moroccan laws have demonstrated inconsistency and created confusion concerning the application of Islamic law. Without a doubt, there have been efforts to limit the application of Islamic law. For example, in the Moroccan Law of Obligations and Contracts, Section 870 affirms that fixed interest in contracts between Muslims is an invalid contractual condition that renders the contract null and void. While this provision is in harmony with Islamic law rulings that prohibit *riba,* sections 871–877 permit fixed interest in commercial transactions, in clear violation of Islamic law.[189] Similarly, Section 1092 of the Moroccan Law of Obligations and Contracts in conformity with Islamic law, upholds that any debt arising from gambling or betting is legally void. However, Section 1095 of the same legislation asserts that a debtor may recover any debt incurred as a result gambling or betting, in violation of Islamic law. In a similar way, Section 1097 violates Islamic law. It creates an

---

[185] Section 42 of 2011 constitution.

[186] Section 56 of 2011 constitution.

[187] Section 30 of 2011 constitution.

[188] Section 60 of 2011 constitution.

[189] Abd al-Salām Aḥmad Fīghū , *ILL - Al- 'Uqud AL-Madaniyah AL-Khassah Fi AL-Qanun AL-Maghribi : Al-Wadiah Al-'Āriyah AlL-Qard Al-Wakalah 'Uqud Al-Gharar*(Dar al-Aman for Publishing and Distribution 2008).

exception to the prohibition of gambling by permitting gambling in select sports, such as horse racing and archery, providing that the gambling did not take place between parties to the sports activities or between spectators. This confusing law is evidence that Islamic law is applied selectively to serve government interests in commercial transactions.

Moroccan Family Law for Muslims is primarily based on Islamic law. However, in recent years, under the influence of political pressure from domestic anti-Islam forces and western States, Morocco has introduced many amendments that conflict with Islamic law. For instance, a bill proposed in 2004 prohibited polygyny as a general rule, unless the husband obtains judicial permission for the second marriage.[190] Courts would permit a second marriage if two conditions are met: [191] 1) the husband must show exceptional circumstances that compel him to seek a second marriage; and 2) the husband must demonstrate the financial competence to equally support two families. To justify these requirements, which are at odds with Islamic law, the legislature cited in the preamble of the legislation a Qur'anic verse that emphasizes the impossibility of providing equal treatment to more than one wife.[192] To be sure, the Moroccan legislature, indeed, confers upon the cited Qur'anic verse a meaning that was never utilized by Muslims. *Qur'an* commentators have unanimously

---

[190] Section 40 of Morocco Family Law. *See Also*, Khalid Birjawi, *Qanun Al-Zawaj Bi-al-Maghrib*, (Menshorat Maktabet Al- Shabab 1999),30-36.

[191] Section 41 of Morocco Family Law.

[192] "You will never be able to do perfect justice between wives even if it is your ardent desire, so do not incline too much to one of them (by giving her more of your time and provision) so as to leave the other hanging (i.e. neither divorced nor married). And if you do justice, and do all that is right and fear Allah by keeping away from all that is wrong, then Allah is Ever Oft-Forgiving, Most Merciful." Qur'an (4:129).

concluded, over the past fourteen hundred years, that the verse refers to the impossibility of reaching equality between wives concerning love and affection because these emotions are beyond the control of human beings.[193] Thus, the *Qur'an* directs Muslims to be fair and provide equality as much as possible but, in the meantime, realizes that emotions may not be subject to human control.

The history of Moroccan law may explain the current state of affairs in Morocco. For centuries, Islamic law, and specifically, the *Malaki* school of thought, was the only source of law in Morocco.[194] The judiciary was staffed by Islamic law scholars who were appointed by the ruler, after recommendation by the local governor or localities.[195] Rulers typically had a council of Islamic scholars for consultation purposes in running state affairs.[196] When imperialistic France invaded many regions in Africa, including Morocco, it imposed French law on the new colonies. In an attempt to change the identity of Morocco, France transformed most of the Moroccan laws, except family law, to French laws. While many aspects of Islamic law remain vivid in Moroccan law today, such as family law for Muslims and *gharar* contracts, the main body of Moroccan law since 1913 is based on French law.[197] The imposition of French law and language

---

[193] See the explanation of the Qur'anic verse 4:129 in Tafsir Ibn Kathir, Tafsir al-Jalalayn, and Tafsir al Tabari.

[194] Mohammed Al-'Agee, Al-Mokhtasar Al-khalele Wa Athrah Fe Al-Darasat Almo'asarah, (Morroco ,Menshorat Wazarah Al-awqaf Wa Alsh'on al-Aslamyiah 2011), 201-10.

[195] Id.

[196] Id.

[197] *Gharar* (uncertain, ambiguous) contracts involve non-existence of the subject matter or ignorance of any material aspect of the transaction. This may occur when a contract's fundamental terms such as price, date of the performance or the subject matter are uncertain/ambiguous. *Gharar* contracts are void under

in Morocco, combined with the emergence of a pro-colonial French sociocultural class, created a national identity that is torn between two competing cultures, Islamic culture infused with local traditions and French culture.[198] This colonial history has dramatically influenced lawmaking, courts' decisions and Islamic identity in modern Morocco.

Although every Moroccan constitution affirms Morocco's Islamic identity, they have never proclaimed the aim of Islamic unity, an Islamic principle mandated in the *Qur'an*.[199] Article 14 of the Fundamental Law of 1961 indicated that Morocco must provide education with an Arab and Islamic national orientation. Article 14, in essence, is a step towards Islamic unity because it brings Morocco closer to its neighboring Muslim-majority states. Nevertheless, article 14 was quickly erased in the 1962 constitution and subsequent constitutions. Later, the 2011 constitution used very mild language to suggest expanding relations with other Muslim states.[200] Since then, no significant change has occurred in the relationship between Morocco and other Muslim-majority states. Conceivably, the omission of Islamic unity as a state goal was intentional given that if Islamic rulings were ever enforced, they would delegitimize the very

---

Islamic law. *See* Frank E. Vogel and Samuel L. Hayes, *Islamic law and Finance: Religion, Risk and Return*, (Kluwer Law international 1998), 91.

[198] Some Muslims, such as Mohammed Al-'Agee, believe that Islamic law scholars with western tendencies pose a greater danger to Islam itself than anything else. See Mohammed Al-'Agee, *Al-Mokhtasar Al-khalele Wa Athrah Fe Al-Darasat Almo'asarah*, (Morroco, Menshorat Wazarah Al-awqaf Wa alsh'on al-Aslamyiah 2011), 224.

[199] Qur'an 21:92. This principle shall be discussed in detail later in this volume.

[200] The constitution only states that the kingdom aimed to strengthen the bonds of togetherness with the Arab and Islamic states.

essence of the current governing system in Morocco. For instance, implementing the Islamic *shura* process to elect the head of state would derail the Moroccan monarchical system of governance. Moreover, Islamic human rights would prevail instead of the more limited rights guaranteed under the current constitution.

It seems that the continuous erosion of Moroccan Islamic identity has extended to its surrounding regions. After gaining independence in 1956, Morocco drafted its first constitution to emphasize a number of constitutional principles to guide the new state. One of these principles, which was declared in the preamble of the consecutive constitutions 1962, 1970, 1972 and 1992, is that Morocco is an African country that envisions African unity. Realizing that Islam is a prominent religion in Africa, African unity would certainly bring Morocco closer to its Islamic identity. Nevertheless, the latest constitution of 2011 diluted the language of African unity declaring that Morocco only aims to strengthen cooperation and solidarity with African states and build a Union of the Maghreb of northwest African states as a strategic option.

CHAPTER 5

Misunderstanding Islamic Law

———————— ༓ ༓ ༓ ————————

5.1   Introduction

One of the pitfalls of Orientalists' research methodology on Islamic law is that they view it through a western lens. They apply whatever knowledge they have acquired to evaluate, compare and accordingly draw conclusions on Islamic law. In essence, they compare unlike norms, i.e., western vs. Islamic, eastern or even African norms, and then they mark any departure from *their* norms as improper or inhumane in an attempt to degrade the different, the other. To avoid the dilemma of misunderstanding Islamic law, one should avoid comparisons based on western values and instead strive to grasp Islamic law theory.

Orientalists' faulty research methodology on Islamic law leads to misunderstanding Islamic law which in turn, generates negative views of Islamic law among non-Muslims. It explains the continuous western states' efforts to alter or "reform" Islamic law in Muslim-majority states and leads to denial of limited Islamic law application within western states' borders.

Since explaining the entire theory of Islamic law is far beyond the scope of this chapter, four controversial topics will be discussed to shed light on the depth of misunderstanding of the Islamic law problem. The application of *Hudud* punishments, women's inheritance, slavery, and non-Muslim *"Dhimmi"* status in the Islamic state under Islamic law will be discussed. It should be noted that slavery is studied from a historical perspective. The discussion does not intend to support slavery by any means, but rather, to clarify facts which were distorted by Orientalists.

5.2   The Application of Hudud Punishments

Islamic law recognizes three categories of crimes: *Hudud, Qisas,* and *Ta'zir. Hudud* and *Qisas* punishments are pre-fixed while the punishment for the *Ta'zir* category of crime is left to the Islamic legislature to define according to the circumstances, e.g., geography, culture, time etc. *Hudud* crimes include theft, slander, a Muslim's voluntary intoxication and *Zina* (fornication or adultery). *Qisas* crimes include homicide and bodily harm. The punishment for *Hudud* and *Qisas* is corporeal, e.g., the punishment for theft is hand amputation, the punishment for adultery is stoning to death.[201]

The corporeal punishment associated with *Hudud* and *Qisas* crimes has been criticized as being unduly harsh, backward and in desperate need of reform in a fashion similar to Christianity's

---

[201] See definition and elements of the offense of Zina (adultery or fornication) in Abdul Qadir Audah, 1 *Al-Tashrai' Al-Jinai' Al-Islami* (Beirut, Muassasah ar-Risalah 2000), 365. See definition and elements of the offense of theft in Hisham M. Ramadan, "Larceny Offenses in Islamic Law", 2006 *MICH. ST. L. REV.*1609.

reformation in the enlightenment era. What is rarely, if ever, mentioned when criticizing Islamic criminal law, is the operational scheme of Islamic penal law. Hence, to illustrate the misrepresentation of Islamic law, some fundamentals of Islamic law jurisprudence must be explained briefly.

i. Offenses of *Hudud* and *Qisas* are both common and the most threatening to society. Accordingly, Islamic law maximizes the employment of the deterrent function of punishment to prevent the common, most threatening future crimes, save lives of the potential innocent victims, and ensure social welfare.[202] For that reason, the punishment for a theft offense, a *Hudud* offense, is hand amputation while the punishment of embezzlement, a *Ta'zir* offense, is left to the legislature's discretion but must be less than hand amputation.[203] Maximum deterrence is required concerning a theft offense because it is more harmful to society; it infuses society with guardedness, fear, and insecurity. In contrast, in embezzlement, the harm is limited to the victim(s). Accordingly, it is understandable, under the proportionality doctrine, to enhance the punishment for offenses that harm the society at large versus those that harm only the victim(s).

---

[202] The language of the Qur'an suggests that deterrence is a punishment rationale. *See, e.g.* (Cut off (from the wrist joint) the (right) hand of the thief, male or female, as a recompense for that which they committed, a punishment by way of example from Allah. And Allah is All-Powerful, All-Wise.) Qur'an 5:38. The Qur'an also indicates that one of the prime rationales for the application of *Qisas* punishment is to save lives. (And there is (a saving of) life for you in Al-Qisas, O men of understanding) Qur'an 2:179.

[203] *See* Muhammad Salim Al-Awa, *Fe Asool Al-Nazzam Al-Jenai' Al-Islami*, (Cairo, Nahadat Misr Publishing 2007), 376-410.

ii. The offenses of *Hudud* and *Qisas* are limited in number and cannot be expanded.

iii. Very few *Hudud* and *Qisas* punishments are executed due to the Islamic law of evidence.   Under the Islamic law of evidence:

   a) The standard of proof in *Hudud* and *Qisas* offenses is beyond <u>all</u> doubt. ***Any*** doubt suffices to preclude *Hudud* or *Qisas* punishment.[204] Notably, under *beyond all doubt*, non-corroborated testimony of the accused *may*, as in *Zina* offense, outweigh the testimony of witnesses because the testimony of the accused alone raises doubt sufficient to preclude the punishment.

   b) Offenders of victimless *Hudud* offenses, e.g., fornication and voluntary intoxication, are strongly encouraged to repent privately and refrain from reporting the offense to

---

[204] Averting *Hudud* and punishment for any doubt is doctrine in Islamic jurisprudence. This unanimously agreed upon doctrine is based on proper interpretation of Islamic law rather than directly authenticated Sunnah or Qur'an. However, there is little authority to support this doctrine. See. e.g. (Aisha Narrated that the messenger of Allah Said "avert the punishment for Hudud for Muslims as much as possible, if (s) he (the accused) has a way out then leave him to his way, for if the Imam (governor/ruler) makes a mistake in forgiving it would be better than making mistake in punishment") Jami At-Tirmidhi Hadith No. 1424. This Hadith and another Hadith of the same meaning mentioned in Sunan Ibn Majah are weak with respect to the authentication. Therefore, these Ahadith, alone without any collaborating jurisprudence, could not be used exclusively to establish legal doctrine. However, the entire scheme of Islamic criminal law supports averting Hudud and punishment for any doubt doctrine. *See also* Ibn Qudamah,10 *Al-Mughni wa'l-Sharh al-Kabir*, (Beirut: Dar Al-Fikr),150-157. Muhammad Abu Zahra, *Al-Garima* (the crime), (Cairo, Dar Al-Fikr Al'Arabi 1998), 150.

the authorities.[205] Individuals who witness victimless *Hudud* offenses are also strongly encouraged to refrain from reporting the offense to the authorities.[206] Once the offense is reported to the authorities, prosecution is triggered, and the punishment must be executed if the offense is proven *beyond all doubt.*[207]

c) Apart from the standard of proof, a very heavy burden of proof is required to prove *Hudud* and *Qisas* offenses. For instance, no less than four credible witnesses who actually saw the act of penetration, or heard the uncoerced confession, shall satisfy the standard of proof for the offense of *Zina* (fornication or adultery).[208] Similarly, no

---

[205] Hisham M. Ramadan, "On Islamic Punishment", In Hisham M. Ramadan (ed.), *Understanding Islamic Law: From Classical to Contemporary* (AltaMira Press 2006), 50-1.

[206] (Abu Hurairah narrated that the messenger of Allah (the Prophet Muhammad) said: "whoever relives a Muslims of a burden from the burdens of the world Allah will relive him of a burden from the burdens of the hereafter. And whoever covers (the fault of) a Muslim, Allah will cover (his faults) for him in the world and hereafter. And Allah in engaged in helping the worshiper as long as the worshiper is engaged in helping his brother (in faith).) ") Jami At-Tirmidhi Hadith No. 1425. *See also* (O ye who believe! avoid suspicion as much (as possible): for suspicion in some cases is a sin: and spy not on each other, nor speak ill of each other behind their backs. Would any of you like to eat the flesh of his dead brother? Nay, ye would abhor it. But fear Allah: for Allah is Oft-Returning, Most-Merciful.) Qur'an 49:11-12.

[207] *See* Hisham M. Ramadan, "On Islamic Punishment", In Hisham M. Ramadan (ed.), *Understanding Islamic Law: From Classical to Contemporary* (AltaMira Press 2006), 50-1.

[208] (And those of your women, who commit illegal sexual intercourse, take the evidence of four witnesses from amongst you against them; and if they testify, confine them (i.e. women) to houses until death comes to them or Allah ordains for them some (other) way), Qur'an 4:15.

less than two credible witnesses or the uncoerced confession shall satisfy the standard of proof for the offense of homicide.[209]

d) Upon receiving an uncoerced confession, authorities shall advise the confessor of possible excuses, the definition of the offense and its elements and be satisfied beyond all doubt that the accused understands the nature and the consequences of the confession.[210] If the confessor pleads any excuse or renounces his confession, at any stage of the trial or prior to the execution of the punishment, authorities shall not proceed in the absence of any other reliable, satisfactory evidence.[211]

---

[209] Anwarullah, *Principles of Evidence in Islam*, (Kuala Lumpur, A.S. Noordeen 2004), 44.

[210] *See* (Jabir Bin Abdullah narrated: "a man from the tribe of Aslam came to the Prophet (Muhammad) and confessed to adultery. He (the Prophet Muhammad) turned away from him, and then he (the man) confessed (again). Then he (the Prophet Muhammad) turned away from him (again) until he (the man) testified against himself four times. So the Prophet said: "are you insane?" he said: "No". He (the Prophet Muhammad) said "are you married?" he said: "yes". So he gave the order and he was stoned at the Musalla. He (the man) ran when he was struck by the stones and he was caught and stoned until he died. So the messenger of Allah spoke well of him but he did not perform the (funeral) prayer for him.) Jami At-Tirmidhi Hadith No. 1429

[211] (Abu Hurairah Narrated: "maiz AL-Aslami came to the messenger of Allah and said that he had committed adultery, so he (the Prophet Muhammad) turned away from him. Then he (Maiz) approached from his other side and said" [O messenger of Allah] I have committed adultery. So he (the Prophet Muhammad) turned away from him. Then he (Maiz) came from the other side and said: O messenger of Allah! I have committed adultery, so he (the Prophet Muhammad) gave the order (for stoning) upon the fourth time. He was taken to Al-harrah and stoned with rocks, he ran swiftly until he passed a man with a camel whip who beat him with it, and the people beat him until he died. They mentioned to the messenger of Allah that he ran upon feeling the rocks at the time of death.

e) Finally, two general rules of evidence play a significant role in ensuring fairness and reducing convictions in *Hudud* and *Qisas* offenses: the presumption of innocence and that "doubt does not avert truth" or, in modern legal terminology, any doubt shall be construed to the benefit of the defendant.

However, it does not follow that failure to satisfy the heavy burden of proof of *Hudud* and *Qisas* offenses, because the defendant successfully raised a fanciful doubt or otherwise, shall exculpate the defendant totally. The flexible category of *Ta'zir* offenses is the "catch net" since it does not require the heavy burden of *Qisas* and *Hudud*. Accordingly, the accused who escapes *Qisas* punishment, e.g., the capital punishment, in an intentional homicide charge might be convicted under the *Ta'zir* category. The punishment for *Ta'zir* is left to the legislature but must be lower than the original *Qisas* offense's punishment. Practically, this means a defendant could be prosecuted for two alternate charges, e.g., intentional homicide under *Qisas* category punishable by capital punishment and intentional homicide under *Ta'zir* category punishable by incarceration. Each charge is subject to a distinct standard of proof; *beyond all doubt* in intentional homicide under *Qisas* category and *to a factual certainty* in intentional homicide under *Ta'zir* category. If the defendant escapes punishment under *Qisas* category, s/he might be convicted under *Ta'zir* category.

In sum, Islamic law balances the strict corporeal punishment of *Hudud* and *Qisas* offenses with a very heavy burden of proof that is in practice very difficult, if not nearly impossible in many cases, to fulfill.

So the messenger of Allah (the Prophet Muhammad) Said: why didn't you leave him?)") Jami At-Tirmidhi Hadith No. 1428.

This approach conforms with the primary purpose of the punishment of *Hudud* and *Qisas* offenses: deterrence. As much as deterrence is best achieved by maximizing the threat of punishment to potential offenders, it does not require many executions of the punishment. As the prominent Islamic law scholar, Muhammad Abu Zahra, pointed out: it is enough and more than enough that the Islamic nation (1.9 billion) has one hand amputation (upon conviction of theft) every year. Those who escaped *Hudud* and *Qisas* punishment because of the difficulty of fulfilling the heavy burden of proof might be subject to a lesser punishment under *Ta'zir* category.

A most critical question in this issue arises. When the punishment of *Hudud* and *Qisas* offenses is criticized, what should a Muslim state do? Should the Muslim state give in to "foreign" criticism and defy Islamic law? Should the Muslim state exercise its sovereignty in enforcing laws in conformity with its faith? Recall the current state of affairs in the world. The United States is still applying the death penalty despite criticism by other Western states. Should the Western world force the United States to abrogate the death penalty because it is contrary to their opinions? Admittedly, this is impossible given that the United States is a superpower. The case is not the same with respect to the weak Muslim-majority states!

5.3 Women's Inheritance Under Islamic Law.

Orientalists repeatedly claim that in Islam, women are worth one-half of men in inheritance.[212] Two important concepts refute such claims.

---

[212] Ann Elizabeth Mayer, "A "Benign" Apartheid: How Gender Apartheid Has been Rationalized.", (2001) 5 *UCLA Journal of International Law and Foreign Affairs*, 237– 338.

The first explains the law of inheritance in Islam. The second explains substantive equality in Islam.

Generally, Islamic law scholars have suggested that Islamic inheritance law is based on two rationales: the degree of relationship between the heir and the deceased and the economic burden of the heirs. In this context, the closer the heir is to the deceased, the greater share the heir receives. The younger generation heirs receive greater shares than older generation heirs because the younger generation typically needs more wealth to establish financial independence. Males in limited circumstances may receive a greater share only if they are burdened with greater financial tasks. These rules translate into the following:

1. Only in four inheritance cases do males receive a greater share than females. For example, a full brother receives double the share of the full sister.
2. In at least eleven inheritance scenarios, females receive a share equal to males. For example, a half-brother and half-sister who share the same mother receive the same inheritance portion.
3. In at least fourteen inheritance scenarios, females receive a greater share than males. For example, a husband of a deceased woman receives a smaller amount of the estate than his daughter(s).
4. In at least five inheritance scenarios, females receive a share from inheritance while their male counterpart does not receive any share. For example, if the deceased had only two heirs, a maternal grandfather and a maternal grandmother, the grandmother receives the entire estate to the exclusion of the grandfather.

Now, it is worth clarifying the concept of equality in Islamic law: Equality may take different forms that lead to uneven outcomes. Equality could mean an equal start/opportunity in which all parties enjoy the same treatment at the starting point notwithstanding the natural differences in all parties. For example, a standardized university entrance exam might be required for all students notwithstanding different high schools' effectiveness in teaching and facilities. On the other hand, equality could mean the provision for 'equal ends' in which society recognizes diversity in the population and natural differences among individuals that preclude the weakest and the most vulnerable from enjoying a dignified life achieved by the wealthy, nurtured and well educated members of society. Society may guarantee equal ends in cases in which basic human necessities of life are at stake. In this context, it can be said that Islam recognizes that women have been exploited throughout history mainly because of their need to obtain the necessary means for dignified living. Thus, Islam has placed women in a preferred position that guarantees social welfare for them as well as their children. In Islamic society, women are not responsible for earning a living. The woman's family or husband bears such responsibility if they can. Again, a woman cannot be compelled to support herself, her family, her husband or her children even if she is wealthy. If a woman's family cannot support her, the State bears the burden of supporting her and her children. In cases in which her family refuses in spite of having wherewithal to support the woman and her children, the State would make the support payment for her and collect payment from the family if necessary. However, it does not follow that a woman cannot work or earn money. On the contrary, she can work, and whatever she earns as well as any inheritance, bequests, and gifts she receives are dedicated only for her joy. Therefore, even in the four inheritance cases in which women receive a lesser share than the male heirs, it cannot be said that Islamic law discriminates against women given that the woman's financial burdens are much lighter than that of the man. Islam promotes substantive equality, not equal starts/opportunity, in which certain individuals may fail to acquire the necessities of life because they are naturally less competitive in the market.

In sum, Islamic law provides equal ends, as distinguished from equal opportunity or equal starts. Women receive higher, equal or lesser inheritance shares, as the case may be, to ensure equal ends are granted those individuals who are the heart of Islamic society, women.

5.4   Slavery Under Islamic Law

The philosophy of Islamic law, its mechanisms and techniques for dealing with issues does not resemble Western thinking. This necessitates further explanation of numerous matters; such as female inheritance shares as explained earlier. Slavery, however, is not a complicated matter in Islam. Nevertheless, slavery has always been misrepresented in the Western recounting of the history of Islamic law. Orientalists' motives to distort Islamic law is, at best, speculative. Perhaps contemporary ill practices in numerous Muslim-majority states have contributed to the Orientalists' confusion between the code, i.e., Islamic law, and its misapplication. Possibly it is the detestation of others. What is certain is that the history of Islam including history of slavery has been misstated. For instance, William Clarence-Smith claims that "slaves [in Islam] were chattels, similar to livestock in many aspects."[213] Clarence-Smith, like many others, never investigated the basic sources of Islamic law on slavery. Rather, he quoted a mistranslation and used an out-of-context statement to support his conclusions. He maintained that the renowned scholar, Abu al-Faraj al-Jawzi, held that "it is incumbent upon a woman to endure her husband's mistreatment as a slave should."[214] To be sure, the original Arabic text never suggested mistreatment of slaves or wives. Instead, Abu al-Faraj in addressing the husband-wife relationship had concluded that a wife is as a slave to her husband strictly in the sense that she should, as slaves do, allow the husband to enjoy her excellent companionship, not to be arrogant or offend him.[215] Surely, the analogy between wives and slaves is offensive to women. However, neither Abu al-Faraj nor other Islamic scholars have suggested ill-treatment of women or slaves in their writings

---

[213] William Gervase Clarence-Smith, *Islam and the Abolition of Slavery* (Oxford University Press 2006),2. Compare Bernard Lewis, who is well known for his unfavorable view of Islam and Muslims, he concluded (Though slavery was maintained. The Islamic dispensation enormously improved the position of the Arabian slave, who was now no longer merely a chattel but also a human being with a certain religious, and hence a social status and with certain quasi legal rights) Bernard Lewis, *Race and Slavery in the Middle East: An Historical Enquiry*, (Oxford University Press 1992),6. Other scholars concluded that Islamic law presented humane treatment to slaves and it was design to eliminate slavery eventually. *See* Amina Wadud, "Alternative Qur'anic Interpretation and the Status of Muslim Women" in Gisela Webb (ed.), *Windows of Faith: Muslim Women Scholar-Activists of North America*, (Syracuse University Press 2000.), 15. *See also* Tamara Sonn, *Interpreting Islam: Bandali Jawzi's Islamic Intellectual History*, (Oxford University Press 1996), 86.

[214] William Gervase Clarence-Smith, *Islam and the Abolition of Slavery* (Oxford University Press 2006),4.

[215] *See* the original text in Arabic, Abū al-Faraj ʿAbd al-Raḥmān ibn ʿAlī Ibn al-Jawzī, *Kitāb Aḥkām al-nisāʾ*, (Beirut: Al-Maktabah al-ʿAṣrīyah 2012), Chapter 64, Bab Wajoob taʾa al Zawj (chapter on Husband Obedience).

elsewhere, apart from William Clarence-Smith's out of context quotes. Misstatements by Abu al-Faraj regarding Islamic law or his failure to accurately convey the intended meaning, should not comprise conclusive evidence against Islamic law. For the purpose of clarifying an important part of Islamic history, it is imperative to explain slavery in Islam.

In the pre-modern world, the practice of slavery had been practiced for centuries at a time when very few human rights were recognized. When Islam emerged fourteen centuries ago, it had to deal with the existing human rights problems including slavery. The slave-owners' view was that slaves represented wealth and were needed to preserve their livelihood. Slaves were ill-treated and deprived of the most precious human right: freedom.[216]

Islam adopts a peaceful, gradual process to deal with social problems and correct common wrongs, such as consumption of alcohol and slavery.[217] For instance, concerning consumption of alcohol, the *Qur'an* initially declared that consumption of alcohol produces benefit *and* harm, but the harm outweighs the benefit.[218]

---

[216] (And if a man smites his servant, or his maid, with a rod, and he die under his hand; he shall be surely punished. Notwithstanding, if he continues a day or two, he shall not be punished: for he is his money.) Exodus 21:20-21. (If a man sells his daughter as a female slave, she is not to go free as the male slaves do.) Exodus 21:7.

[217] (Jarir Narrated that the messenger of Allah said: (he who is deprived of *refeq* (kindness and /or leniency) is in fact deprived of every good) Mokhtaser Sahih Muslim,Bk. of virtue, No. 1783. (Aishah , the wife of the prophet narrated that the prophet said "*refeq* (kindness and /or leniency) is not to be found in anything but it adds to its beauty; and it is not withdrawn from anything ,but it makes it defective.) Mokhtaser Sahih Muslim,Bk. of virtue, No. 1784.

[218] (They ask you (O Muhammad) concerning alcoholic drink and gambling. Say: "In them is a great sin, and (some) benefit for men, but the sin of them is

Later, the *Qur'an* prohibited performing prayers while intoxicated.[219] As a final stage, the *Qur'an* prohibited intoxicants entirely.[220] By the time the prohibition of alcohol became evident in the *Qur'an*, the unshakeable faith of the Islamic community had led to the total abandonment of consuming intoxicants. It was a gradual but sure method to enforce a prohibition. Comparatively, societies that introduced a sudden prohibition of alcohol - e.g., the United States in the early 20th century - without altering the prohibitory norms by enforcing new moral standards, failed to enforce the prohibition and eventually abandoned the attempt.[221] Likewise, the sudden abolition of slavery in America was the leading cause of a civil war where hundreds of thousands were killed.

Similar to the Islamic scheme of the gradual prohibition of alcohol, the scheme to eliminate slavery in Islam followed two gradual steps. First, Islam eradicated the sources of slavery. In the pre-modern world, sources of slavery varied from kidnapping to selling one's own children. Islam prohibited all sources of slavery save one: prisoners of

---

greater than their benefit." And they ask you what they ought to spend. Say: "That which is beyond your needs." Thus Allah makes clear to you His Laws in order that you may give thought.") Qur'an 2:219.

[219] (O you who believe! Approach not As-Salât (the prayer) when you are in a drunken state until you know (the meaning) of what you utter...) Qur'an 4:43.

[220] (O you who believe! Intoxicants (all kinds of alcoholic drinks), gambling, Al-Ansâb, and Al-Azlâm (arrows for seeking luck or decision) are an abomination of Shaitân's (Satan) handiwork. So avoid (strictly all) that (abomination) in order that you may be successful) Qur'an 5:90.

[221] *See* generally David Kyving, *Repealing National Prohibition*, (Kent State University Press 2000).

war.[222] Additionally, this sole source was subjected to very restrictive regulations. Prisoners of war in Islam may be:

a) Released with a ransom; or

b) Released without a ransom;.[223] or

c) Killed, this is especially true for those who have committed heinous crimes such as murder.[224]

d) Taken as slaves as practices suggest.[225]

According to sequences of choices listed in the *Qur'an*, the most favorable choice is release without ransom, then release with ransom if it is in the interest of the Islamic State. Taking prisoners of war as slaves is subject to two conditions. A) It should be in the interest of the Islamic State. B) Only the government of the Islamic State can take slaves. Individuals cannot act on their own to take slaves. Taking

---

[222] *See e.g.* Islam prohibited selling free people. See (On the authority of Abu Hurayrah (may Allah be pleased with him), who said that the Messenger of Allah (peace be upon him) said that Allah the Almighty said: There are three (types of men) whose adversary I shall be on the Day of Resurrection: a man who has given his word by Me and has broken it; a man who has sold a free man and has consumed the price; and a man who has hired a workman, has exacted his due in full from him and has not given him his wage. Sahih Al-Bukhari, Hadith No. 19.

[223] (So, when you meet (in a fight, Jihad in Allah's Cause), those who disbelieve smite at their necks till when you have killed and wounded many of them, then bind a bond firmly (on them, i.e. take them as captives). Thereafter (is the time) either for generosity (i.e. free them without ransom), or ransom (according to what benefits Islam), until the war lays down its burden.) Qur'an 47:4.

[224] (It is not for a Prophet that he should have prisoners of war (and free them with ransom) until he had made a great slaughter (among his enemies) in the land.) Qur'an 8: 67. Note that this verse addresses the Prophet only, thus it is subject to interpretation with respect to its applicability after the death of the Prophet.

[225] Abdullah Naseh Elwan, *Nezam Al-Raaq Fe Al-Islam* (Slavery under Islamic ruling), (Riyadh, Dar-us-Salam Publications 2004), 12.

prisoners of war as slaves can be beneficial to the Islamic State to exchange prisoners of war between the Islamic State and its enemies.

Islam's second step to eliminate slavery manifested in the employment of good and bad individuals' traits including human infirmity, faith, and benevolence to free slaves. For those with firm religious beliefs, freeing a slave, whether owned or bought to be emancipated, is a great charity.[226] Others who are not interested in charitable deeds will eventually commit wrongs which, in turn, result in freeing slaves given that the Islamic expiation for numerous wrongs includes freeing a slave.[227] Ultimately, if a slave seeks emancipation

---

[226] *See e.g.* (It is not Al-Birr (piety, righteousness, and each and every act of obedience to Allah, etc.) that you turn your faces towards east and (or) west (in prayers); but Al-Birr is (the quality of) the one who believes in Allah, the Last Day, the Angels, the Book, the Prophets and gives his wealth, in spite of love for it, to the kinsfolk, to the orphans, and to Al-Masâkin (the poor), and to the wayfarer, and to those who ask, and to set slaves free, performs As-Salât (Iqamat-as-Salat), and gives the Zakat, and who fulfill their covenant when they make it, and who are As-Sabirin (the patient ones, etc.) in extreme poverty and ailment (disease) and at the time of fighting (during the battles). Such are the people of the truth and they are Al-Muttaqûn (pious)). Qur'an 2:177. *See also* (Narrated Abu Dhar: I asked the Prophet, "What is the best deed?" He replied, "To believe in Allah and to fight for His Cause." I then asked, "What is the best kind of manumission (of slaves)?" He replied, "The manumission of the most expensive slave and the most beloved by his master." I said, "If I cannot afford to do that?" He said, "Help the weak or do good for a person who cannot work for himself." I said, "If I cannot do that?" He said, "Refrain from harming others for this will be regarded as a charitable deed for your own good.") 3 Sahih AL-Bukhari, No. 694.

[227] *See e.g.* (It is not for a believer to kill a believer except (that it be) by mistake, and whosoever kills a believer by mistake, (it is ordained that) he must set free a believing slave and a compensation (blood money, i.e. Diya) be given to the deceased's family, unless they remit it. If the deceased belonged to a people at war with you and he was a believer; the freeing of a believing slave (is prescribed), and if he belonged to a people with whom you have a treaty of mutual alliance, compensation (blood money - Diya) must be paid to his family, and a believing

in return for paying the owner a certain amount of money, the *Qur'an* orders Muslims to grant such a request.[228] In this context, the slave owner and society, in general, must provide financial aid to secure emancipation money.[229]

In the transition period, between slavery and emancipation, Islamic law mandated that a slave enjoy full honor, dignity and a "brethren" treatment until the full process takes effect and he is freed.[230] In essence, permissible slavery was similar to a long-term

---

slave must be freed. And whoso finds this (the penance of freeing a slave) beyond his means, he must fast for two consecutive months in order to seek repentance from Allah. And Allâh is Ever All-Knowing, All-Wise.) Qur'an 4:92. *See also* (And those who make unlawful to them (their wives) (by Az-Zihâr) and wish to free themselves from what they uttered, (the penalty) in that case (is) the freeing of a slave before they touch each other. That is an admonition to you (so that you may not return to such an ill thing). And Allâh is All-Aware of what you do.) Qur'an 58:3.

[228] (And such of your slaves as seek a writing (of emancipation), give them such writing, if you know that they are good and trustworthy. And give them something yourselves out of the wealth of Allah which He has bestowed upon you) Qur'an 24:33.

[229] Id. Notably, Islamic law scholars, pursuant to the guidelines in Qur'an and Sunnah concluded that any act involving the uttering of words that may be interpreted as freeing a slave mandates unconditional emancipation. It seems that they tried to find any excuse to free slaves. See Muhammad ibn 'Abd al-Wahid Ibn al-Humam, 3 *Sharh Fath al-Qadir*, (Beirut, Dar Sadir), 356-60.

[230] (Narrated Al-Ma'rur bin Suwaid: I saw Abu Dhar Al-Ghifari wearing a cloak, and his slave, too, was wearing a cloak. We asked him about that (i.e. how both were wearing similar cloaks). He replied, "Once I abused a man and he complained of me to the Prophet. The Prophet asked me, 'Did you abuse him by slighting his mother?' He added, 'Your slaves are your brethren upon whom Allah has given you authority. So, if one has one's brethren under one's control, one should feed them with the like of what one eats and clothe them with the like of what one wears. You should not overburden them with what they cannot bear, and if you do so, help them (in their hard job)." Sahih AL-Bukhari, No. 721.

labor relationship. If a slave owner abuses his labor rights, e.g., abuses the slave, the labor relationship is terminated, and emancipation shall take effect immediately.[231]

Once slavery was abolished in Muslim-majority states, neither Islamic scholars nor the general Muslim population objected to such a move. In fact, Islamic Law scholars encouraged banning all forms of slavery, a ban which is in accordance with the spirit of Islam. As the ideal role model for Muslims, the Prophet Muhammad, in his last words before death, ordered Muslims to treat slaves with full dignity and brethren-like treatment.

5.5   The Status of Non-Muslims Under Islamic Law

Two distinct accounts on the treatment of non-Muslims in the Islamic State have been presented historically. One positive view has been introduced by Islamic scholars, as well as some renowned Western historians such as Sir Thomas Arnold and Adam Mez. This view portrays Islamic society as a virtuous society in which tolerance,

---

[231] (Malik related to me from Hilal Ibn Usama from Ata Ibn Yasar that Umar Ibn al-Hakam said, "I went to the Messenger of Allah, may Allah bless him and grant him peace, and said, 'Messenger of Allah, a slave girl of mine was tending my sheep. I came to her and one of the sheep was lost. I asked her about it and she said that a wolf had eaten it, so I became angry and I am one of the children of Adam, so I struck her on the face. As it happens, I have to set a slave free, shall I free her?' The Messenger of Allah, may Allah bless him and grant him peace, questioned her, 'Where is Allah?' She said, 'In heaven.' He said, 'Who am I?' She said, 'You are the Messenger of Allah.' The Messenger of Allah, may Allah bless him and grant him peace, said, 'Free her.' ") IMAM Malik, Muwatta, Bk. 38, No. 38.6.8. *See also* (Malik related to me that he had heard that a slave-girl came to Umar Ibn al-Khattab (who had been beaten by her master with a red hot iron) and he set her free.) IMAM Malik, Muwatta, Bk. 38, No. 38.5.7.

justice, and mutual understanding is the norm that governs the relationship among citizens of various religions or no religions.[232] A contrary view advanced by Islamophobia's mighty machine against Islam, particularly in recent years, has suggested that Islamic law is archaic, intolerant and biased. Nadia Yakoob & Aimen Mir, have claimed, without providing any supporting evidence, that non-Muslims residing in the Islamic State are not full citizens and that non-Muslims who reside outside the Islamic State, in the absence of a treaty granting them personal security, can be killed with impunity.[233] Along the same lines of analysis, Bernard Lewis and Bat Ye'or in an attempt to rewrite history by relying upon the ignorance of Islam among Western readers have falsely claimed humiliating and unfair obligations on non-Muslims residing in the Islamic State.[234] These contradictory descriptions of the status of non-Muslims inside and outside the Islam State require clarification. The following analysis shall reveal how Muslims understand Islamic law as it relates to the treatment of non-Muslims within an Islamic State or within Muslim-majority states under Islamic law. Islam strives to achieve a fair distribution of duties, enhance social harmony by means of establishing a social welfare system, eradicate hate crimes against

---

[232] See Adam Mez, *Die Renaissance des Islams*, (University of Michigan Library 1922). See also Sir Thomas W. Arnold, *The preaching of Islam* (London, 1898) & Sir Thomas W. Arnold, *The Caliphate*, (Oxford, 1924).

[233] Nadia Yakoob & Aimen Mir "Improving Asylum Law and Practices in the Middle East in Yvonne Y. Haddad and Barbara F. Stowasser (ed.), *Islamic Law and the Challenges of Modernity* (AltaMira Press, 2004), 109 -127.

The authors' claims are clearly contrary to clear direction of Qur'an. See Qur'an 17:33-5.

[234] Bat Ye'or, *The Dhimmi: Jews and Christians Under Islam*, (Fairleigh Dickinson University Press, 1985). Bernard Lewis, The *Crisis of Islam,* (Random House, 2004).

religious groups and sustain a graceful, tolerant environment mandated by a modern civilized nation.

5.5.1 Categories of Non-Muslim

Classically Islamic law scholars, during the past fourteen centuries under Islamic state rule, have divided Non-Muslims residing in the Islamic state into three categories: *Dhimmi, Mo'ahed* and *Harbi*. Historically the treatment of the Non-Muslim residing in Islamic law depends on this classification. Hypothetically, the ideal Islamic State ought to treat non-Muslims according to this classification. The following analysis is based on reliable evidence only. Orientalists' work on many Islamic law topics including this one is incorrect and seems to aim at infusing hatred between Muslims and non-Muslims especially those who reside in non-Muslim-majority states.

A. *Dhimmi/* Non-Muslim Citizen

The Islamic State encompasses various cultures and religions by the very nature of the universality of the message of Islam. The *Qur'an* directs Muslims to establish bridges of understanding between various cultures, civilizations, and religions. The *Qur'an* reminds humanity that we share one origin; we are brothers and sisters; we comprise diverse nations that we may know and learn from each other.[235] The *Qur'an* directs Muslims to forgive those with bad

---

[235] O mankind! We created you from a single (pair) of a male and a female, and made you into nations and tribes, that ye may know each other (not that ye may despise each other). Verily the most honored of you in the sight of Allah is (he who is) the most righteous of you. And Allah has full Knowledge and is well-acquainted (with all things). Qur'an 49:13, O mankind! Reverence your Guardian-Lord, who created you from a single Person, created, of like nature, his mate, and

intentions towards Muslims and towards the Islamic State.[236] The proper Islamic State is founded on mutual respect, understanding, and tolerance between various cultures and religions.

Because diversity is a reality in the establishment of the Islamic State, common ground is necessary upon which laws and customs are to be instituted. Nations create their constitutions, whether written or unwritten, to be the supreme law of the land. The Islamic state is not an exception. Muslims, by confessing to Islam, accept the Islamic fundamentals, i.e. the *Qur'an*, and *Sunnah*. Non-Muslims living in an Islamic State or who intend to live in an Islamic State need an understanding, agreement or a covenant with the Muslim population and the Islamic government to lay the foundation of laws that govern their relationship within the Islamic State. This agreement is the social contract of the Islamic State which respects and allows the practice of all religions, beliefs, and customs so long as they do not harm the State or infringe upon the fundamentals of the State constitution. This agreement is known as *Dhimmah Contract*: a contract that protects the minority from the tyranny of the majority, popular unfair social trends or an unjust government. The *Qur'an* and *Sunnah*, as the basis of the Islamic constitution, mandate *Dhimmah Contract* to protect minorities from the tyranny of potentially unjust rulers of the Islamic State.

---

from them twain scattered (like seeds) countless men and women Qur'an 4:1. We have honored the sons (and daughters) of Adam. Qur'an 17:70.

[236] Many of the people of the Scripture (Jews and Christians) wish that if they could turn you away as disbelievers after you have believed, out of envy from their own selves, even after the truth has become manifest unto them. But forgive and overlook, till Allah brings His Command. Verily, Allah is Able to do all things. Qur'an 2: 109.

A Non-Muslim citizen of the Islamic State is termed, *Dhimmi*, meaning "person of the covenant." The term refers to the contract between the non-Muslim and the Islamic State.[237] On this basis, *Dhimmi* is the non-Muslim citizen who becomes the subject of the Islamic State upon entering a covenant with the Islamic State or obtains *Dhimmi* status by residing permanently in the Islamic State and intends to accept the general covenant terms between the Islamic State and *Dhimmi*.[238] The intent to reside in the Islamic State can be explicit, by entering into a covenant with the Islamic State, or implicit by residing in the Islamic state and participating in citizenship activities, such as buying property, paying real-estate taxes or seeking a means of livelihood for an extended period. [239]

The covenant between Muslims and non-Muslims, i.e., *Contract of Zimah/ Dhimma*, is a manifestation of the power of the executive branch of government. It falls exclusively within the power of the ruler of the State or one of his subordinates.

Individuals in the *Dhimmi* category, generally speaking, owe the same duties and enjoy the same rights as Muslims residing in the Islamic State.[240] However, there are some exceptions which will be illustrated later. Naturally, any Muslim who enters the Islamic State is not required to join the *Dhimmi*/Islamic State agreement because by confessing Islam one is anticipated to accept Islamic law

---

[237] *See* Ibn Qayyim al-Jawziyyah, 2 *Ahkam Ahl adh-Dhimah*(Dhimmi's adjudications),(Cairo, Dar al-Hadith 2005), 873.

[238] Muhammad Abu Zahra, *Usul Al-Fiqh* (Basis of Jurisprudence), (Dar al-Fikr al-Arbi 2004), 97.

[239] Muḥammad ibn al-Ḥasan al-Shaybānī, 5 *Sharḥ kitāb al-Siyar al-kabīr*, (Beirut, Dar Al Kotob Al-Ilmiyah 1997),241-2.

[240] Ibn Hajar Al-Asqalani, *Fath Al-Bari Sharh Sahih Al-Bukhari*, (Riyadh, Dar al-Salam Publishing 2000), (Ketab Al-Sharakah), 245.

unconditionally and therefore owes the duties and the enjoys the rights shared by all Muslims.

Some scholars have suggested that *Dhimmah* contract exposes non-Muslims to the teachings of Islam and Islamic lifestyle in the Muslim majority State. They may, therefore, convert to Islam. On this basis, those scholars have suggested that the Islamic State must grant *Dhimmah* contract to any non-Muslim who expresses a desire to join the Islamic State.[241]

B. Temporary Visitor (Mosta'men/ Mo'ahed)

A temporary visitor may enter the Islamic State under the *Aman* (safety) contract.[242] The Safety contract is a mutual contract between the Islamic State and the visitor that explains the rights and the obligations of both parties.[243] The Islamic State may rescind the contract if there is a reasonable fear of security concerns or war with the visitor's State.[244] Otherwise, the Safety contract may include any equitable condition(s) that does not contradict Islamic law. Examples of inequitable conditions contradicting Islamic law would include

---

[241] Awni Farsakh, al-*Aqalliyat fi al-Tarikh al-Arabi* (Minorities in Arabs History), (Raid El-Rayyes Books 1994),73.

[242] Muhammad Abu Zahra, *Usul Al-Fiqh* (Basis of Jurisprudence), (Dar al-Fikr al-Arbi 2004),97-8.

[243] It should be noted that an agreement between the Islamic State and another state, an individual or group of individuals is limited in its scope. Granting the right of entry under safety contract to a citizen of a state never means granting the same right to the whole population of this state or even to the visitor's ethnic group, his friends or family. The agreement must be narrowly construed after giving full effect to the literal and natural meanings of the agreement's words. *See* Muḥammad ibn al-Ḥasan al-Shaybānī, 2 *Sharḥ kitāb al-Siyar al-kabīr*, (Beirut, Dar Al Kotob Al-Ilmiyah 1997), 3-10.

[244] See Qur'an 8:58, see also Ibn Qudamah,10 *Al-Mughni wa'l-Sharh al-Kabir*, (Beirut: Dar Al-Fikr), 514.

refraining from selling alcohol to Muslims or fighting Muslims.[245] Invalid conditions are void and null while the contract on the whole remains valid.[246]

Islamic Law scholars have divided Safety contract into two main categories: limited and general. The distinction between limited and general Safety contracts is based upon the geographical jurisdiction of the Islamic State representative. A Muslim, as a citizen of the Islamic State, has limited powers. Accordingly, he may grant, expressly or implicitly, a limited Safety contract to a visitor providing that such a contract will not harm the Islamic State or Muslims.[247] A general Safety contract can occur between large groups of non-Muslims or an entire nation and the Islamic State. At a lesser level of government, the governor of a province or mayor of a city may also enter into a Safety contract with the residents of a province or city respectively.[248]

Non-Muslim residence in the Islamic State for an extended period may result in significant consequences including gaining citizenship of the Islamic State.[249] This might occur when a non-Muslim's acts, expressly or implicitly, show an intention to join the social contract between the State and non-Muslims. The implied intention of the non-Muslim to become a citizen may occur by various means including purchasing real estate in the Islamic State and paying real

---

[245] Ibn Qudamah,10 *Al-Mughni wa'l-Sharh al-Kabir*, (Beirut: Dar Al-Fikr),572

[246] *Id.*

[247] Ministry of Awqaf of Arab Republic of Egypt (Egypt's Islamic Trust Ministry), 26 Mawso'ah al-Fiqh al-Islami (Islamic Fiqh Encyclopedia), 5-8. Ibn Qudamah,10 *Al-Mughni wa'l-Sharh al-Kabir*, (Beirut: Dar Al-Fikr), 548.

[248] Id.

[249] Ibn Nujaym, 5 *Al-Bahr ar-Raiq Sharh Kanz ad-Daqaiq*, (Beirut, Dar Al Kotob Al-Ilmiyah 1997),170.

estate taxes on time. Accordingly, classical Islamic law scholars repeatedly asserted that the Safety contract is limited to a renewable, specified period.[250] The renowned scholar, al-Nasaqui, suggested that the visiting period should be less than one year[251]. Others suggested that it could be extended up to ten years.[252]

A modern theory of the Islamic State would necessarily include only one type of Safety contract, a general contract between the Islamic State and the visitor. It is not plausible to allow non-officials, or municipalities' executives, with limited powers, the right to grant a Safety contract to visitors. It would be chaotic to have random persons issuing safety contracts in a large population as currently exists in modern Muslim-majority states. Modern States should confer the power of granting non-nationals the right of entry to the proper department of the executive branch of the government exclusively. The modern designation of the Safety contract is the entry permit/visa. Thus, the entry permit/visa is a reciprocal contract between the visitor and the Islamic State upon which the visitor is under obligation to respect and uphold the Islamic State's laws as long as he is in the Islamic State. In return, the Islamic State guarantees the visitor's rights including Islamic human rights. Gaining the Islamic State's citizenship should be regulated, subject to Islamic law, as the State sees fit.

Attacks on tourists that have occurred in recent years are never justified under Islamic law and are in clear violation of the Islamic

---

[250] Ibn Qudamah,10 *Al-Mughni wa'l-Sharh al-Kabir*, (Beirut: Dar Al-Fikr),509-11.

[251] Ibn Nujaym, 5 *Al-Bahr ar-Raiq Sharh Kanz ad-Daqaiq*, (Beirut, Dar Al Kotob Al-Ilmiyah 1997),170.

[252] Mansur al-Buhuti, 3 *Kashshāf al-Qinā' 'an Matn al-Iqnā'*,(Beirut, Dar Al Kotob Al-Ilmiyah 1997), 118.

Safety Contract. This is true even if the tourists are nationals of a State at war with the Islamic State so long as the visitor(s) holds a valid visa/entry permit/Safety contract. However, this does not necessarily mean that those who enter the Islamic State illegally have no rights. Islamic Human Rights remain applicable to everyone including the right to live with dignity.

Correspondingly, the *Qur'an* has ordered Muslims to fulfill their covenants.[253] Accordingly, a Muslim who enters a non-Islamic State with an entry permit must fulfil its obligations including the obligation to respect and uphold the non-Muslim State laws. If the Muslim believes that he cannot respect and uphold the non-Islamic State laws because it contradicts Islamic law or otherwise, he ought to depart immediately. Therefore, acts of terrorism committed against non-Islamic States by visa holding individuals not only violate the *Qur'an* and Islamic law in general but in addition, invoke the toughest punishments in Islam under the law of *Hirabah*.[254]

C. Harbi

Non-Muslims who neither reside in the Islamic State nor are party to the Safety contract with the Islamic State are *Harbi*. The status of *Harbi* is governed by Islamic law. In particular, the *Qur'an* explains general Islamic State's rights and obligations towards *Harbi*(s) as follows:

> "Allah forbids you not, with regard to those who fight you not for (your) Faith nor drive you out of your homes, from dealing kindly and justly with them: for Allah loves those who are just. Allah only forbids you, with regard to those who fight you for

---

[253] Qur'an, 17:33-5.

[254] Hirabah is a category of offenses that includes highway robbery.

*(your) Faith and drive you out, of your homes, and support
(others) in driving you out, from turning to them (for friendship
and protection)".* [255]

These clear Qur'anic guidelines establish that peace, with
graceful, just dealing is the norm while war is permitted to fight
oppression. Elsewhere in the *Qur'an*, Muslims are ordered to favour
peace over war if the enemy so desires. [256] More specifically, contrary
to many Orientalists' unfounded claims, *Harbi* enjoy Islamic human
rights including the right to life and the right to asylum by virtue of
the *Qur'an*. [257]

5.5.2   Rights of Non-Muslims in The Islamic State

As stipulated earlier, Islamic human rights guarantee fundamental
rights to all people, Muslims and non-Muslims alike. Non-Muslims
should receive identical treatment as Muslims in the Islamic State.
However, there are some rights and obligations commanded by the
contract of *Dhimmah*, the social contract between non-Muslims and
the Islamic State that have to be explained in detail given that non-
Muslims rights are constantly misrepresented by numerous
Orientalists as well as by violent groups such as the Islamic State of
Iraq and Syria or ISIS, which has been unfairly branding itself as an
Islamic State.

The specific rights emphasized under *Dhimmah* contract are:

---

[255] Qur'an 60:8-9.

[256] Qur'an 8:61.

[257] Qur'an 17:33-5 &9:6.

A. The Right to Life and Security of A Person

Dhimmah social contract ensures that non-Muslims, like Muslims, have the right to life and security of person from domestic or foreign aggression.[258] The renowned Islamic law scholar of the Middle Ages, *Imam* al-Shaybānī, suggested that a distinction ought to be made between a non-Muslim citizen and a visitor.[259] The visitor to the Islamic State, that is a national of another State, is offered only protection from harm occurring inside the Islamic State by the nationals of the Islamic State provided that the visitor's State is able to protect its citizens from outside aggression. A citizen or permanent

---

[258] The Prophet Muhammad said "those who commit an act of aggression against a member of the non-Muslims, who usurp his rights, who makes any demand upon him which is beyond his capacity to fulfill, who forcibly obtain anything from him against his wishes, I will be his (the oppressed's) advocate on the day of judgment." This Hadith was listed in Abu Dawood Hadith book and Baihaqi, As-Sunan Al-Kobra book. In the same meaning see Hadith "who harms a non-Muslim harms me, and he who harms me , harms Allah." Imam At-Tabarani, Al Awsat Hadith collection. See Also Yusuf al-Qaradawi, *Non-Muslims in the Islamic Society*, (Khalil Muhammad Hamad & Sayed Mahboob Ali Shah Trans.), (American Trust Publications 1985),4. *See also* Hadith listed in Sahih Al-Bukhari Collection, Hadith Number 3166, The book of Jihad. Narrated 'Abdullah bin Amr: "the Prophet said, whoever killed a person having safety covenant with the Muslims, shall not smell of paradise though it is smelled from a distance of forty years". See Hadith in Sahih Al-Bukhari collection, Hadith Number 3052 the book of Jihad :"Narrated Amr Bin Maimun: Umar (the *Caliph* of the Muslims, after he was mortally stabbed) instructed (his would be successor) saying, I urge him (the New *Caliph*) to take care of those non-Muslims who are under the protection of Allah and his Massager in that he should observe the convention agreed upon with them, and fight on their behalf (to secure their safety) and should not overtax them beyond their capability". Also Yusuf al-Qaradawi, *Non-Muslims in the Islamic Society*, (Khalil Muhammad Hamad & Sayed Mahboob Ali Shah Trans.), (American Trust Publications 1985),4-8.

[259] Muḥammad ibn al-Ḥasan al-Shaybānī, 5 *Sharḥ kitāb al-Siyar al-kabīr*, (Beirut, Dar Al Kotob Al-Ilmiyah 1997), 110-112.

resident of the Islamic state, whether Muslim or non-Muslim, enjoys the state's duty of protecting him from unjustified harm inside the Islamic State and abroad.[260] Thus, if a hostile State attacks the Islamic State, killing and abducting individuals, it is the duty of the Islamic State to seek the release and protection of permanent residents and citizens only and not the visitors.[261] The burden of protecting a visitor, the national of another State, from a harm caused by a third party State rests upon the visitor's State. There are two exceptions to this rule. 1) A Stateless visitor, with no protection from another State shall enjoy the Islamic state's full protection from harm caused by either the Islamic State or a foreign State, so long as the harm occurred while the Stateless person was in the Islamic State.[262] 2) When a visitor enters the Islamic State on a condition that s/he will receive the status of a citizen upon entry into the Islamic State with respect to the rights and duties or rights only, such a condition must be fulfilled.[263]

---

[260] Historical incidents are the prime example for equal protection of Muslims and Non-Muslim Dhimmi resident in the Islamic State. The renowned scholar Ibn Taymiyya, as a representative of the Islamic State, went to Qatlo Shah, the Tarter invader of Syria, to negotiate the release of the prisoners of war. Qatlo Shah refused the release non-Muslims and accepted the release of Muslims. After Ibn Taymiyya's insistence on release of all prisoners indiscriminately, Qatlo Shah released all prisoners of war, Muslims and Non-Muslims. See Also Yusuf al-Qaradawi, *Non-Muslims in the Islamic Society*, (Khalil Muhammad Hamad & Sayed Mahboob Ali Shah Trans.), (American Trust Publications 1985),4.

[261] Muḥammad ibn al-Ḥasan al-Shaybānī, 5 *Sharḥ kitāb al-Siyar al-kabīr*, (Beirut, Dar Al Kotob Al-Ilmiyah 1997), 110-112.

[262] Muḥammad ibn al-Ḥasan al-Shaybānī, 5 *Sharḥ kitāb al-Siyar al-kabīr*, (Beirut, Dar Al Kotob Al-Ilmiyah 1997), 134-7.

[263] " It is not righteousness that ye turn your faces towards East or West; but it is righteousness to believe in Allah and the Last Day, and the Angels, and the Book, and the Messengers; to spend of your substance, out of love for Him, for your kin, for orphans, for the needy, for the wayfarer, for those who ask, and for the ransom of slaves; to be steadfast in prayer, and practice regular charity, <u>to</u>

Due to the limited control of the Islamic State outside its territories, Islamic law scholars have developed a territorial jurisdictional theory. The theory is based on the factual realization that the Islamic State cannot be responsible for or protect other nationals of foreign nations from the actions committed by non-Muslim residents/citizens of the Islamic State outside its territories. However, the Islamic State may act as an advisor, moderator or referee, as the circumstances require, on the basis of its moral obligation to forbid wrong deeds, but not as a State exercising its sovereign power.[264] In this context, when a non-Muslim commits an offense in a foreign territory, he will not be prosecuted or punished for such an offense in the Islamic State.[265] Similarly, a civil wrongs court order issued by a foreign court shall not be enforced in the Islamic State.[266] However, the Islamic State authorities may issue an advisory statement to foreign nations urging them to comply with equitable foreign judgments. Nevertheless, if the Islamic State is a party to a treaty that requires extradition and/or enforcement of foreign judgments that do not contradict the foundation of Islamic law, the terms stipulated in the treaty shall be honored and enforced.[267]

The right to life and security of a person extend to cover economic security. The Islamic State guarantees social welfare for every

---

fulfill the contracts which ye have made; and to be firm and patient, in pain (or suffering) and adversity, and throughout all periods of panic. Such are the people of truth, the God-fearing" Quran 2:177.

[264]"Ye are the best of Peoples, evolved for mankind, enjoining what is right, forbidding what is wrong, ..." Quran 3:110.

[265] Muḥammad ibn al-Ḥasan al-Shaybānī, 5 *Sharḥ kitab al-Siyar al-kabīr*, (Beirut, Dar Al Kotob Al-Ilmiyah 1997), 100-2.

[266] Id.

[267] Qur'an 5:1 & 23:8.

individual in the Islamic State. Capital collected from the mandatory charity imposed on Muslims, *Zakat,* and the tax imposed on non-Muslims, *Jizya,* are among the major sources funding the Islamic social welfare system. Entitlement of non-Muslims to social welfare was reaffirmed historically on a number of occasions.[268]

B. Autonomous Rights

Islamic law recognizes the worth of free will, human autonomy and the right to be governed by rules fashioned by that free will: the autonomous rights for non-Muslims and Muslims. Perhaps the most important autonomous right for non-Muslims in the Islamic state is the freedom of embracing and exercising a religion. History testifies that Islamic law pioneered the freedom of embracing a religion, or no religion, in an era marked by extreme religious intolerance. [269] For instance, the Roman Empire, at the time a world superpower, gave its citizens the choice between embracing the state religion or death.[270]

---

[268] Yusuf al-Qaradawi, *Non-Muslims in the Islamic Society*, (Khalil Muhammad Hamad & Sayed Mahboob Ali Shah Trans.), (American Trust Publications 1985),9. See Right to Social Security in Universal Islamic Declaration of Human Rights (1981). See also article 17 of The Cairo Declaration on Human Rights in Islam (1990).

[269] Guglielmo Ferrero & Corrado Barbagallo, 2 *Short History of Rome,* (Capricorn Books 1964), 431 -458.

[270] Id. A distinction must be made between Islamic law, as a code, and intolerant practices that constituted undue hardship to the practice of religion that sporadically occurred in the modern history of the Islamic states. A number of those incidents targeted a particular religion. On other occasions, it targeted all religious practices alike including Islamic practices. *See* Qasem Abdu Qasem, *Ahl El Zimmah Fe Misr men al Fath al-Islami heta Nahyat al-Mamaleek* (Dhimmi people in Egypt from the time when Islam conquered Egypt till Mamluk era), (Cairo, Ein for Human and Social studies 2003), 31-80. Ill practices against non-Muslims were primarily due to the *Caliph's* (ruler) disobedience of Islamic law.

More than 1400 years ago the *Qur'an* ordered Muslims: "Let there be no compulsion in religion: Truth stands out clear from Error…"[271] This Qur'anic rule is well rooted in Islamic jurisprudence given that Islam recognizes that all Mankind, regardless of their faith, color or otherwise, is entitled to the benefit of honorable and dignified treatment.[272] A facet of the right of honorable treatment is the Freedom of Embracing and Exercising a Religion. This freedom is immensely important especially to minorities who reside in the Islamic state, to protect them from the tyranny of the majority. If a ruler of a Muslim majority state mistreats non-Muslims because of their religious beliefs, they can invoke their guaranteed freedoms including the freedom to practice their faith, or not to practice any religion, freely.

For example, the *Caliph* Abdul-Malik confiscated the Church of John and made it part of a mosque. Christians complained to Umar Bin Abdulaziz, the successor of Abdul-Malik, for the loss of their church. Umar order the Governor of the province where the incident occurred, to offer a monetary settlement or, if the Christians were unsatisfied, to return the church to them. *See* Yusuf al-Qaradawi, *Non-Muslims in the Islamic Society*, (Khalil Muhammad Hamad & Sayed Mahboob Ali Shah Trans.), (American Trust Publications 1985), 32.

[271] Qur'an (2:256), See also "If it had been thy Lord's Will, they would all have believed, all who are on earth! Wilt thou then compel mankind, against their will, to believe!" Qur'an 10:99. One of the main characteristics of Islamic human rights is that it is eternal and mandatory in nature as opposed to other human rights instruments such as the Universal Declaration of Human Rights (1948) or subject to constitutional limitations imposed by courts e.g. S. 1 in the Canadian Charter of Rights and Freedoms (1982). Recently, the freedom to embrace and exercise a religion was reaffirmed in the Universal Islamic Declaration of Human Rights Articles. X (Rights of Minorities), XII (Right to Freedom of Belief, Thought and Speech) and XIII (Right to Freedom of Religion). http://www.alhewar.com/ISLAMDECL.html.

[272] We have honored the sons of Adam…) Qur'an 17:70

The right to embrace and exercise religion in Islam blossomed to include many freedoms. Non-Muslims in the Islamic state enjoy the freedom of implementing their religious law of personal status. The rationale is that laws of personal status are closely associated with, if not a fundamental part of, one's religion. Imposing foreign law of personal status, e.g., Islamic law, which stands at odds with the non-Muslim's beliefs, is a violation of Islamic human rights, the right of embracing religion. In general terms, the right to practice religion also includes a policy of non-intervention in the internal religious affairs of non-Muslims such as electing the Pope, the hierarchy of the religious leader, or building places of worship.[273]

Under freedom to practice religion in Islamic law, religious minorities in the Islamic State established religious courts to settle disputes among individuals who adhere to the same religion so long as the disputes are not related to public order, e.g., criminal offenses, basic civil transactions. This typically limits the application of religious law to family law matters. Christian courts that applied Canon law and Rabbinical courts that applied *Halakhah* (Jewish law) thrived under the Islamic regime.[274] Interestingly, family law for non-

---

[273] See Qasem Abdu Qasem, *Ahl El Zimmah Fe Misr men al Fath al-Islami heta Nahyat al-Mamaleek* (Dhimmi people in Egypt from the time when Islam conquered Egypt till Mamluk era), (Cairo, Ein for Human and Social studies 2003), 31-80.

[274] See Yusuf al-Qaradawi, *Non-Muslims in the Islamic Society*, (Khalil Muhammad Hamad & Sayed Mahboob Ali Shah Trans.), (American Trust Publications 1985),25(citing the historian Adam Mez), *See also*, Joel, Beinin, *The Dispersion of Egyptian Jewry; Culture, Politics, and the Formation of a Modern Diaspora*, (University of California Press 1998), 36-37.

Muslims has been applied even when it offends the moral and religious norms of Islam.[275]

Recognizing the legal autonomy of religious minorities, leading to the creation of parallel court systems, has created conflict of laws challenges. Individuals from religious minorities may not share the same religion and accordingly not share the same law, e.g., a Jew married to a Christian or an atheist, a Muslim married to a Jew or a Christian, or even individuals from the same religion who are dissatisfied with the law of their religion. In all these instances, the general law of the land, i.e., Islamic law, shall apply.[276]

At this point, one ought to realize that free exercise of a religion under Islamic law is much broader than its counterpart in Western societies. Indeed, free exercise of religion in Western societies has an unduly restrictive meaning, in comparison to Islamic law. While most of the modern day constitutions affirm free exercise of religion, most of Western States, except the United Kingdom, has forbidden implementation of the law of personal status for religious minorities

---

[275] During the reign of the Muslim *Caliph* Umar Ibn Abd Al Aziz, Umar asked the renowned scholar Al-Hassan Al-Basri for a *fatwa* (religious opinion) regarding permitting non-Muslims, residing the in the Islamic State, to marry regardless of consanguinity.[275] Al-Hassan advised the *Caliph* to allow non-Muslims to practice their family law although it is repulsive to Muslims. Compare the status of orthodox Mormons who are persecuted for practicing polygamy which is a part of orthodox Mormons religious teachings and remains a fundamental part of a number of religious sects. See Edwin Brown Firmage and Richard Collin Mangrum, *Zion in the Courts: A Legal History of the Church of Jesus Christ of Latter-day Saints, 1830-1900*, (University of Illinois Press 2001), 59-236.

[276] Muhammad Sharif Chaudhry, *Non-Muslim minorities in an Islamic state*, (Impact Publications International 1995), 34.

in the domestic courts or utilizing religious law to settle family disputes in a religious quasi-judicial forum, e.g., arbitration.[277]

In addition, free exercise of religion under Islamic law encompasses exercising religion free from harassment and degradation due to one's faith. If there is conflict between any right and the free exercise of religion, the latter prevails. For example, in defamation of religion, there two competing rights; freedom of speech and freedom to practice a religion devoid of undue harassment/defaming of one's religion. The international community is sharply divided on this issue.[278] Numerous Western countries favor

---

[277] See (Congress shall make no law respecting an establishment of religion, or prohibiting the free exercise thereof…) First Amendment, U.S. Constitution., See also (2. Everyone has the following fundamental freedoms: a) freedom of conscience and religion; b) freedom of thought, belief, opinion and expression, including freedom of the press and other media of communication…) section 2 of The Canadian Charter of Rights and Freedoms. Mormons historically have been and still are persecuted, especially with respect to polygamy. Polygamy is a part of Mormons religious teachings and remains a fundamental part of a number of religious sects. See Edwin Brown Firmage and Richard Collin Mangrum, *Zion in the Courts: A Legal History of the Church of Jesus Christ of Latter-day Saints, 1830-1900*, (University of Illinois Press 2001), 59-236. Recently the Ontario provincial government rejected a proposal to allow the use of Islamic law to settle family disputes in arbitrations. See http://www.foxnews.com/story/0,2933,169125,00.html. Recently U.K. allowed Islamic family law tribunals see http://www.timesonline.co.uk/tol/news/uk/crime/article4749183.ece.
[278] U.N. Human Rights Council adopted resolution on religious defamation. See U.N. Human Rights Council Resolution Combating Defamation of Religions, Resolution 7/19 (March 27, 2009). Countries that voted in favor of the resolution: Azerbaijan, Bangladesh, Cameroon, China, Cuba, Djibouti, Egypt, Indonesia, Jordan, Malaysia, Mali, Nicaragua, Nigeria, Pakistan, Philippines, Qatar, Russian Federation, Saudi Arabia, Senegal, South Africa, Sri Lanka. Countries that voted against the resolution: Canada, France, Germany, Italy, Netherlands, Romania, Slovenia, Switzerland, Ukraine, United Kingdom of Great Britain and Northern

freedom of speech at the expense of cross-cultural and interfaith harmony.[279] In contrast, several Muslim-majority states, representing the Islamic view, favor the freedom to practice religion free of defamatory persecution at the expense of freedom of speech.[280]

Another right that has arisen from the right to embrace and exercise religion freely in Islam is the right to be free from the Islamic lifestyle and trade practices that are based solely on the Islamic faith. For example, both alcoholic beverages and pork are prohibited items for Muslims to buy, sell or consume.[281] Non-Muslims may buy, sell or consume alcohol freely in the Islamic State so long as they do not sell or serve it to Muslims. Moreover, Islamic law does not recognize the right of ownership of alcoholic beverages or pork for Muslims, while it does for non-Muslims. A Muslim who damages alcoholic beverages or pork owned by another Muslim is not liable for his actions and may be rewarded.[282] If a non-Muslim owns the alcoholic beverages or pork, the Muslim who damages them is liable for his actions civilly and criminally.[283] Here, Muslims, the dominant group in the Islamic State do not impose their religious standard upon the non-dominant

---

Ireland. See http://ap.ohchr.org/documents/E/HRC/resolutions/A_HRC_RES_7_19.pdf.

[279] Id.

[280] Id.

[281] "O ye who believe! intoxicants and gambling, (dedication of) stones, and (divination by) arrows, are an abomination of Satan's handiwork: eschew such (abomination), that ye may prosper." Qur'an 5:90. "Forbidden to you (for food) are: dead meat, blood, the flesh of swine (pork)…" Qur'an 5:3.

[282] Shams al-Din al-Sarakhsi ', 5 *Kitab al-Mabsut*, (Beirut, Dar Al Fikr 2000), 131-161. *See also*, Yusuf al-Qaradawi, *Non-Muslims in the Islamic Society*, (Khalil Muhammad Hamad & Sayed Mahboob Ali Shah Trans.), (American Trust Publications 1985),7.

[283] Id.

group; instead, an objective standard contradicting the formal equality was mandated to achieve substantive fairness.

Autonomous rights for non-Muslims, like other rights, are subject to reasonable limitation in a civil society. The rationale for setting a limitation is that allowing every group of individuals to create their religion and laws would lead to lawlessness and disorder in that every person or group could set their own law. For instance, a religious group could claim that paying taxes is prohibited by their religion or that torturing animals is an integral part of their religious practice. A primary uniform law and legal system is a fundamental necessity to establish a State. On this basis, Islamic law scholars concluded that most civil transactions would be subject to Islamic law to create economic harmony, stability, and equitable commercial transactions. Thus, gambling, *Riba* (roughly translated, usury) ought to be prohibited for *all* citizens and residents of the Islamic State. However, activities that do not impinge upon the socio-economic structure of the Islamic State, i.e., buying, selling and consuming alcohol or pork are permitted to non-Muslims *only*.

Similarly, Islamic criminal law, with some exceptions, shall apply to every individual who resides or visits the Islamic State.[284] Only the renowned scholar, Abu Hanifa, on the basis of his theory of personal jurisdiction, as distinguished from territorial jurisdiction theory, suggested that Islamic criminal law should not apply to non-Muslims residing or visiting the Islamic State.[285] Barring Abu Hanifa, scholars have unanimously supported this all-encompassing application of Islamic criminal law.

---

[284] Id.

[285] Id.

Several Islamic law scholars have drawn theoretical guidelines to assess the permissibility of creating an exception to non-Muslims concerning the Islamic legal norms in the Islamic State.[286] The prominent Islamic philosopher, al-Shatibi, argued that five main interests ought to be protected, namely, the protection of religion, life, intellect, procreation, and property.[287] Conduct that does not encroach upon one of these social interests and is not expressly prohibited in the primary sources of Islamic law, i.e., *Qur'an* and *Sunnah*, ought to be permitted.[288] If there is a conflict between two or more interests, Islamic law strikes a balance by averting the greater of two harms by the assumption of the lesser harm, or by preferentially averting harm over procuring benefits or averting public harm by the private assumption of loss.[289] The application of these guidelines is straightforward. Sale or consumption of alcohol by non-Muslims may cause harm to the non-Muslim consumer, and it infringes upon the Islamic State's right to protect intellect and life. However, a non-Muslim might be required to consume alcohol as a religious ritual. Accordingly, depriving non-Muslims of trade or consumption of alcohol infringes upon one of Islamic law's objectives, namely, protection of religion providing that freedom to practice a religion is

---

[286] Rashad Hassan Khalil, 2 *Nazaryat al-Mossawah Fe Al-Shariah al-Islamia* (Equality theory in Islamic Law), (Cairo, Dar al-Farouq publishing),324-326.

[287] Muhammad Khalid Masud, *Shatibi's Philosophy of Islamic Law*, (Kitab Bhavan 1998), 151-152.

[288] Id. Sunnah can be defined as, (That of the spoken and acted examples of the prophet (Muhammad). It includes what he approved, allowed or condoned when under prevailing circumstances). Cyril Glasse, *The New Encyclopedia of Islam* (3rd ed.), (Rowman & Littlefield Publishers 2008), 504.

[289] Hisham M. Ramadan, "On Islamic Punishment", In Hisham M. Ramadan (ed.), *Understanding Islamic Law: From Classical to Contemporary*, (AltaMira Press 2006), 44.

a guaranteed right in Islam. Hence, Islamic law assumes the lesser evil, i.e., potentially causing harm to the non-Muslim consumer, thus allowing the sale and consumption of alcohol for non-Muslims. In contrast, *Riba* is both prohibited under the *Qur'an* and infringes upon the protection of property interest, because *Riba* creates an unjust financial system, according to Islam.[290] Because there is no recognizable right, religious right or otherwise, attached to the practice of *Riba* and since *Riba* causes harm to society at large, the Islamic legislature ought to avert the harm by forbidding the practice of *Riba* to Muslims and non-Muslims alike.

Remarkably freedom to exercise religion is so fundamental in Islam that numerous Muslims believe limiting such a right jeopardizes world peace. The eminent scholar Muhammed Abu Zahra suggested suppressing the practice of a religion is justification for launching a war against the oppressive regime.[291] The history of the early Islamic state supports this proposition. The Islamic state launched a war against the Roman Empire after the Romans

---

[290] (O you who believe! Be afraid of Allah and give up what remains (due to you) from Riba (usury) (from now onward), if you are (really) believers. And if you do not do it, then take a notice of war from Allah and His Messenger but if you repent, you shall have your capital sums. Deal not unjustly (by asking more than your capital sums), and you shall not be dealt with unjustly (by receiving less than your capital sums). Qur'an 2:278-279.

[291] Muhammed Abu Zahra, *al-'Alaqat al-Duwaliyya fi al-Islam* (international relationships in Islam), (Cairo, Dar al-Fikr al-Arabi 1995), 53. The source of Professor Abu Zahra proposition is this Quranic text: Allah forbids you not, with regard to those who fight you not for (your) Faith nor drive you out of your homes, from dealing kindly and justly with them: for Allah loves those who are just. Allah only forbids you, with regard to those who fight you for (your) Faith, and drive you out, of your homes, and support (others) in driving you out, from turning to them (for friendship and protection). It is such as turn to them (in these circumstances), that do wrong.) Qur'an 60:8-9.

slaughtered Muslims and Jews who practiced their religion in al-Sham region.[292] Once the Islamic state captured al-Sham, freedom to embrace and exercise religion was protected.[293]

5.5.3 Duties of Non-Muslim In The Islamic State

A. General Taxes (*Jizya*)

The Islamic State employs its financial system to foster social justice and eradicate negative feelings generated by financial status differences among its citizens. Muslims residing in the Islamic State pay the obligatory charity, *zakat,* that supports the weak, ill and needy and accordingly eliminates the negative feelings of social class envy and injustice.[294] Mandatory charity, *zakat,* is a religious duty and a

---

[292] Id. AL-Sham region currently includes Syria, Lebanon, and Palestine. See also Guglielmo Ferrero & Corrado Barbagallo, 2 *Short History of Rome,* (Capricorn Books 1964), 431 -458.

[293] The following paragraph is an excerpt from the treaty of surrender of Jerusalem. The treaty was signed by the patriarch of the city on behalf of the Christians and the Islamic state ruler (the *Caliph*). The treaty reads … (The *Caliph*) guarantees for them (the Christians) the safety of their persons, of their goods, of their churches and Crosses- whether in good state or repair or otherwise- and generally of their religion. Their churches will not be changed into dwellings, nor destroyed. Neither they nor their properties will suffer any damage whatsoever. In matters religious, no coercion will be exercised against them. Nor will any of them be hurt. See Ismail Raji al-Faruqi, *Islam and Other Faiths,* (Ataullah Siddiqui (ed.), (The Islamic Foundation 1998), 295.

[294] See (…and establish regular Prayer and give regular Charity; and loan to Allah a Beautiful Loan. And whatever good ye send forth for your souls, ye shall find it in Allah's Presence, yea, better and greater, in Reward, and seek ye the Grace of Allah: for Allah is Oft-Forgiving, Most Merciful.) Qur'an (73:20). See the distribution of charity is means to achieve social harmony (Alms are for the poor and the needy, and those employed to administer the (funds); for those whose hearts have been (recently) reconciled (to the truth); for those in bondage and in

right for those in need that ought to be collected by force if necessary.[295] Because *zakat* is a religious duty for Muslims, non-Muslims that reside in the Islamic State are not required to pay it.[296] Instead, they are required to pay *Jizya* Taxation.[297]

Jizya tax is a per capita annual obligation levied on all adult, sane men who can earn their livelihood and are capable of being a combatant for the Islamic State.[298] Women, children, poor men and the mentally ill are entirely exempt from *Jizya* Payment.[299] There is no consensus on the amount due; rather it is up to the Islamic State government, at a particular time and place, to determine the tax amount. Historically, *Jizya* amount has always been much less the *Zakat* obligation on Muslims. However, under no circumstances should *Jizya* be excessive that non-Muslims would to convert to Islam

---

debt; in the cause of Allah; and for the wayfarer: (thus is it) ordained by Allah, and Allah is full of knowledge and wisdom) Qur'an 9:60.

[295] Ibn Rushd (Averroës),1 *Bidayat al-Mujtahid wa-Nihayat al-Muqtasid*, (Cairo, Al-Maktabah al-Tawfiqia), 446-460.

[296] Ibn Rushd (Averroës),1 *Bidayat al-Mujtahid wa-Nihayat al-Muqtasid*, (Cairo, Al-Maktabah al-Tawfiqia), 714.

[297] "Fight those who believe not in Allah nor the Last Day, nor hold that forbidden which hath been forbidden by Allah and His Messenger, nor acknowledge the Religion of Truth, from among the People of the Book, until they pay the Jizya with willing submission, and feel themselves subdued." Quran 9:29. The original text in Arabic speak of Dhimmis paying Jizya while "Saghron". The word Saghron is never meant to humiliate Dhimmi, as a number of Orientalist scholars have maintained. Rather it denotes surrendering, laying down of arms and accepting the laws of the Islamic State. See Yusuf al-Qaradawi, *Non-Muslims in the Islamic Society*, (Khalil Muhammad Hamad & Sayed Mahboob Ali Shah Trans.), (American Trust Publications 1985).

[298] S. Abul A'al, Maududi, *The Islamic Law and Constitution*, (Khurshid Ahmad Trans. &ed.) (12th ed.), (Lahore, Islamic Publications 1997), 282.

[299] God puts no burden on any person beyond what he has given him. Quran 65:7.

just to avoid *Jizya*. In fact, imposition of any burden on non-Muslims, such as excessive taxation, that virtually forces them to convert to Islam violates freedom of embracing and exercising a religion.

The eminent Islamic scholar, Al Mawardi, suggested taxes should vary depending on the wealth of the *Dhimmi* taxpayer. The Islamic State may divide *Dhimmi* individuals into four main categories: wealthy, average wealth person, least wealth person, and poor person.[300] A person of average wealth should pay double what the least wealthy person pays.[301] A wealthy person should pay double what an average wealth person pays.[302] A poor person is exempt from paying *Jizya*.[303]

Paying *Jizya* tax triggers *Dhimmi* rights such as protection, e.g. enjoying the ownership of property without interruption or interventions.[304] If the State fails to offer the rights associated with paying *Jizya*, the State must refund *Jizya* in full. The similarity between *Jizya* tax and the local tax systems in non-Islamic States is

---

[300] Abu'l Hasan al-Mawardi, *Kitab Al Ahkam As Sultaniyyah* (The laws of Islamic Governance), (Beirut, Dar al-Fikr), 144.

[301] Abu Hanifa suggested that a wealthy person should pay forty-eight Durhams, an average wealth person pay twenty-four Durhams and the least wealthy person should pay 12 Durhams. See Abu'l Hasan al-Mawardi, *Kitab Al Ahkam As Sultaniyyah* (The laws of Islamic Governance), (Beirut, Dar al-Fikr), 144. However, other scholars suggested different amounts and it seems that the amount due is subject to change depending on time and place. See Ibn Qudamah,10 *Al-Mughni wa'l-Sharh al-Kabir*, (Beirut, Dar Al-Fikr), 566-8.

[302] Id.

[303] "Let the man of means spend according to his means: and the man whose resources are restricted, let him spend according to what Allah has given him. Allah puts no burden on any person beyond what He has given him. After a difficulty, Allah will soon grant relief." Quran 65:7.

[304] S. Abul A'al, Maududi, *The Islamic Law and Constitution*, (Khurshid Ahmad Trans. &ed.) (12th ed.), (Lahore, Islamic Publications 1997), 281.

noteworthy. Residents of a city are typically required to pay property tax that funds social services such as schools, roads maintenance, and police. Likewise, *Dhimmi* receives various rights in return for paying *Jizya*, including social welfare.

In sum, *the Jizya* tax system is employed to assure the *Dhimmi* contribution to the general revenue, though it might be much less than the Muslims' contribution, to access many entitlements such as social welfare, policing, protection from non-Islamic State external aggression and other social services.

B. Agricultural Land Tax (*Kharaj*)

Kharaj, a state general revenue source, is the productive agricultural land taxation of land that was *once* owned by a non-Muslim. Accordingly, *Dhimmi* may also be required to pay this tax.[305] Conversion of *Dhimmi* into Islam does not cease the payment of *Kharaj*.[306] Nor does sale to a Muslim of the land upon which *Kharaj* is levied cause cessation of the payment of *Kharaj*.[307] This sort of taxation varies depending upon certain factors including the nature of the land, e.g., highly productive land, average production land, crop type, whether the crops are grown annually, semiannually or every two years.[308]

---

[305] Abu'l Hasan al-Mawardi, *Kitab Al Ahkam As Sultaniyyah* (The laws of Islamic Governance), (Beirut, Dar al-Fikr), 148-56.

[306] Yusuf Al-Qaradawi & A. Azhar Nadvi, *Islam: Muslims & Non-Muslims*, (India, Adam Publishers & Distributors 2000), 136.

[307] Id.

[308] It is worth noting that a new convert into Islam, according to Imam Malek, Al-Shafi' and Ibn Hanbel, must pay Zakat, instead of Jizya, *Kharaj* and 5% or 10 % of his land's yield. Imam Abu Hanifa disagreed with this opinion. *See* Yusuf al-Qaradawi, *Non-Muslims in the Islamic Society*, (Khalil Muhammad

C. Commercial Tax

During the reign of the *Caliph* Umar Ibn al-Khattab, the Islamic State, pursuant to Umar's orders, imposed a commercial tax on *Dhimmi* upon movement of their goods from one region to another.[309] There is no reference to this type of taxation in the primary sources of Islamic law, i.e., the *Qur'an* and *Sunnah*. Therefore, scholars theorize possible justifications for such a tax. Some scholars suggested that the commercial tax was based upon an agreement between *Dhimmi* and Umar.[310] Others concluded that this tax is equivalent to a customs duty levied on imported goods.[311] Nevertheless, since the only source of this tax is the *Caliph* Umar Ibn al-Khattab's order, the modern Islamic State may be required to examine the justification for this tax in current times and possibly eliminate it.

Apart from the Orientalists' unsupported and unauthenticated assertions that many forms of taxation have been imposed on non-Muslims, *Jizya*, *Kharaj* and commercial taxes are the only taxes ever known to have been levied on non-Muslims in the Islamic State. [312]

Hamad & Sayed Mahboob Ali Shah Trans.), (American Trust Publications 1985),20.

[309] Abu 'Ubayd al-Qasim ibn Salam, *The Book Of Finance (Kitab al-Amwal)*,(Delhi, Adam Publishers 2007).

[310] See Yusuf al-Qaradawi, *Non-Muslims in the Islamic Society*, (Khalil Muhammad Hamad & Sayed Mahboob Ali Shah Trans.), (American Trust Publications 1985),23-4.

[311] Id.

[312] See Bat Ye'or, *The Dhimmi: Jews and Christians Under Islam*, (Fairleigh Dickinson University Press, 1985),54-5.

5.5.4 State, Muslim and Non-Muslim Duty to Promote a Tolerant Society

Islam as a universal religion that aims to unite individuals from different cultures and backgrounds. The Islamic State is open to individuals of all faiths, or no faith, to reside and prosper. Thus, striving to achieve social harmony is an essential goal of the Islamic State.[313] To promote harmony in a diverse society, two restrictions are imposed, one on the state and the other on individuals.

First, the Islamic State must refrain from imposing obligations on Muslims and non-Muslims that conflict with their religious beliefs or interfere with free exercise of religion.[314] Accordingly, for instance, Jews are not to be compelled to work or be at a disadvantage if they refrain from working on Saturdays, to allow them to observe their Sabbath.[315] Correspondingly, Christians are not to be compelled to work or be at a disadvantage if they refrain from working on Sundays during the time allocated for their prayer services.[316]

Second, Muslims and non-Muslims alike are required to refrain from defaming others' religions in order to maintain social

---

[313] Indeed, social harmony is a true goal of every civilized state especially if the state encompasses various religions and cultures. States are destined to find mechanisms that encourage social harmony. For instance, in the United States, Kenneth Karst realized that: "Americans have always attached importance to the social boundaries dividing us along the lines of race, religion, and ancestral nationality. Yet, also from the beginning, those dividing lines have been eroded by the process of culture assimilation", Kenneth L. Karst, *Belonging to America: Equal Citizenship and the Constitution*, (Yale University Press 1989), 174.

[314] Yusuf al-Qaradawi, *Non-Muslims in the Islamic Society*, (Khalil Muhammad Hamad & Sayed Mahboob Ali Shah Trans.), (American Trust Publications 1985),29. Compare, R. v. Big M Drug Mart Ltd., [1985] 1 S.C.R. 295.

[315] See Id.

[316] See Id.

harmony.[317] Islamic law encourages civility in discussion, and endeavors to eliminate religious tension by prohibiting religious hate speech.[318] The primary source of legislation in Islam, i.e., the *Qur'an*, directly orders Muslims not to defame other faiths.[319] Similarly, the social contract between Muslims and non-Muslims in the Islamic State, *Dhimmi* contract, mandates that non-Muslims refrain from offending Islam.[320] This position might be viewed as an unfavorable encroachment upon freedom of speech, a fundamental freedom mentioned in some international human rights statements as well as

---

[317] See, for Example, Pakistan courts affirmed that Muslims and Non-Muslim alike should refrain from committing acts intended to provoke or insult other religions to foster social harmony. It was held "Ahmadis [a religious group] like other minorities are free to profess their religion and no one can take away that right of theirs either by legislation or by executive orders. Ahmadis, however, are obliged to honor the constitution and the law and should neither desecrate nor defile the personage of any other religion including Islam". PLD 2000 Lah 364.

[318] And dispute ye not with the People of the Book, except with means better (than mere disputation), unless it be with those of them who inflict wrong (and injury); but say, "We believe in the Revelation which has come down to us and in that which came down to you; our God and your God is One; and it is to Him we bow (in Islam). Qu'ran 29:46.

[319] Revile not ye those whom they call upon besides Allah, lest they out of spite revile Allah in their ignorance. Thus have We made alluring to each people its own doings. In the end will they return to their Lord, and we shall then tell them the truth of all that they did) Sura Al-An'am 6:108. Muslims also ordered to discuss any subject, including religion, gracefully. See (And dispute ye not with the People of the Book, except with means better (than mere disputation), unless it be with those of them who inflict wrong (and injury); but say, "We believe in the Revelation which has come down to us and in that which came down to you; our God and your God is One; and it is to Him we bow (in Islam)." Qur'an 29:46.

[320] Abu'l Hasan al-Mawardi, *Kitab Al Ahkam As Sultaniyyah* (The laws of Islamic Governance), (Beirut, Dar al-Fikr), 145, Ibn Qudamah,10 *Al-Mughni wa'l-Sharh al-Kabir*, (Beirut: Dar Al-Fikr), 563. See Also Mansur al-Buhuti, 3 Kashshāf al-Qinā' 'an Matn al-Iqnā' (Beirut, Dar Al Kotob Al-Ilmiyah 1997), 133.

in Islamic human rights instruments.[321] Nevertheless, rights are never limitless. As explained earlier, restrictions on freedom of speech in order to combat defamation of religion involve two competing rights; the freedom of speech and the freedom to practice religion devoid of undue social and psychological religious harassment. The Islamic law view is that in assessing the benefits generated by implementing unlimited freedom of speech, we must also consider foreseeable harm. Harms may include social disharmony, encouragement of hate crimes and disenfranchisement of social and religious sects. Weighing the harm and benefit, it is clear that the benefit significantly outweighs the harm. Accordingly, Islamic law may sacrifice unlimited freedom of speech to eliminate future harm.

5.5.5 A Response to Orientalists On *Dhimmi* Under Islamic Law.

Many Orientalists have claimed that *Dhimmi* is not full citizenship status because *Dhimmi* have to pay *Jizya* and *Kharaj* while Muslims do not, and that *Jihad* (serving in the military) is an obligation upon Muslims only. This proposition is erroneous in principle because it fails to appreciate fundamental facts. Every sovereign nation has the exclusive power to legislate the laws of citizenship that regulate conditions of acquiring citizenship. States may classify their citizens into any number of categories, e.g., citizen by birth, citizen by naturalization. States may impose restrictions on one class of citizens

---

[321] *See* the preamble and article 19 of Universal Declaration of Human Rights (1948) and article 22 of The Cairo Declaration on Human Rights in Islam (1990). You may notice that in the Cairo Declaration, the freedom of expression is limited by the principles of Islamic law. Article 22 (a) reads: Everyone shall have the right to express his opinion freely in such manner as would not be contrary to the principles of the Sharia's.

by depriving them of specific rights.[322] States may also refuse to grant citizenship to individuals with a particular ideology.[323] Similarly, the Islamic State is an ideological state. It classifies its citizens according to their ideology: citizen Muslim, citizen non-Muslim (*Dhimmi)* and visitor. *Zakat* is a religious duty upon Muslims only, and is subject to mandatory enforcement. *Zakat* is used to cover the expenses of the State including social welfare, State officials' salaries, and the military. To ensure that non-Muslim citizens pay their fair share of military expenses and social welfare, *Jizya* is imposed. However, the *Jizya* amount is much less than *Zakat*. For instance, during the Islamic State's early dynasties of Umayyad and Abbasid, the amount of *Jizya* was one to four Dinars ($4.75 to $19.00) per year depending on the income of the payee. The *Zakat* amount is, at least, 2.5% of one's unused wealth. This basically means that Muslims' contributions in *zakat* to the general revenue is much higher than non-Muslims' contributions. To increase the revenue of the Islamic State, non-Muslims owning agricultural land, Muslims who bought land upon which *Kharaj* is levied and a landowner who recently converted to Islam ought to pay *Kharaj*. In essence, *Kharaj* is levied on land once owned by a non-Muslim to compensate for the non-Muslim citizen's

---

[322] For example, naturalized citizens of U.S.A. cannot run for the highest office in the nation. See "No person except a natural born Citizen, or a Citizen of the United States, at the time of the Adoption of this Constitution, shall be eligible to the Office of President; neither shall any Person be eligible to that Office who shall not have attained to the Age of thirty-five Years, and been fourteen Years a Resident within the United States." Section 1 United States Cons.

[323] A person who has been member of, or connected with, the communist party –or any similar party inside or outside of the United States-within 10 years prior to his or her application for naturalization, is disqualified from becoming a citizen", See Margaret C. Jasper, *Becoming a citizen*, (Oxford University Press 2004), 16.

lack of contribution to the State's general revenue. In this context, levying *Kharaj* was never intended to place the non-Muslim at a disadvantage or to promote Islam since the conversion to Islam or purchase by a Muslim of agricultural land once owned by a non-Muslim will not relieve the burden of paying *Kharaj*.

Authentic, reliable historians' texts that are typically ignored by Orientalists affirm that when the Islamic State conquered the Roman and Persian empires, there was pre-existing massive divisiveness and oppression among those populations. Forced religion and overwhelming taxation was the norm. These practices ended when Muslims conquered the Roman and Persian provinces: *Jizya* and other taxes were much lower than those imposed by the Romans and the Persians.[324] Non-Muslims, particularly Christians, served in prestigious Islamic State positions.[325] For instance, Mansur bin Sargon, a Christian, held the office of the treasury.[326] His son and grandson succeeded him in the Umayyad dynasty. Ibn Athal, another Christian, was the *Kharaj* tax collector in the city of Homs. Freedom of speech was also fostered to the extent that various religious groups were permitted to discuss religious matters with Muslims and non-Muslims. This Islamic practice was so tolerant to be almost unimaginable in the old world given the traditional religious intolerance practiced within the Roman and Persian Empires.

---

[324] See 'Izz al-Dīn Ibn al-Athīr, *al-Kāmil fī al-Tarīkh* (the complete history), (Beirut, Dar Ṣadir 1965-1967).

see Ibn Khaldun, *Tarikh Ibn Khaldun*, (Beirut, Dar Al-Kotob Al-Ilmiyah)., see also Muḥammad Ibn 'Idhārī, *Kitab al-bayān al-mughrib fī akhbār al-Andalus wa-al-Maghrib*, (Beirut, Dār al-Thaqāfah, 1967).

[325] Id.

[326] Id.

Having said that, the general rule of good and honorable treatment of non-Muslims has been tainted by isolated incidents in history, which are entirely contrary to Islamic law principles. One such incident involved the expansion of al-Amawi mosque in Damascus at the expense of a neighboring church which had been built at the site of a pagan temple. When the *Caliph* al-Walid Ibn Abd al-Malik decided to expand the mosque, he offered a very generous compensation in return for the confiscation of the church. When the Christians refused, he nevertheless demolished the church to expand the mosque. Also, under the Umayyad dynasty, the non-Muslim deceased were not allowed to be buried until the taxation due was fully paid. Later, the succeeding *Caliph* Umar Ibn Abdulaziz abolished all unfair conditions imposed on non-Muslims. Throughout history, especially during the Mamluk dynasty, Muslims and non-Muslims alike were subject to oppressive and unfair treatment. However, Orientalists frequently mention only the unfair treatment of non-Muslims to imply disadvantageous treatment of non-Muslims which is contrary to the historical facts.[327]

Joining the military of the Islamic State is a sacred task; therefore, non-Muslims cannot be ordered to join the military. However, non-Muslims, contrary to some Orientalists' conclusions, may serve in the military. The *Sunnah* testifies that the Prophet allowed the Jewish people of Banu Qaynuqa to join the Islamic army in the *Battle of*

---

[327] Qasem Abdu Qasem, *Ahl El Zimmah Fe Misr men al Fath al-Islami heta Nahyat al-Mamaleek* (Dhimmi people in Egypt from the time when Islam conquered Egypt till Mamluk era), (Cairo, Ein for Human and Social studies 2003),187.

Khyber.[328] The Prophet also allowed Safwan bin Umayyah, then a non-Muslim, to join the *Battle of Hunayn.*[329]

All these rules commanded by the Islamic State are a typical exercise of State sovereignty as understood and practiced by various States worldwide. Except as pertains to the Islamic State, no one has ever suggested that placing political restrictions on a particular citizen class, e.g., naturalized citizens, renders this class as "less than full citizenship status" or second-class citizens. If restricting a class of citizens, e.g., naturalized citizens, is unjustifiable discrimination then every Western democracy is equally guilty. However, such allegations are made when the State issuing similar restrictions is an Islamic State. In fact, Islamic law guarantees the equal dignity of humanity notwithstanding religion, ethnicity, gender, citizenship background or any other individual characteristics.[330] Accordingly, it is unimaginable to treat a citizen of the Islamic State, as a second-class citizen for any reason whatsoever.

Finally, concerning non-Islamic ill practices towards non-Muslims, a clear distinction should be made between Islamic law and ill practices. When Muslims violate Islamic law and ill-treat non-Muslims, it does not mean that **Islam** ill-treats non-Muslims.

---

[328] See Abu Bakr Al-hamzany, Kitab al-at'bar fe al-Nasikh wal-Mansukh Men al-Athar.

[329] Id.

[330] (We have honored the sons of Adam; provided them with transport on land and sea; given them for sustenance things good and pure; and conferred on them special favors, above a great part of Our Creation) Qur'an 17:70. This verse suggests that mankind, including all races, cultures, religious and non-religious have been honored by God; accordingly, the Islamic State is bound to treat every person with honor and dignity under all circumstances.

CHAPTER 6

Islamic Self-Governing Theory

———— ༄༅༄༅ ————

6.1   Introduction

Conceivably the most significant problem that has adversely affected Muslim-majority states from the inception of Islam until current times is the selection process of rulers and people's representatives. Citizens are captives to the circumstances that lead to good or bad rulers. Without a doubt, the correlation between proper Islamic law application and prevalence of justice and prosperity in Muslim majority state is noticeable. On the contrary, when unjust rulers twist Islamic law directives in order to serve their interests, oppression, despair, and poverty become the norm. During the reign of Umar Ibn Al Khattab (579- 644), the *Caliph* well-known for his sense of justice and well-regarded among Muslims, the national treasury was so full of gold and silver that *Caliph* Umar ordered that all debts of the citizens be paid by the state. Every citizen who sought marriage was awarded financial aid from the state. In contrast, during the reign of the unelected and unjust tyrant, al-Mustansir Billah (1029-1094) who had inherited the rulership from his father, calamity struck resulting in famine and plagues.

Suppression of free Islamic speech about the Islamic system of governance has led to a common status of public ignorance. Dictators in Muslim-majority states often employ "government-collaborating scholars" to justify their actions and eradicate Islamic speech not in their favor. Muhammad Ali Pasha (1769- 1848) was appointed governor of Egypt following the demands of the Egyptian *Ulema* (Islam Scholars) to the Ottoman Empire. He later exiled these *Ulema* once he had a firm grip on power. Abd al-Rahman al-Kawakibi (1855–1902), speaking on the relationship between oppression and religion, realized that political oppression is either generated by religious oppression or accompanied by it.[331] Accordingly, the best and most direct approach to restoring good political life is by restoring religion itself. He concluded that Islam fights oppression by every means and he gave examples of best-governing practices including the mandatory use of *Shura*/public consultancy in the decision-making process.[332] Nevertheless, oppressive rulership always recruits scholars to justify oppression. He exclaimed:

> *What is the authority (the legal foundation for an opinion in Islam) upon which scholars who support oppression, command people to shed holiness on rulers to exempt them from liability so when rulers do justice people thank them and when rulers became unjust, people have to be patient and that any resistance*

---

[331] Abd al-Rahman al-Kawakibi, *Taba'i' al-istibdad wa-maṣari' al-isti'bad* (The Nature of Despotism), (Muhammad Umara ed.), (Cairo, Dar al-Sharouk 2009).

[332] See Qur'an 27: 32-34 &3:159.

> to oppression constitutes a crime of *baghy* which calls for
> bloodshed of the resistance.[333]

Likewise, foreign powers that invade Muslim-majority states attempt to control free Islamic speech that aims to combat oppression. Recall imperialistic colonial France's crack-down on the Association of Algerian Muslim *Ulema*/scholars to eliminate anti-oppression speech. Apart from the colonial period, at present, many Muslims believe that foreign powers utilize various means to control free Islamic speech to serve its interests. Foreign powers have utilized Islamophobia to falsely claim cultural and religious superiority over Muslim-majority states and thereby demand that Muslim-majority states follow their footsteps.[334] To be sure, Islamophobia is alive and well trying to rewrite the history of Islam and redefine Islamic law. Islamophobia also sparks fear of anything Islamic, derailing any rational, informed discussion of Islamic law including the Islamic system of governance.

Despite resistance to a fair discussion of the Islamic system of governance and negative representations of Islam engendered by entities such as ISIS, open discussion of the Islamic system of governance is inevitable for the benefit of humankind, both Muslim and non-Muslim nations. The discussion shall involve elections, representation of Muslims, non-Muslims and women in Islam in light of the primary sources of Islamic law, the *Qur'an*, and *Sunnah*. Practices of the initial four *Caliphs*, known as the rightly guided *Caliphs*, shall be discussed, when relevant, to explain how Muslims

---

[333] Abd al-Rahman al-Kawakibi, *Taba'i' al-istibdad wa-maṣari' al-isti'bad* (The Nature of Despotism), (Muhammad Umara ed.), (Cairo, Dar al-Sharouk 2009),36.

[334] See, Edward Said, *Orientalism*, (Vintage Books 1979).

understood directives of Islam in its golden era. This discussion may illuminate a pathway for peaceful change in many of the dictatorial systems of current Muslim-majority states.

6.2   Shura Principle in The *Qur'an*

The concept of *Shura* (consultation) has been delineated in the *Qur'an* twice. Each instance has unique significance and serves a particular purpose. The *Qur'an* declares:

> *And by the Mercy of Allah, you (the Prophet Muhammad) dealt with them gently. And had you been severe and harsh-hearted, they would have broken away from about you; so pass over (their faults), and ask (Allah's) Forgiveness for them; and consult them in the affairs. Then when you make azm (when you have taken a decision), put your trust in Allah, certainly, Allah loves those who put their trust (in Him).[335]*

This verse and its historical application shed light on the mandatory nature of *Shura*, the mutual consultation, its process, and rationale. The obvious observation is that the verse creates an atmosphere that focuses on the Prophet Muhammad as a role model for Islamic leadership, exemplifying the ideal pattern of behavior in administering Muslims affairs. It directs leaders to be lenient, tolerant of unintentional mistakes and to make decisions after engaging in full consultation with the people. Once the consultation has taken place, the leader must follow the recommended resolution by the *Shura* Council.[336] This conclusion stems from the *Qur'an* explanation, *Tafsir Ibn Kathir*, which maintained that the *Caliph* Ali Ibn Abi Talab

---

[335] Qur'an 3: 159.
[336] See Qur'an 27: 32-34.

concluded that the word 'azm,' which was mentioned in this verse, means mandatory following of the recommended resolution.

The best practice of *Shura* as modeled by the Prophet Muhammad shows that he created a *Shura* council with up to seventy members. The *Shura* Council was neither a symbolic nor an artificial entity; the council's decisions were enforced if there was no divine order on the matter. In the Battle of Uhud, the Meccan army was about to attack the Muslims in Medina. Prophet Muhammad consulted the Muslims as to the best approach in confronting the imminent threat. A group of Muslims, including the Prophet, thought that they should defend themselves from within the boundaries of Medina. However, the majority stance suggested that they should meet the Meccan army outside Medina. Prophet Muhammad enforced the majority opinion, though it was contrary to his own opinion and ultimately it was proven to be the wrong technique; the Muslims lost that battle. This instance, among many others, demonstrates the process of *Shura*. First, all qualified individuals are entitled to vote notwithstanding their rank or status. Second, the majority opinion prevails in the decision-making process. Third, if the enforced majority opinion produces an undesirable result, the individuals who proposed the minority opinion should not blame the majority but rather should accept the majority opinion outcome with grace and tolerance. This point can be easily inferred since the *Qur'an* links tolerance of unintentional faults and seeking forgiveness with the *Shura* (consultation) process to signify that both *Shura* and its consequences should be held in a peaceful and tolerant environment.[337] The outcome of the *Shura* process is obvious; it introduces peace and comfort in a society given that the decision is made after consultation

---

[337] Qur'an 3:159.

with the people and thus the people should bear the consequences of their collective choice gracefully.

The concept of *Shura* is central in Islam given that the *Shura* concept was revealed in the *Qur'an* in Mecca at a time when Islam was a new and peculiar religion to Arabs. All verses of the *Qur'an* that were revealed in Mecca were aimed at establishing the foundation of the new faith and defining the basic features of the emerging Islamic society. Thus, according to Islamic scholars, the timing of the revelation of the *Shura* process stresses its indispensability within the Islamic State.

The fruit of making *Shura* and electing officials is conspicuous throughout Islamic history. Most of those who ascended to power without an election, except an unusual few such as Umar ibn Abd al-Aziz, tarnished their reign with oppression. Early Muslims appreciated the importance of *Shura* in governance and applied it accordingly.[338]

---

[338] "Jarir Said: While I was at Yemen, I met two men from Yemen called Dhu Kala and Dhu `Amr, and I started telling them about Allah's Messenger Dhu `Amr said to me, "If what you are saying about your friend (i.e. the Prophet) is true, then he has died three days ago." Then both of them accompanied me to Medina, and when we had covered some distance on the way to Medina, we saw some riders coming from Medina. We asked them and they said, "Allah's Messenger has died and Abu Bakr has been appointed as the *Caliph* and the people are in a good state.' Then they said, "Tell your friend (Abu Bakr) that we have come (to visit him), and if Allah will, we will come again." So they both returned to Yemen. When I told Abu Bakr their statement, he said to me, "I wish you had brought them (to me)." Afterwards I met Dhu `Amr, and he said to me, "O Jarir! You have done a favor to me and I am going to tell you something, i.e. you, the nation of 'Arabs, will remain prosperous as long as you choose and appoint another chief whenever a former one is dead. But if authority is obtained by the power of the sword, then the rulers will become kings who will get angry, as

Interestingly, Sura Ash-Shura and, in particular, the verses immediately preceding the command of making *Shura*, creates a psychological state of mind to prepare new Muslims to accept the command with grace and the desire to follow it. The *Qur'an* reads:

> So whatever you have been given is but (a passing) enjoyment for this worldly life, but that which is with Allah (Paradise) is better and more lasting for those who believe and put their trust in their Lord. And those who avoid the greater sins, and Al-Fawahish (illegal sexual intercourse), and when they are angry, forgive. And those who answer the Call of their Lord, and perform the prayers, and who (conduct) their affairs by Shura (mutual consultation), and who spend of what We have bestowed on them (charity).[339]

These verses start with an inspirational statement; a promise that believers will go to paradise whose joys are everlasting and much better than worldly joys. The verses then list the qualities of true believers including making *Shura*. In essence, *Shura* was framed as a mandatory pattern of behavior and a distinctive characteristic of the "believers." On the other hand, the *Qur'an* elsewhere condemns rulers who greedily grip power and thus abandon *Shura*.[340] Similarly, the *Qur'an* criticizes nations who accept dictatorial regimes without attempting to change or, at least, denounce them. In this context, the *Qur'an* employs faith, a keystone value in Islamic society, to implement the *Shura* doctrine. The psychological effects of framing *Shura* as a characteristic of believers who will receive a substantial reward, i.e., paradise, are indeed overwhelming. It creates an

kings get angry, and will be delighted as kings get delighted." Sahih al-Bukhari Book of Maghazi (Military Expeditions led by the Prophet).

[339] Qur'an 42:36.

[340] Qur'an 11:97 & 43:54.

irresistible motive to implement *Shura* in the Islamic society. If such a reward is an insufficient motive, then the threat of punishment in the hereafter may drive Muslims, who believe in the *Qur'an*, to act and enforce *Shura*.

6.3   The Exercise of Shura During the Life of The Prophet and The Reigns of Initial Four *Caliphs*

Prophet Muhammad, the role model for Muslims, utilized *Shura* extensively in war and in peace. He listened, discussed, and sometimes followed, the opposing view. In the Battle of Badr, when the Prophet ordered Muslims to position themselves at a particular location, a Muslim asked whether such a proposition was a divine order or just the Prophet's opinion; the Prophet replied that it was his opinion. This Muslim was thus empowered to suggest a better location. The Prophet accepted his proposal and ordered the Muslims to be positioned as was suggested. After the battle, the Prophet consulted his fellow Muslims concerning the prisoners of war. Some suggested that they should be released for ransom. Others believed that they should be killed for the crimes that had been committed against Muslims. The Prophet preferred release with ransom.

The practice of the Prophet shows that he was reluctant to impose his leadership vision on the Muslims, leaving the leadership selection process to *Shura* principle. Before his death, the Prophet refused to appoint a successor leaving the Muslims to elect their own leader. If representation were needed from a particular group, such as Al-Ansar, he would typically ask groups to elect their representatives. When a matter arose, he consulted a group of 10 members of the earliest converts to Islam, belonging to the most prominent families of Quraysh tribe. This historically renowned group is known as *Al-Muhajireen Al-Awaleen* (early immigrants from Mecca to Medina). This group played a leading supervisory role over the executive branch, represented by the Islamic ruler, and served as consultants during the rightly guided *Caliphs'* reigns. One of the most significant examples of *Al-Muhajireen Al-Awaleen's* supervisory powers is their calling for a revolt against the third *Caliph*, Osman when they believed that several of his actions were questionable.

The number of Al-*Muhajireen Al-Awaleen*, the Islamic State board of trustees, declined after the death of the Prophet. In addition to the vast expansion of the State, a new reality, this invited a call for an increase in the number of the consultancy group and for broader representation. Ali, the fourth rightly guided *Caliph*, believed that the consultancy group should be limited to *Al-Muhajireen Al-Awaleen* while his opponent, in the leadership of the Islamic State, Mu'āwiya Ibn Abī Sufyān, suggested that broader representation, including Mu'āwiya supporters, was required. Unfortunately, this conflict resulted in a battle between Ali and Mu'āwiya which led to the most dramatic adverse change in the Islamic State, the death of Ali and the death of *Shura* in the reign of Mu'āwiya. The death of Ali, Prophet Muhammad's cousin and son-in-law, in a battle between Muslims created a deep scar in the Muslims' consciousness with far-reaching adverse consequences. A group of Muslims believed that Ali and the house of the Prophet Muhammad, to the exclusion of others, were the rightful rulers of the Islamic State. This group developed a distinctive jurisprudential approach to Islam and became known as *Shia*. The rest of the Muslims became known as *Sunni* Muslims. Numerous *Sunni* Muslim scholars forbid contesting Muslim State rulers' authority or actions so long as an elementary form of Islamic law is applied in the State. Admittedly, this approach was profoundly influenced by, if not a direct result of, the Muslim civil war that divided Muslims and created generational agony. Unfortunately, Mu'āwiya, who suggested that broader representation was needed for the election of the Muslim State's ruler, subsequently ignored his own proposition and appointed his son as the ruler of the Islamic State. Thus, the seed of a genuine democratic process that was nurtured by the Prophet in appointing a consultancy council died, and the Islamic State missed a golden opportunity to apply this approach to modern practice.

In addition to use of the *Al-Muhajireen Al-Awaleen* council, decision-making only after mutual consultation among Muslims continued and flourished in every aspect of governance within the Islamic State during the reigns of the four rightly guided *Caliphs*. Whenever a dispute arose, Abu Bakr, the first *Caliph*, would initially search for resolution within the teachings of the *Qur'an*. If none was found and he was unaware of a rule in *Sunnah* on the issue, he would ask the Muslims for a *Sunnah* addressing the issue. If no *Sunnah* precedent was found, he would then consult the Muslims for a resolution. Even in major executive decisions, Abu Bakr consulted the Muslim community. For example, he consulted Muslims over the decision whether to fight Muslim tribes who refused to pay *Zakat* (mandatory charity) after the death of the Prophet. Umar, the second *Caliph*, would commonly consult Muslims in various affairs including the adjudication of appropriate punishment for infanticide, consumption of alcohol and the strategy for battling the Persian Empire. At a grassroots level, the Companions of the Prophet, who enjoyed great respect and trust of all Muslims, would periodically meet the people at large and offer advice to the *Caliphate*.

6.4   The Concept of Shura in Application.

6.4.1   Islamic Parliament/Shura Council

6.4.1.1   The Delegation of Authority: Principle and Scope

Direct or self-representation in large societies is impossible due to its complex and costly logistics. It requires nationwide referendums on every issue. Its economic and social burden may become overwhelming. For that reason, all societies, including Islamic society, recognize the necessity of delegated or indirect representation. In this context, the Islamic system of governance recognizes the concept of a *Naqeeb* (leader/representative) who is responsible for aiding his constituents to fulfill their social obligations, communicating the constituents' will to the governing body, and calling for and organizing regular meetings with his constituents to solve their problems. The *Qur'an* and *Sunnah* give examples of elections of a *Naqeeb*. The *Qur'an* speaks of appointment of twelve *Naqeeb* from the Jewish people at the time of the Prophet Moses.[341] The Prophet Muhammad had practiced free elections in the second pledge/ Covenant at al-Aqabah, at which time the Prophet asked various groups of Muslims to elect twelve deputies/representatives, each to represent his clan.

---

[341] Indeed, Allah took the covenant from the Children of Israel (Jews), and We appointed twelve leaders among them. And Allah said: "I am with you if you perform As-Salat (duly prayers) and give Zakat (mandatory charity) and believe in My Messengers; honor and assist them, and lend to Allah a good loan. Verily, I will remit your sins and admit you to Gardens under which rivers flow (in Paradise). But if any of you after this, disbelieved, he has indeed gone astray from the Straight Path. Qur'an 5:12.

The scope of delegation is limited by several boundaries; 1) The delegates cannot exceed the power delegated to them, 2) Islamic law defines the scope of the power delegated, 3) The customary practices within a community cannot contradict Islamic law.

Delegates, in exercising their powers, in lawmaking, entering into a covenant, supervising the executive branch or otherwise must work within the framework of Islamic law principles. The underpinning of this thesis is that Muslims upon confessing into Islam accept the Islamic principles unconditionally including the supremacy of Islamic law. Non-Muslim citizens of the Islamic state are also bound by the Islamic law limit when they become members of the Islamic State and accept its social contract. This issue has been explained in detail in previous chapters.

Accordingly, delegates, in exercising their power in law-making, may uphold local custom so long as it does not contradict Islamic law. Indeed, Islam, under no circumstances, intends to erase or eradicate cultures, customs or good pre-Islamic human traits so long as it does not contradict Islamic law. Instead, Islam, Muslims believe, is meant to preserve and enhance the best traits and customs of humanity.[342]

6.4.1.2   Role of Islamic Parliament/ Shura Council

Some Islamic law scholars have suggested that the *Shura* council's task is limited to offering noncompulsory advice to the ruler. They have relied on a Qur'anic statement affirming that the majority opinion

---

[342] The Prophet Muhammad said: "The only reason I have been sent is to perfect good manners." Sahih Al-Bukhari. He also said: The Prophet said: "The believers who have the most perfect faith are those who have the best character, and the best of them are those who are best to their womenfolk." Sunan al-Tirmidhī

may not be correct. Accordingly, the government ought not to be bound to the majority opinion. The following is a sample of the Qur'anic verses from which this opinion is derived:

> (And if you obey most of those on the earth, they will mislead you far away from Allah's Path. They follow nothing but conjectures, and they do nothing but lie.).[343]

Obviously, this interpretation is fundamentally erroneous because it institutes a rule from a bad fit context. The verses only suggest that obedience of an entire people of the earth may mislead one. The Muslim State is a different and distinct community, whereupon any general rule addressed to the general population of earth, may not apply. Likewise, what applies to the Muslim State may not be applicable to the people of the earth at large, many of whom are not Muslim. What is more, numerous hadith and the practice of the initial four *Caliphs*, the representatives of the golden era of Islam, indicate that the majority opinion shall prevail, so long as it is consistent with fundamental sources of Islamic law, i.e., the *Qur'an* and *Sunnah*. Prophet Muhammad commanded Muslims to adhere to the *Jam'ah* (main group of Muslims) opinion and avoid divisiveness.[344] The initial four *Caliphs* also followed the footsteps of the Prophet. For example, the election process that was invented by Umar Ibn Al Khattab, the second *Caliph*, to elect a ruler, which shall be discussed in detail later in this volume, suggests that majority opinion shall prevail. We have seen the positive role of Al-*Muhajireen Al-Awaleen* in the early Islamic State in representing the collective consciousness of Muslims and their unique supervisory power over the *Caliphs'* affairs. The legacy of Al-*Muhajireen Al-Awaleen* reflects the best

---

[343] Qur'an 6:116.

[344] At-Tirmidhi.

Islamic democratic practices in which consultation among Muslims was sought, and the majority opinion prevailed.

Indeed, if there is a single reason that the Islamic State deteriorated dramatically leading to its total collapse, it is the failure to continue the democratic process as delineated in *Shura* principles which require majority governance combined with respect of minority rights. After the death of the fourth *Caliph* Ali, Mu'āwiya bin Abi-Sufyan, the fifth *Caliph*, established an absolute monarchy, refused to follow general *Shura* principles, made *Shura* exclusive to his clans and appointed his son as the sixth *Caliph*. Notably, Mu'āwiya's ruler succession practice ought to be distinguished from Abu Bakr's, the First *Caliph*, who had appointed Umar Ibn Al Khattab as the second *Caliph*. Umar was a close companion of the Prophet, with an unblemished character and was brilliant in supporting Islam from the moment of its birth. Muslims throughout the centuries from the time of Abu Bakr until now have approved Abu Bakr's actions. Indeed, the common belief among Muslims is that Abu Bakr had only one consideration, the interests of Muslims, unlike Mu'āwiya who preferred his son, 'Yazīd, to be his successor. In any case, the character, the qualities, and righteousness of the close companions of the Prophet Muhammad, such as Umar Ibn al-Khattab, are unique and unrepeatable. Therefore, ignoring *Shura* principle or denying the need for the majority rule based on Abu Bakr's practice of appointment of Umar Ibn al-Khattab without majority consensus is objectionable.

Having established that the role of *Shura* council exceeds that of an advisory power, a logical question follows. What are the powers of the *Shura* Council in the light of the *Qur'an* and *Sunnah*? By process of elimination, if the ruler of the Islamic State, his subordinates, and his agents perform the executive function of the government and judges fulfill the judicial duties, then the *Shura* council is left with the duty to legislate and supervise the government. The *Qur'an* conveys the concept that individuals cannot perform two duties that may have conflicting interests.[345] As a result, neither the role of adjudication vested in the judiciary nor the role of enforcement of the law vested in the executive branch of the government can be combined with the role of lawmaking since that lawmaking may conflict with the interests of the judiciary or executive branches. A judge should not be permitted to make a law and then apply it because judges are not authorized representatives of the national will in lawmaking nor do judges consult the nation before law-making. Combining the judiciary and law-making runs the risk that a judge becomes law unto himself. If a judge is allowed to make law **and** apply it, the judge may create unfair laws that contradict Islamic law with impunity. It seems that this is what the *Qur'an* warned against: an individual cannot perform two duties that may have conflicting interests; in this case, law-making and law-applying. Similarly, the executive branch of the government should not be permitted to make laws that open the door for executives to escape accountability and perhaps favor themselves, under the laws they make.

Concerning the supervisory power of the *Shura* council, the *Qur'an* and *Sunnah* speak of Muslims' duty to enjoin good deeds and forbid wrongdoing.[346] This general duty cannot be performed by

---

[345] Allah (God) has not put for any man two hearts inside his body. Qur'an 33:4.

[346] You [Muslims] are the best of peoples ever raised up for mankind; you enjoin Al-Ma'ruf (good deeds) and forbid Al-Munkar (wrongdoing), and you believe in Allah. Qur'an 3:110. The Prophet Muhammad said "Whoever of you sees an evil must then change it with his hand. If he is not able to do so, then [he

every citizen of the Islamic state with ease particularly in governmental actions. Indeed, governmental actions can be complicated with consequences unforeseeable to ordinary, average individuals. Therefore, the *Shura* Council, as authorized representatives of the people, should shoulder the burden of enjoining good deeds and forbidding wrongdoing especially with regard to governmental actions.

Furthermore, the *Shura* council's vested supervisory and legislative powers stem from its role as elected representatives of the people. In this context, these representatives are trustees who owe fiduciary duties, as delineated in the *Qur'an*, to the trust beneficiaries, the people.[347] Trustees are bound to serve the trust beneficiaries as delineated in the trust contract. Muslims, by confessing to Islam as their religion, implicitly accept all rights, duties, and restrictions enumerated in Islam including their right and duty to be governed by Islamic law. Accordingly, representatives, in dispensing their fiduciary duties, may create legal rules, based on the fundamental sources of Islam, i.e., the *Qur'an* and *Sunnah*, to govern the relationship between individuals, between individuals and the State, and to supervise the executive branch of the government. Representatives also are under the general Islamic burden to dispense their legislative and supervisory duties justly, steadfastly and

---

must change it] with his tongue. And if he is not able to do so, then [he must change it] with his heart. And that is the slightest [effect of] faith." (Sahih Muslim). Notably the Qur'an verse (3:110) makes Muslims best people raised up for mankind conditional on 1) command good deeds and forbid wrongdoing. 2) Believing in God. So Muslims are not the best because of race, culture but rather for the good qualities above mentioned, if performed.

[347] Qur'an 4:58.

tirelessly, as well as demonstrate capability and trustworthiness.[348] These are not only prerequisites to serving but also form the basis for removal from Parliament if a representative becomes incapacitated physically or mentally and is unable to dispense his duties or if a representative shows a lack interest or indolence in dispensing trustee duties. The mechanism for the removal of a Parliament member is flexible; however, two main features guide the removal process. Fairness to the representative while stressing the supremacy of the collective social interest over an individual representative's interest. Secondly, representatives are liable as trustees who owe a fiduciary duty to the trust beneficiaries: the people. Once these guidelines are taken into consideration, the Islamic State Parliament may craft the tools and the mechanism for removal.

6.4.2   The Composition of Shura Council/Islamic Parliament

6.4.2.1   Representation of Women

The *Qur'an* utilizes neutral language, concerning gender, in addressing Muslims' duty to conduct their affairs with mutual consultation.[349] Since the *Qur'an* is very precise in its terms, as Muslims believe, this generalization necessarily suggests that all Muslims, men and women alike, are qualified to serve in the *Shura* council. Any alternative proposal based on gender discrimination to determine eligibility to *Shura* Council membership is contrary to clear *Qur'an* direction. Furthermore, regarding legislative functions, Parliament's main functions are legislating and monitoring

---

[348] Qur'an, 5:8 & 28:26.
[349] Qur'an 42:38 &3: 159.

government performance. Legislating in the Islamic State entails creating rules of conduct, mutable resolutions that are either based directly on the *Qur'an* and *Sunnah* or derived through utilization of other *Ijtihad* methods. Because women have always been, and still are, excellent scholars, they are fully capable of creating rules of conduct. Perhaps the best-known examples of women scholars are *Aisha* and *Ḥafṣah bint Umar,* the Prophet Muhammad's wives. The Prophet Muhammad's actions testify that he encouraged women's scholarship. The Prophet consulted his wife, *Umm Salamah,* and followed her advice. The renowned Islamic Scholar *Imam al Shafi'i* had suggested that the Prophet's consultation intended not only to seek advice but also to explain best practices in governance. Since the *Qur'an* has imposed a duty upon Muslims, men and women alike, to enjoin the good and prohibit wrongdoing, both genders are required to serve the same function in Parliament through monitoring the governmental actions.[350]

Although women's right to serve as Parliament members seems logical and a direct application of Islamic law principles, a heated discussion in some Muslim-majority states arose between two competing ideologies. A conservative perspective suggests that women should not be representatives in Parliament. A more compelling perspective emerged, led by a prominent contemporary scholar Yusuf al-Qaradawi, advocating women's right to serve in Parliament. al-Qaradawi observed that the *Qur'an's* commands are typically gender neutral.[351] It then follows that, by virtue of the *Qur'an,* men and women are partners in fulfilling their religious

---

[350] See Qur'an 3:104.
[351] See Qur'an 22:77& 2:153.

obligation to enjoin good deeds and to forbid evil.[352] Accordingly, the best tool to achieve this objective is to engage in the parliamentary process to fulfill these obligations. Moreover, to better serve the needs of women in particular with issues related specifically to women, such as marriage, child custody, and violence against women, they ought to have the right to voice their opinions during the law-making process. Moreover, Muslims have always looked to the Prophet Muhammad as the ideal role model for Muslims. He acknowledged the need for representation of women and their engagement in the consultancy process.

Those who object to women's representation in Parliament adduced some objections. They cite a command in the *Qur'an* for women to stay at home, as a general rule, leaving their homes only in necessity.[353] al-Qaradawi, in his rebuttal to this claim, explained that this interpretation of that Qur'anic verse takes the command out of context.[354] The verse immediately preceding this verse shows that this command clearly addresses only the wives of the Prophet, not the public at large. Indeed, Islam recognizes the wives of the Prophet as being unlike any other women.[355] The *Qur'an* testifies that their rewards and penalties in the hereafter are double that of other women. Accordingly, what applies to the wives of the Prophet may not apply to other women. Even though this command addresses the wives of the Prophet, this did not preclude them from fulfilling their duties

---

[352] Qur'an 9:71.

[353] Qur'an 33:33.

[354] Qur'an 33:33

[355] Some aspects of the Prophet Muhammad and his wives should not be generalized such as the Prophet fasting for a few days continuously without breaking fasting at sunset.

outside their homes. *Aisha*, the Prophet's wife, participated in the Battle of Jamal because she firmly believed she must do so.

Moreover, Islamic history shows the necessity of women's representation in Parliament to explain issues women know best. For instance, during his reign, *Caliph* Umar Ibn al Khaṭṭāb ordered financial benefits to all citizens providing they have passed the weaning phase. Later when *Caliph* Umar was walking in Mecca, he had heard a child crying vigorously. Upon inquiry, he learned that the child's mother had weaned the child prematurely in order to be eligible for the financial benefits. He regretted his decision of excluding newborn infants from the benefits and ordered that all citizens, notwithstanding age, be eligible for benefits. If women had been consulted regarding the financial benefits, perhaps *Caliph* Umar would have crafted a financial benefit system for all citizens that was fair and satisfactory to all in the first instance.

The conservative view also invoked a doctrine, which is widely accepted by Muslims scholars, that the Islamic State must block the means to the forbidden. According to this approach, the conservative view suggests that a woman going out to work may incur harm to herself or to society in general and could encourage the forbidden, i.e., neglect of children, incitement of violence against women, extramarital sexual intercourse. Apparently, the application of the doctrine "blocking the means to the forbidden" in this manner is undeniably over-sweeping and will cause unfair and undesirable outcomes. Under the guise of the strict application of this doctrine, States can prohibit activities and commercial transactions unfairly and unnecessarily. The internet is an excellent tool for communication, commercial activity, and learning. The internet also can be misused for a variety of illegal purposes. If we apply this doctrine without examining the outcomes and the impact on society in general, the internet would be prohibited. This simple analogy shows the risk of the blind application of this doctrine. A better approach to this doctrine is to subject it to a harms/benefits analysis which is commonly accepted in Islamic jurisprudence. General prohibition is unjustifiable under Islamic law unless there is an explicit command in the *Qur'an* or authentic *Sunnah* or a consensus on the interpretation of the *Qur'an* and authentic *Sunnah* that establishes such a prohibition. Women, like men, in *individual* cases might be banned from working, temporarily or permanently, for a good cause showing a valid social objective such as child welfare or categorically unsuitable work environment for women. Again, this ban for women should not be a product of discriminatory practices or the whim of a government. Nothing less than a valid social objective recognized under Islamic law or a direct prohibition in the *Qur'an* or *Sunnah* suffices to preclude women from working freely. Comparatively, men also might be banned from some jobs if there is a valid social objection or prohibition in the *Qur'an* or *Sunnah* under Islamic law that would justify such ban. Even in these individual cases, the burden of establishing the grounds for banning employment, whether for men or women, is on the State. Ultimately, women in Muslim-majority states have received education, worked successfully and have become valuable contributing members with more benefit than harm to society.

In recent years, the conservative approach has rapidly declined in most of the Muslim-majority states. King Abdullah of Saudi Arabia, in his address to *Al-Shura* council on September 25, 2011, approved the participation of women in the *Al-Shura* council as members in accordance with the Sharia guidelines. Women also were given the right to nominate themselves for membership of Municipal Councils and participate in the nomination of candidates according to Islamic guidelines. This wind of change is indeed significant in Saudi Arabia, a State that is dominated by conservative scholars, and raises speculation as to the cause of this historic move bearing in mind that the rules of *Shura* have not changed since the time of the Prophet Muhammad. Perhaps Western political powers influenced Saudi regime to change the role of women in Parliament in 2011.

Notably, moderate approaches advocating women's employment, including Parliament membership, have been adopted by emerging Islamic democracies such as Ennahda Islamic Party in Tunisia. This trend along with recent developments in Saudi Arabia shows that the Arab spring might blossom into greater freedom for women and a promising future for human rights in general. Regrettably, the future of women's representation, and human rights in general, in Arab countries, have become unclear after major political setbacks in the recent years in Yemen, Egypt, Syria, and Libya.

6.4.2.2   Representation of The Non-Muslim In Parliament

Islamic law scholars have been divided on the issue of representation of non-Muslims in the Islamic State Parliament. One major school of thought suggests that Muslims should not take non-Muslims as *Aulyia' (supporters, helpers)*. Accordingly, non-Muslim citizens of the Islamic State ought not to serve in Parliament. This approach often cites two verses in the *Qur'an* in support of this view:

> *Let not the believers take the disbelievers as Aulyia' instead of the believers, and whoever does that will never be helped by Allah in any way, except if you indeed fear a danger from them.*

> *And Allah warns you against Himself (His punishment), and to Allah is the final return.*[356]

> *O you who believe! Take not for Auliya' disbelievers instead of believers. Do you wish to offer Allah a manifest proof against yourselves?*[357]

An alternative interpretation of these *Qur'anic* verses suggests that the former proposition creates an over-sweeping generalization of the role of the non-Muslim in the Islamic State. Exclusion of non-Muslims, as *Aulyia'*, ought to be construed narrowly. Muslims are forbidden to blindly follow non-Muslim laws and lifestyle as a substitute for Islamic teachings. Certainly, the intention is not to bar all levels of cooperation with non-Muslims. The Prophet Muhammad praised non-Muslims' pre-Islamic *Hilf al-Fudul* (non-Muslims Alliance of al -Fudul), which was designed to aid the oppressed, and expressed his desire to have joined the alliance if he had witnessed its establishment. If the intention was to ban all cooperation with non-Muslims, the Prophet Muhammad would not have endorsed the *Hilf al-Fudul* concept.

Furthermore, it is wrong to isolate some verses out of the entire context of the *Qur'an*. Other verses in the *Qur'an* have delineated the limits of cooperation with non-Muslims indicating that Muslims should not take non-Muslims as *Aulyia'* only if they have expressed enmity to Muslims, to Islam in general or fought to occupy Islamic territories.[358] The *Qur'an's* guidelines for cooperation with non-Muslims are defined as follows:

---

[356] Qur'an 3:28.
[357] Qur'an 4:144.
[358] Qur'an 60:1 & 58:22.

Allah does not forbid you to deal justly and kindly with those who fought not against you on account of religion nor drove you out of your homes. Verily, Allah loves those who deal with equity. It is only as regards those who fought against you on account of religion, and have driven you out of your homes, and helped to drive you out, that Allah forbids you to befriend them.[359]

This verse explicitly commands that, so long as non-Muslims neither fight Muslims nor attempt to occupy Islamic territories unjustly, they should be treated justly and kindly. It follows that all sorts of cooperation with non-Muslims is possible including parliamentary representation, especially to protect their genuine interests. Non-Muslim citizens of the Islamic state might have skills, knowledge or expertise that may benefit the Islamic state and guide the Islamic Parliament in the decision-making process. There is no Islamic rationale for depriving the Islamic state of the meaningful contribution of non-Muslims to the Islamic state. Also, non-Muslim citizens of the Islamic State need fair representation in the Islamic Parliament especially in matters related to their rights or that impact their economic status.

However, this conclusion faces some practical difficulties. First, should non-Muslims be entitled to vote on matters governed by Islamic law, which may contradict their (non-Muslim) beliefs? Would the general public of Muslims trust non-Muslims to vote on matters related to Islamic law? Indeed, it might be challenging to craft rational support for the proposition that non-Muslims should have a role in deciding Muslim affairs governed by Islamic law. In other matters, especially those that do not involve Islamic law and that are of

---

[359] Qur'an 60:8-9.

common interests to both Muslims and non-Muslims, non-Muslims should not be deprived of their right to participate in decision-making, as Parliament members, voting if so desired.

6.4.2.3   Diversity of Representation.

The Islamic State of a*l-Khulfa-Al-Rashidin*, during the reigns of the initial four *Caliphs'*, recognized scholarly diversity in the interpretation of the *Qur'an* and *Sunnah*, which led to numerous methodologies in *Ijtihad*/Islamic lawmaking. This legacy continued after the end of their era with the emergence of many schools of thought.   Each   school   offers   a   distinctive   methodological interpretation of the *Qur'an* and *Sunnah*, ranking supplementary sources of Islamic law differently which leads to a unique technique of rule creation. This diversity creates competing opinions, of Islamic origin, that enriches the social and political life of the State. On these bases, groups that adopt various methodological interpretations may establish political parties that represent its views. Correspondingly, groups and classes within society such as women, workers, non-Muslims, or others may join or form a political party to advance their interests.

Most importantly, forming political parties is an effective tool to achieve Islamic democracy. When individuals adopt a perspective, believe in its rationales, and aim for an outcome, they shall endorse it. Such endorsement takes the form of *bay'ah*, a contract, between the political party and its supporters to fulfill the goals of the party by an appropriate means, in return of full support of party members and supporters. If a political party deviates from its contractual agreement with its supporters or employs inappropriate means to achieve its goals, the contract is deemed void unless the political party's supporters ratify the change in the contractual agreement expressly or implicitly. In practical terms, this takes place either in periodic elections by voting against the party that failed to fulfill its contractual obligations, voting "no confidence" in the party leadership in an internal party electoral process or by another innovative approach that can be crafted in the State constitution.

Notably, political party membership does not necessarily require an automatic vote to the party; instead, a party's members and supporters are under religious, moral and legal obligation to scrutinize the party's actions to ensure its conformity with Islamic law. Indeed, under Islamic law, allegiance is to Islam alone which requires individuals to act according to what is in the best interest of the Muslim State even though that might be contrary to one's party's interests.[360] Logically, it follows that no allegiance is given to those who are openly inimical to Islamic fundamentals or Muslims.[361]

It is important to emphasize that political parties are entirely independent of the State. Each party must distinguish itself by its own values, interpretation technique of Islamic law or by stressing particular ideologies. For example, it would be valuable to have an Islamic socialist party to represent and promote the interest of unfortunate citizens of the State. It would also be valuable to have parties that represent various industries such as farmers, workers etc. The diversity in representation along with independence from the State are the best tools for the Islamic Parliament to achieve its objectives.

---

[360] See Quran 5: 55-6.
[361] Qur'an, 60:1.

6.4.3   Matters Subject to Shura

Prefixed adjudications delineated in the *Qur'an* and *Sunnah* are the immutable part of Islamic law. Accordingly, they are not subject to interpretation, discussion or voting. Apart from these limitations, all other Islamic state citizens' affairs, whether of Muslims or non-Muslims and including the creation of new legislation are mutable and shall be conducted by *Shura*. Practically, this means that state 's legislature is free to enact legislations on mutable adjudications so long as the general principles outlined in *Qur'an* and *Sunnah* are followed.

For instance, when the Muslim state legislature considers prohibiting attempted murder it should investigate general principles of *Qur'an* and *Sunnah*. These principles dictate the following: since murder is prohibited, the lesser included offense of attempted murder is also prohibited. The general Islamic doctrine of justice, measured to the slightest degree, submits that punishment must be proportionate to the crime, an eye for an eye and tooth for tooth, unless the victim, or the victim's heirs, forgive the offender.[362] Accordingly, attempted murder is a prohibited act, and its punishment is less than that of the completed crime, murder.

Islamic law scholarship accumulated over the past fourteen centuries plays a dynamic role in the law-making process. It offers an invaluable discussion of the *Qur'an* and *Sunnah*, an extensive practical examination of various mutable rules and creates a historical contextual interpretation of the *Qur'an* and *Sunnah*. It also provides

---

[362] So whosoever does good equal to the weight of an atom (or a small ant), shall see it. And whosoever does evil equal to the weight of an atom (or a small ant), shall see it. Qur'an 99:7-8.

an exhaustive list of rules of conduct, a precedent to follow, ready for adoption by the State seeking to function successfully under Islamic law. These rules of conduct, established over the past fourteen centuries, are subject to the presumption of continuity unless the Parliament finds that such mutable rules are not appropriate due to disparity in time and place between its inception and present times.

Notably, a number of Orientalists have proposed wholesale abandonment of the wealth of Islamic law scholarship created over the past fourteen centuries, since the birth of Islam, in favor of creating new, modern Islamic law.[363] Those who have made such a proposal did not offer any rationale short of claiming that the established scholarship is archaic and not in conformity with the contemporary world. In more explicit terms, these Orientalists demand that a nation of 1.9 billion Muslim abandon their Islamic culture, belief system and legal history because they do not like it. Such a proposal was summarily dismissed by the overwhelming majority of Muslims.

6.5   The Ruler of The Islamic State

Classical Islamic scholarship used the titles *Imam, Amir al-Mu'minin* (the commander of the faithful) or *Caliph* interchangeably to refer to the ruler of the Islamic State. Classic scholarship recognized the indispensability of a ruler in performing the executive functions of upholding Islamic law, guarding people's right to practice their religion freely, managing Islamic state affairs and carrying out the objectives of Islamic law, i.e., protection of life, religion, progeny,

---

[363] See Abdullahi Ahmed An-Na'im, Toward an Islamic Reformation: Civil Liberties, Human Rights and International Law. (Syracuse University Press 1990).

intellect, and property/wealth.[364] Classic scholars advanced several rationales to demonstrate the need for a ruler. First, the Muslim nation throughout the centuries has unanimously agreed upon the necessity of having a ruler. Immediately after the death of the Prophet Muhammad, Muslims elected Abu Bakr as the first ruler. The legacy continued; Muslims had rulers, sometimes chosen by a defective process, who performed their functions adequately with limited exceptions in modern times. A notable example is of Ataturk who totally overturned the Islamic law objective of protection of the religion, rendering Turkey an anti-Islamic state. Second, the *Qur'an* orders Muslims to obey rulers so long as the ruler's command is compatible with Islamic law.[365] If the ruler's command contradicts Islamic law, then his command is obsolete and not obeyable.[366] The *Quran's* command to obey the ruler implicitly commands selection of a ruler. Three, the Prophet Muhammad commanded Muslims to have a ruler.[367] Four, selection of a ruler is inevitable in order to avoid the

---

[364] See Ahmad Al-Raysuni, *Imam Al-Shatibi's Theory of the Higher Objectives and Intents of Islamic Law*, (Nancy Roberts trans.), (International Institute of Islamic Thought 2005), 108. See also Abu'l Hasan al-Mawardi, *Kitab Al Ahkam As Sultaniyyah* (The laws of Islamic Governance), (Beirut, Dar al-Fikr),3.

[365] O you who believe! Obey Allah and obey the Messenger (Muhammad), and those of you (Muslims) who are in authority. (And) if you differ in anything amongst yourselves, refer it to Allah and His Messenger, if you believe in Allah and in the Last Day. That is better and more suitable for final determination. Qur'an 4:59.

[366] Prophet Muhammad said: Listening and Obedience are binding on a Muslim whether he likes or dislikes, so long as he is not commanded for disobedience (to Allah). If he is commanded to disobedience (to Allah), no listening and disobedience are binding (on him). Sunan Abu Dawud hadith #2626.

[367] The Prophet, said, "Verily, the leader is only a shield behind whom they fight and he protects them. If he fears Allah the Exalted and enjoins justice, then

potential harm of lawlessness and disorder caused by lack of leadership. The renowned scholar, ʿAḍad al-dīn al-ʾĪjī accurately concluded that the absence of a ruler who represents law and order would have a devastating effect on society such that people would spend all their time protecting their lives and wealth to the exclusion of performing daily activities; eventually, the entire society would collapse.[368]

Having established the necessity to have a ruler, the logical question is: what are the mechanisms and the process of selection of a ruler? There is no short answer to this question; rather one should review Islamic history and Islamic law guidelines. After the death of Prophet Muhammad, Muslims struggled to create an appropriate ruler selection process for the emerging Islamic State. The *Qur'an* and *Sunnah* provided broad guidelines, but the selection mechanism was left to Muslims to adapt to their ever-changing needs and circumstances. Two central guidelines control the ruler selection process under Islamic law; *Shura* doctrine and the contractual relationship between the ruler and the people (*bay'ah*). *Shura* doctrine was been discussed earlier. Concerning the contractual relationship, Islam, since the time of the Prophet, has recognized the concept of *bay'ah* upon which individuals make an oath of allegiance to a person in return for, or without, fulfillment of specific terms. Various groups of early Muslims made *bay'ah* to the Prophet Muhammad, sometimes conditional upon fulfillment of specific terms. The Muslim ruler is subject to *bay'ah* in which he acts as an

---

he will have a reward. If he enjoins other than that, then it will return upon him."
Sahih Muslim.

[368] ʿAḍud al-Dīn al-Ījī, Kitāb al-Mawāqif fī ʿIlm al-Kalām, (ʿAbd al-Raḥmān ʿUmayra ed.), (Beirut, Dār al-jeel 1997), 400.

agent representing the Islamic State in return for fulfillment of his contractual relationship obligations including upholding Islamic law, defending the borders of the State, being fit and of good moral character so long as he is in power.

Because *bay'ah* is a mutual contract, people have the power to revoke it if the ruler breaches the contractual agreement or becomes unfit to govern. The *bay'ah* contract is also subject to Islamic law. Accordingly, in case of violation of fundamental Islamic law rules that are not subject to interpretation, people may revoke the contract immediately and call for a new election. The mechanism for this procedure is not precisely delineated in the *Qur'an* or *Sunnah* nor is the election process of the Islamic ruler clearly illustrated. However, since one of the aims of this volume is to refute the notion that Islam permits authoritarian regimes, these issues are worthy of profound analysis, guided by the practices of initial four *Caliphs*. It should be noted that the practices of the initial four *Caliphs* are considered by Muslims as an ideal model to follow. This period represents the golden era of Islam.

6.5.1 The Election of A Ruler

6.5.1.1 Transfer of Power at The Time the Initial Four *Caliphs*: The Role Model in The Golden Era

Three models of a succession of rulers during the reigns of initial four *Caliphs* occurred.

A. Imperfect Election Process

After Prophet Muhammad's death, a peaceful transfer of power, compliant with the Islamic law, was the first challenge that faced the emerging Islamic State. Since the primary sources of Islamic jurisprudence, the *Qur'an* and *Sunnah* did not specify a mandatory political process that guaranteed the peaceful transfer of power after the death of the Prophet Muhammad, the early Islamic state utilized the doctrine of *Shura* and *Bay'ah* contract in succession of power.[369] However, the general principles of *Shura* and *Bay'ah* contract offer no procedural guidelines or model to follow. As a result, after the death of the Prophet Muhammad, Muslims had to be innovative to fill the vacant ruler of state position and ensure a peaceful transfer of power. A group of Muslims, *Al-Ansar*, held a meeting at *Saqifa Benu Sa'idah* to elect one of them to be the new leader. Only three of *Al-Muhajereen*, Muslims who migrated from Mecca to Medina, rushed to the meeting to join the election process driven by fear that *Al-Ansar*, who were only a portion of the population, might make a decision notwithstanding the rest of Muslim votes in the succession process. The meeting ended with the election of the closest companion of the Prophet Muhammad, Abu Bakr, as the new ruler. Objectively, this election process was far from perfect because numerous Muslims neither voted nor were consulted in the election process. However, this imperfect procedure did not stir the Muslim community's disapproval at the time for a number of reasons including the elite status of Abu Bakr, who was the closest companion to the Prophet Muhammad and that Prophet Muhammad had asked Abu Bakr to lead the Muslims in prayer shortly before the Prophet's death, which may have persuaded many Muslims to believe that the Prophet desired to appoint Abu Bakr as the first *Caliph*. Those who believed in this symbolic appointment of Abu Bakr as *Caliph* (by leading the prayers) suggested that the Prophet Muhammad stopped short of making an unequivocal declaration of appointment of Abu

---

[369] Qur'an 42:38 & 3:159.

Bakr because Muslims might understand such an appointment as endorsing an Islamic monarchy starting with Abu Bakr and his family after his death. In this environment, Muslims' implicitly ratified the election of Abu Bakr -the first Muslim *Caliph*- without much disagreement.

Another example of the imperfect election process was the election of the fourth *Caliph*, Ali Ibn Abi Talib. After the assassination of the third *Caliph*, 'Uthman, the majority of the people of Medina, the current capital of the Islamic state, elected Ali as the fourth *Caliph*. Most of the people of Iraq and the Arabian Peninsula concurred with the people of Medina's decision and ratified the election of Ali. Nevertheless, Ali was not as lucky as Abu Bakr whose election was ratified by the entire Islamic state. The people of al-Sham region refused to ratify Ali's election.[370] Ali, believing that he was the legitimate ruler of the Islamic state, attempted to unify the Islamic state and subdue the al-Sham region to the central authority of Medina by force. This chain of events culminated in the assassination of Ali. To this day, the majority of Sunni Muslims, as well as all Shia, believe that Ali was the legitimate ruler of the Islamic state. It seems that the unfortunate events that led to dissention by Al Sham region can be attributed entirely to the lack of a tight, well-designed mechanism of the election process.

B. Predecessor Ruler Appointment of Successor

Abu-Bakr, before his death, appointed Umar Ibn al-Khaṭṭāb as his successor. Umar was a close companion to the Prophet and was well regarded, known for his impartiality, sense of justice and sympathy

---

[370] al-sham region now includes, Syria, Lebanon, Palestine and Jordan.

toward the weak and the needy. Like Abu Bakr, Muslims approved the appointment of Umar contentedly.

C. Electing One of The Ruler Nominees

Several factors dominated the election process of third *Caliph*, 'Uthman Ibn Afan. Initially, there was no formal election process in place as yet in the Islamic State. There was fear that Muslims might fall into a divisive succession process that would threaten the unity of the emerging Islamic State. Additionally, reluctant to make the wrong choice, Umar, then the *Caliph*, refused to appoint his successor as Abu Baker had done. Umar Ibn al-Khaṭṭāb was asked, "Would you appoint your successor?". He replied, "If I appoint a *Caliph*, it is true that somebody who was better than I (i.e., Abu Bakr) did so, and if I leave the matter undecided, it is true that somebody who was better than I (i.e., the Prophet Muhammad) did so." Then he was quoted as saying "people are of two kinds: either one who is keen to take over the *Caliphate* or one who is afraid of assuming such responsibility. I wish I could be free from its responsibility in that I would receive neither reward nor retribution. I will not be able to bear the burden of the *Caliphate* whether I am living or dead.[371] Eventually, Umar created an innovative process that provided guidelines for succession to prevent unqualified or unsatisfactory rulers from taking power and avoided imposing a ruler upon the Muslims. The succession process involved his nomination of six community leaders. He ordered them to hold a closed meeting to select one from amongst themselves within a time period not exceeding three days in which the majority vote shall prevail. In case of a tie (3-3) vote, the group shall consult Abd Allah Ibn Umar. If the counseling was not successful, the cluster

---

[371] Sahih Al-Bukhari, Hadith # 325.

that included Abd al-Rahman Ibn Ouf shall prevail. Under this process the third *Caliph*, 'Uthman Ibn Afan was elected.

6.5.1.2 Evaluating the Ruler Electoral Process in The Time of Rightly Guided *Caliphs*

Although the ruler succession process in the golden era of the rightly guided *Caliphates* shed light on the various possibilities of transfer of power, it lacked comprehensive guidelines that were both workable and in conformity with Islamic law. The first model involving the election of Abu Bakr, overlooked the general public's right to vote in that only those who attended the meeting at *Saqifa Benu Sa'idah* were engaged in the election process. Indeed, what saved this flawed process is the estimable status of Abu Bakr, as the closest companion of the Prophet Muhammad. Similarly, the status of Umar Ibn al-Khattab, the second *Caliph*, and his renowned reputation for justice and mercy saved the second model from causing political unrest in the Islamic state given that it contradicted the fundamental *Shura* principle. Because the cornerstone of the first and the second models was the unique and unrepeatable character of the proposed ruler, these methods cannot be followed in the future. No potential candidate for Muslim leadership can claim to be comparable, in character or in qualities, to Umar Ibn al-Khattab or Abu Bakr. If such a claim were ever made, the public would denounce and immediately reject it. Undeniably, any attempt to follow these models poses a severe and unjustified risk to the State's interests. Muslims throughout the centuries have agreed that both Umar and Abu Bakr are incomparable, and accordingly, a self-imposed ruler rising to power under circumstances similar to the rise of Umar and Abu Bakr would result in political and civil unrest. Such a proposition is especially true in the twenty-first century after the Muslim population has repeatedly experienced the negative consequences of undemocratic succession processes. Also because the Muslim population at the time of Abu Bakr and Umar was small, the implicit ratification of the ruler was an indisputable fact free from any doubt or coercion. No one contested the authority of Umar or Abu Bakr to rule nor did any object to their leadership. Nowadays, realities such as the enormous increase of the State's population and the increasing complexity of society shall refute any claim of implicit ratification of a ruler succession and shall be tainted by doubt of coercion notwithstanding ignoring the individual's right to choose his ruler under *Shura* and *bay'ah* doctrines.

Nevertheless, the first and third model, the election of a qualified candidate, with improvements to make it suitable for our time, is worthy of endorsement providing that the proposed improvement is both in accordance with Islamic law jurisprudence and responds to the current social needs.

6.5.2   Multiple Rulers vs. One Ruler

Classic scholarship has raised the question of multiple rulers to govern the Islamic nation. Generally speaking, the vast majority of scholars have suggested that the Muslim nation should be governed by only one ruler. This proposition stems from the notion that the Islamic nation is a unified universal nation. Accordingly, the notion of having more than one ruler defeats the principle of a unified universal nation. Moreover, several verses in the *Qur'an* mandate the unity of the Islamic nation.[372] The Islamic state, as an ideological state, is confined to any limitations or principles enumerated in the *Qur'an*.

---

[372] For example: "indeed, this nation of yours (Muslims nation) is one nation, and I am your Lord, so fear Me." Quran 23:52.

An exception can be made when the Islamic state is so vast that one ruler cannot manage its affairs or if a natural geographical barrier, such as a sea, prevents the central authority of the government from protecting its territories or exercising any function of the government adequately.[373] As to classic scholarship's uncertainty about exercising the central government's control and protection over vast territories, it is plausible that nowadays with the advancement of science and technologies, as well as better organization of governmental powers, central governments are capable of running any state regardless of its size.

6.5.3   Towards Contemporary Islamic State Ruler Electoral Model

Because there are no exhaustive procedural guidelines that explain the Islamic State's ruler selection process, scholars have presented several theories. Mainstream classic Islamic law scholars including al-Mawardi and Ibn-Khaldun limited the process of selecting the ruler either by election or by appointment by the previous ruler. Typically, they refer to the appointment of the second *Caliph*, Umar by Abu Bakr as a precedent to this model of succession. Numerous problems may arise from this proposition. As explained previously, the appointment of Umar was indeed a unique experience that cannot be generalized. It denies people's unalienable right of conducting their affairs via *Shura*. It may lead to social unrest if people collectively reject the appointment of the new ruler. It may also create an enormous injustice to the Muslim state. For instance, Mu'āwiya bin Abi-Sufyan, the fifth *Caliph*, had established an absolute monarchy

---

[373] See Abu Mansur 'Abd al-Qahir al-Baghdadi, *Usul al-Din*, (Beirut Dar Al Kotob Al-Ilmiyah, 2002).

contrary to the Islamic principle of *Shura* and appointed his son, 'Yazīd, to be his successor. To be sure, 'Yazīd has been portrayed very negatively by the majority of Islamic historians, and his reign was considered to be a dark era in Islamic history. In any event, rulership in the Islamic State is a contract between the people and the ruler. Appointing successors devoid of contractual agreement permits the ruler to conduct State affairs free from contractual obligations or liabilities.

An alternative rulership succession mechanism involves utilization of an election process, directly or indirectly. The indirect election process has been presented in classic Islamic scholarship under the model of the committee of *Ahl Al Hall Wa Al-Aqd*. This committee is comprised of a group of intellectuals with outstanding qualities that represent the interests of the Islamic state in a variety of ways including the appointment of the ruler. The root of the indirect election through *Ahl al-Hall wa'l-Aqd* can be traced to Islamic medieval political theory that was influenced by particular rulers' succession practices such as the election of Abu Baker at *Saqifa Benu Sa'idah*. The scholars who presented *Ahl Al Hall Wa Al-Aqd* theory never explained how the *Ahl Al Hall Wa Al-Aqd* committee is appointed or elected nor did they explain the Islamic jurisprudential foundation for their theory.[374] Nevertheless, these theorists have asserted that *Ahl Hall Wa Al-Aqd* are the people's representatives who came to power consensually. In any case, *Ahl Hall Wa Al-Aqd's* empowerment to elect a ruler on behalf of the people is subject to Islamic law fundamentals including that *Ahl Al Hall Wa Al-Aqd* must act within their limited delegatory power otherwise their selection of

---

[374] See Abu'l Hasan al-Mawardi, *Kitab Al Ahkam As Sultaniyyah* (The laws of Islamic Governance), (Beirut, Dar al-Fikr).

the ruler is not binding to the nation. Any condition can be imposed on their delegatory power to select a ruler, particularly requiring mandatory public ratification of the selection. This ratification is known in Islamic scholarship as *bay'ah* contract, a public oath of allegiance to the ruler in return for the ruler's fulfillment of the contractual conditions of *bay'ah*.

A possible contemporary addition to the theory of *Ahl al-Hall wa'l-Aqd*, if ever adopted in the Islamic state, is that *Ahl Hall Wa Al-Aqd* can be an independently elected body, a committee comprised of a group of Parliament members or the entire Parliament. The ratification by the people of the committee's selection indisputably assures compliance with the Islamic law principle that *bay'ah* contract is a consensual agreement between the ruler and the people.

Nevertheless, there is nothing in Islamic law that precludes a direct election process so long as essential Islamic doctrines are respected and upheld. *Shura*, consultation, must take place among all eligible voters. Necessary minimum qualifications of the ruler must be met. Any other condition that does not violate Islamic law is permitted. For instance, periodic election of the ruler is a valid objective given that periodic elections strengthen the accountability of the ruler. Listing the circumstances that give rise to the impeachment of the ruler is also a useful objective. Limiting rulers' powers in relation to specific State affairs and vesting those powers to other elected bodies can be a handy tool to distribute governance powers and enhance accountability.

In any case, whether the ruler is elected indirectly by the *Ahl Al Hall Wa Al-Aqd group* or through direct public election, the people's approval is a must. Islamic law needs to be followed including its doctrine of *Shura* and both the ruler and the people are bound to the terms of the *Bay'ah,* the electoral agreement, to its minute detail.

It is imperative to distinguish between these theoretical foundations explaining the ruler election process and the current practices of some Muslim-majority states. In Saudi Arabia, an absolute monarchy State, *Hay'at al-Bay'ah*, the Allegiance council, elects the Crown Princes from among the heirs of the founding King, Abdul-Aziz al-Saud. Membership in that council is limited to King Abdul-Aziz al-Saud's heirs. This practice is far removed from Islamic law. The doctrine of *Shura* mandated by the *Qur'an* speaks of mutual consultation among Muslims that is either directly practiced by the entire population through a voting process or via real representation of society of *Ahl Al Hall Wa Al-Aqd.* In Saudi Arabia, the Allegiance council cannot be classified correctly as *Ahl Al Hall Wa Al-Aqd* since its membership is limited to the royal family to the exclusion of the entire population. Neither the Prophet Muhammad nor the rightly guided *Caliphs* limited the exercise of *Shura* to a family. Also, as a general rule in Islam, there is no superiority based on heritage, race, family or otherwise. Righteousness is the only ground for superiority. If so, why should the royal family claim such superior status as to serve as *Ahl Al Hall Wa Al-Aqd* and elect a ruler from amongst themselves? For that reason, Saudi Arabia's model of governance cannot be branded as an Islamic one.

In the wake of the Arab spring, revolutions brought intense discussion regarding the permissibility of revolt against tyrannical regimes and the rulers' succession process in the light of Islamic principles. Al-Azhar, perhaps the oldest and most prestigious Islamic institution in the Islamic world, made a public statement suggesting that democracy, with Islamically mandated limitation, is the modern formula for the ruler succession process. As well, Al-Azhar had suggested that Muslim nations may peacefully revolt against authoritarian rulers. It seems that the statement abandoned the classical electoral model of indirect election process/representative election through *Ahl Al Hall Wa Al-Aqd*. The significance of this statement, especially if coupled with a successful exercise of peaceful transfer of power in post-revolutionary Muslim-majority states, shall change not only world history but also Islamic scholarship. Muslim-majority states including Egypt, Tunisia, Libya, Syria, and Yemen could have -but did not-create new models of the succession process in close alignment to Islamic law given that Islamic political forces are dominant in all these States. It was anticipated that these models would interact and compete for a period until each State finds its way into a better future guided by Islamic law. These models could have exposed the deficiencies in the autocratic, non-Islamic systems of governance in the Middle East and inspired further revolutions. Unfortunately, at the moment, the Muslim-majority states that have experienced the Arab spring face enormous opposition from within, from the deeply corrupt state, and from other dictatorial Muslim-majority states out of fear that the correct model of Islamic governance poses a severe threat to their authoritarian regimes existence.

6.5.4   Ruler Qualifications and Impeachment

The first Muslim *Caliph*, Abu Bakr in his inaugural speech emphasized the doctrine of impeachment if the ruler diverted from Islamic law as follows:

> *"O, People! I have been put in authority over you, and I am not the best of you. So if I do the right thing then help me and if I do*

*wrong then put me straight. Truthfulness is a sacred trust, and
lying is a betrayal. The weak amongst you is strong in my sight.
I will surely try to remove his pain and suffering. The strong
amongst you is weak to me I will – Allah willing – realize the
right from him fully. When obscene things spread among any
nation, calamities generally continued to descend upon them.
As long as I obey Allah and His messenger, you should obey me,
and if I do not obey Allah and His messenger, then obedience to
me is not incumbent upon you"*

Abu Bakr, in this speech, highlighted two main qualities for those
in places of authority that were mentioned in the *Qur'an*; capability
and trustworthiness in terms of Islamic law obedience.[375] These
qualities branch into several characteristics including justice,
knowledge of Islamic law, general fitness (physical and mental
competences), and track record of trustworthiness. Sometimes
finding a candidate for Islamic rulership that possesses both required
qualities, capability and trustworthiness, is difficult. Candidates may
show excellent capability in leadership but with a blemished
reputation of Islamic trustworthiness and vice versa. Here, the
renowned Islamic political science scholar, Ibn Taymiyya, suggested
that the selection of a ruler ought to be guided by a harm/benefit
analysis.[376] The candidate for rulership who is expected to produce
more benefit and less harm to the state is preferred over the more
pious candidate who may produce less benefit and incur more harm.
Being pious, without a doubt, is an excellent characteristic but if it
only benefits the candidate for rulership without visible benefit to the

---

[375] Qur'an 28:26.

[376] Ibn Taymiyya, *al-Siyasah al-shar`iyah fi islah al-ra`i wa-al-ra`iyah*,
(Sharia system of governance to produce a righteous ruler and people), (Kindle
Edition 2017).

state, it should be discounted. On the other hand, a candidate for rulership with personal infirmity, some tendency of personal disobedience of Islamic law, but expected to produce maximum benefit and less harm to the state, is favored. Ibn Taymiyya correctly illustrates that the Prophet Muhammad created these rules in selecting leadership. The Prophet Muhammad denied Abū Dhar al-Ghifari a leadership position although, as the Prophet Muhammad testified, the righteousness of Abū Dhar was exemplary. In the meantime, the Prophet Muhammad appointed Khalid Ibn al-Walid as a leader of the Muslim army though he disagreed with some of his acts.

Once the ruler assumes office, he is bound to fulfill *bay'ah*, contractual obligations including strict obedience to Islamic law as mandated in the *Qur'an* and to protect the interests of the State.[377] Understandably, strict obedience to Islamic law is a superimposed condition to the *bay'ah* contract. Neither the people nor the ruler can avoid this condition so long as the State maintains its Islamic identity. The *Qur'an* suggests that adhering to Islamic law is independent of any other cause, while obedience toward the people in power is subject to their obedience to Islam.[378]

When a ruler loses one of the two mandated qualities, capability and trustworthiness, he might be subject to impeachment. This may occur in a number of situations including:

i.   The ruler fails to adopt Islamic law as the constitution of the land or introduces laws or practices inconsistent with Islam.

---

[377] See Qur'an 4:59.
[378] Qur'an 4:59.

ii. The ruler fails to dispense his duties, e.g., maintain peace and order in the society.

iii. Substantial clear injustice by the ruler

iv. Failure or refusal to protect the State

v. Physical Unfitness.

vi. Ruler captured by the enemy

It cannot be overemphasized that any of these situations must occur ***beyond all doubt*** before the question of impeachment takes place. Any doubt precludes impeachment of a ruler. For instance, many provisions of Islamic law are subject to interpretation. The ruler in administering State affairs may adopt any possible interpretation.[379] Here, Islam strikes a balance between the people's right to revolt if the ruler violates the terms of *bay'ah* contract or boldly, without any doubt, violates Islamic law and maintaining peace and order in the society. Fanciful allegations are insufficient to initiate the impeachment process while preserving the people's right to revolt against oppression. This delicate balance is, indeed, challenging. The assassination of 'Uthman, the third *Caliph*, at the hand of the dissidents, who wrongfully believed that 'Uthman violated Islamic law, created a scar in the consciousness of the Islamic nations. Many Muslims may be horrified at revolting out of fear that they might be wrong in judging the ruler's actions. Also, the political struggle may create a power vacuum which in turn undermines peace, order and the rule of law in society.

---

[379] The Prophet Muhammad said: "A Muslim has to listen and obey (the order of his Muslim ruler) whether he likes it or not, as long as he does not order to commit a sin (Islamically illegal conduct). If he does, he should neither listen nor obey" Sahih Muslim.

Such a state of affairs might explain why many Islamic political theorists were reluctant to issue a *fatwa*, religious opinion, allowing revolt against tyrannical rulers. On the other hand, Muslim-majority states' tyrants, throughout history, have utilized fear from wrongful resistance to strengthen their grip on power. Nevertheless, it does not follow that Muslim nations ought to submit to injustice and refrain from opposing tyranny. To achieve the proper balance, some scholars have attempted to create a mechanism to oppose rulers who deny or refuse to apply one of the fundamentals of Islamic law or seize power by illegitimate means. A scholarly opinion, including reports on the renowned scholars Malik and Abu Hanifa, propagates passive resistance to the ruler who boldly violates Islamic law.[380] Others, relying on some *hadith* that prohibit any resistance to the ruler, even when the ruler boldly ignores the law of the land and spreads injustice, forbid revolution. *Imam* al-Nawawī (1233-1277) concluded that revolting against an unjust ruler produces more harm than benefit as regards to possible bloodshed and seditions.[381] Slim minority scholarship, including Muʿtazila and Zaidiyyah, allowed bearing arms to oppose tyranny.[382]

From recent experiences with violent opposition to tyranny in Muslim-majority states, it is evident that violent resistance may not succeed in changing oppressive regimes while the resulting harm and collateral damage are inevitable. In spite of violent opposition, the

---

[380] Abu Bakr al-Jassas , 1 *Ahkam Ul Quran* ,(Beirut, Dar Ihya' al-Turath al-'Arabi 1992), 86.

[381] Muhammad Umara, Al-Islam wa-Falsafah al-hukm (philosophy of governance in Islam), (Cairo, Dar al Shorouk 2009),499.

[382] Id, 500.

tyrannical Syrian regime has killed at least hundreds of thousands of people and destroyed many villages in order to ensure its survival.

Passive resistance, especially if supported by the majority of the population can cripple tyrannical regimes successfully. The 2011 Egyptian revolution is the best example of passive resistance. On February 11, 2011, former President Mubarak stepped down while about eighteen million Egyptians marched in the streets in protest of the regime.[383] No regime is capable of containing this number, even by use of force. Perhaps this is what was envisioned by Malik and Abu Hanifa to be the model of revolt against tyranny. Also, this model is apparently in harmony with Islamic principles that highly value the sanctity of life, the duty to follow Islamic law even against the will of the ruler and the duty to uphold justice actively. Moreover, this model ensures that the majority of the population shares the belief that the ruler has violated the *Bay'ah* contractual obligations. It eliminates the possibility that a limited fraction of the population would impose their will on the majority under the allegation of tyranny. For all these reasons, this model is worthy of endorsement.

6.6 The Islamic Form of Democracy: Comparative Prospective

In Western democracies, the concepts of democracy and fundamental human rights have evolved throughout the centuries resulting in a very distinct ideology from that initially practiced in ancient Greece, the Roman Empire or in common law countries. Rights of the "other,"

---

[383] Notably, the setback that occurred in Egypt in the summer of 2013 when the Egyptian army orchestrated a military Coup under the guise of 'the people revolt against the elected ruler' has nothing to do with passive resistance model of rebellion; rather, it was a product of a deeply corrupt state in Egypt.

who is not a member of the dominant group, have always been defined by those in power. This occurred by crafting constitutional and ordinary laws that serve the dominant group's interests and ensure its continued superiority. An example of constitutional rules that favor the dominant group is the right to vote which was limited to white males only. Women, people of color and slaves had no voting rights. Likewise, the dominant group utilized their legislative power to create ordinary laws that reflected their views and desires. For instance, common law for centuries required any alleged rape victim to prove that she resisted the sexual intercourse to her utmost ability.[384] A woman's failure to cry out when she was being attacked was evidence of consent.[385] Accordingly, those terrified victims of rape, women who failed to prove "utmost resistance" had no legal recourse. This rule protected many white rapists from prosecution.

It has taken centuries to improve the life of the "other" and for his voice to be heard. Today, women and minorities in Western democracies have gained many rights. Nevertheless, the dominance of the elite group persists, and the "other" has to fight continuously to receive humane, dignified treatment comparable to that of the dominant group. For example, even now, women still strive to attain equal pay for equal work.[386] African-Americans in the United States are struggling to achieve equal justice for blacks.[387] To further muddy the waters, lobbies are created to defend group and corporate interests

---

[384] State v. Cowing, 99 Minn. 123, 108 N.W. 851 (1906); Prokop v. State, 148 Neb. 582, 28 N.W.2d 200 (1947).

[385] People v. Morrow, 132 Ill. App. 2d 293, 270 N.E.2d 487 (1971).

[386] For example, in 2016 Statistics Canada reported that a woman working full time in Canada makes 73.5 cents for every dollar a man makes.

[387] In fact, the National Association of Blacks in Criminal Justice was established to achieve this goal.

regardless of merit. Money and power create lobbies that influence the decision-making process and define the limits of rights. In sum, Western democracies are best described as unfettered democracies in which the democratic process and the limitation of rights and freedoms are evolving. However, this evolution can be hijacked by the dominant group and fall victim to special interest lobbies whose sponsors possess enough money and power to influence decision making.

In contrast, in the Islamic system of governance, Islamic democracy, the people's right to govern is limited by Islamic law. Recall that the basics of Islam, the foundations of Islamic law, the *Qur'an* and *Sunnah,* are inviolate. The unchangeable rules delineated in the *Qur'an* and *Sunnah*, prevent negative influence by lobbies since a lobby cannot demand preferential treatment that is not justified under the *Qur'an* or *Sunnah*. Rights and freedoms remain fixed from the time of revelation of Islam till the end of days. The majority cannot subdue the minority's rights since the rights are firm, unchangeable and inflexible. The rights of non-Muslims, women, and non-citizens are acknowledged and guaranteed. There is no "other" who is subject to the whim of the dominant group; everyone in the Islamic state knows his rights and obligations. Issues such as equal pay for equal work or equal and fair justice for people of color would never arise under proper Islamic rule.

The parameters to the Islamic democracy are, without a doubt, self-imposed. Muslims by joining Islam accept all obligations and benefits of Islam. Muslims are accountable for following the good ethical manners of the Prophet Muhammad, for paying the mandatory annual charity *Zakah* and for upholding human rights. It follows that Muslims, by joining the Islamic faith, accept all Islamic commands. For instance, they have to contribute to social welfare through paying *Zakah,* and they cannot discriminate or alienate the "other" because of race, origin, sex and the like. Likewise, non-Muslims in the Islamic state by joining the Islamic social contract, *Dhimmah* contract, accept the parameters of Islamic law. They ought to pay *Jizya* (*Zakah* equivalent for the non-Muslim) to contribute to social welfare and should refrain from discriminating against the "other." Some of the restraints on Muslims and non-Muslims are immutable such as paying Zakah and upholding Islamic human rights. The Islamic state, however, can create mutable restraint(s), subject to Islamic law guidelines, in response to social need. The Islamic state may impose further taxation on its citizens, beyond *Zakah* and *Jizya*, to fund state needs or social services. Here, because Islamic law is vibrant, dynamic and capable of responding to social needs by creating new legal rules through *Ijtihad*, the Islamic state may modify its democratic practices or impose further rules so long as it does not contradict basic sources of Islamic law, i.e., the *Qur'an* and *Sunnah*.[388]

In sum, the difference between Western and Islamic democracy is that in Western democracies, the majority govern and minority is sometimes the voiceless, "other" that shall be at the mercy of the dominant group which controls the government, makes laws and imposes socially acceptable rules of conduct. For example, when the majority elected Donald Trump, the "others" suffered the consequences. If the majority elects a good President, the "others" shall enjoy many benefits. In contrast, under Islamic law, immutable Islamic human rights and rules of governance are not subject to

---

[388] Ijtihad is the process of finding a solution to a legal question through interpretation of Qur'an and Sunnah.

interpretation or majority control. The dominant group, existing in the ideal Islamic state, is restrained by immutable Islamic law rules that protect the weakest and the voiceless in the society from the tyranny of the majority.

6.7 Autonomous Islamic Democracy

By definition, Islamic democracy requires that law making, as a form of democratic exercise, should be limited by Islamic law guidelines and free from foreign influence. Nevertheless, Islamic democracy has been subject to great criticism and is under pressure to conform to Western ideals. Many Western states demand that various Muslim-majority states that only partially follow Islamic law, abandon their heritage, laws, and customs and adopt Western laws. For instance, Western states have not only prohibited polygyny, a practice that is permitted under Islamic law but has incited several Muslim-majority states to abolish or restrict it. Under French influence, Morocco recently restricted polygyny.[389] Western countries have presented various claims to prohibit polygyny going so far as to claim that polygyny violates universal international human rights.[390] The merit or demerit of such claims is not the issue. The impetus for such claims, whether motivated by Christian theologians who condemn polygyny or by women's lobbies who may believe that polygyny undermines women's rights, is also irrelevant. Furthermore, that polygyny in Islam is a consensual relationship, and a wife cannot forcibly be kept in a marriage relationship, whether polygamous or monogamous, is

---

[389] See the discussion in this volume explaining the recent changes in Moroccan's laws regarding Polygyny.

[390] For example, Canada's department of Justice in 2006 issued a statement that claimed that Polygyny is a violation of the universal international human rights. See http://www.justice.gc.ca/eng/rp-pr/other-autre/poly/chap3.html.

immaterial as well. The pertinent question is whether one nation can/should force its will on another nation. Can a Western nation justifiably claim that there is an international consensus that polygamy violates universal international human rights while polygyny is widely practiced in Africa and many Asian countries, and permitted by the Islamic religion which has 1.9 billion followers? Are the norms of the Christian West the universal norm? The answer is no. Suppose the Christian West utilized its financial, military and scientific power to claim superiority over world affairs. Should the Islamic world follow the current Western norms blindly and abandon its sovereignty, autonomy, and individuality? Suppose the Islamic world did so and blindly follow whatever norms were imposed upon them by the West. What should the Islamic world do when the Western norms change? Should the Islamic world automatically follow such changes as the slave follows his master? For example, in the past women were not allowed to vote in many Western states and now they can. Suppose that a fascist political movement prevailed in the Western states and rescinded women's suffrage. Should the Islamic world follow this ban? When would the Islamic world gain its emancipation? These questions with their unapologetic sarcastic tone are frequently raised by Muslim thinkers that demand respect for the individuality, uniqueness, and sovereignty of Muslim-majority states. The Western world should realize that in the Islamic system of governance, the people's right to govern, limited by Islamic law, ought to be respected and even admired in some instances although it may not be compatible with all Western values. It should be respected from the point of view that Muslim-majority states are sovereign nations with a deeper, older civilization than the culture of numerous Western nations. It should be admired in the sense that Islamic law, the restraint to Islamic democracy, stands as a barrier to prevent tyranny by the majority that is a typical byproduct of unrestrained Western democracy where the majority defines the limits of the minority's rights.[391] It should be admired because unrestrained democracies can produce dictatorial and authoritarian regimes that bring nothing but misery to humanity. Perhaps the best example is of the Nazis who rose to power through a democratic process and cost humanity tens of millions of innocent lives, spreading devastation and despair across the world. One may argue that the modern, Western form of democracy includes constitutional guarantees for minority rights and that state institutions prevent majority tyranny. It is unfortunate to see that the current practices of Western democracies negate such a claim. We have seen the courts restrict the minority's legal rights even when the minority is comprised of the native people of the land who supposedly enjoy inextinguishable legal rights.[392] We have seen former United States President Donald Trump, in January of 2017, approve torture as a method of interrogation notwithstanding the long-established United States Supreme Court

---

[391] For Example, see, Jack and Charlie v. The Queen (Jack and Charlie v. The Queen, [1985] 2 S.C.R. 332.). In this case the defendants, native Canadians, were convicted on the charge of hunting outside the hunting season on land that their tribe historically hunted. The Supreme Court of Canada concluded that if Indians wish to exercise their historic religious practices, there are ways within the bounds of the provincial statute in which to exercise those religious practices. The Court, representing the majority opinion, affirmed that it is the duty of minority natives to adapt to majority norms, notwithstanding that the natives are the original land owners of the land and that they have practiced their religion freely thousands of years before the arrival of the Europeans.

[392] See, Jack and Charlie v. The Queen, [1985] 2 S.C.R. 332.

jurisprudence since 1936 that denies the admission of evidence obtained through use of torture in interrogations.[393]

Finally, it is worth noting that Islamic principles, including the Islamically restrained form of democracy, has never been scientifically proven to have diminished human rights in Muslim-majority states. On the contrary, Daniel Price after conducting substantial scientific research on the relationship between Islam and democracy, concluded that although lack of democracy is the most significant factor influencing human rights issues in developing countries, Islam itself does not adversely affect human rights in Muslim-majority states.[394] What actually generates poor human rights practices in many Muslim-majority states is the state's intentional denial of Islamic human rights listed in the *Qur'an* and *Sunnah* as well as the refusal to adopt Islamic human rights implementation tools. These tools include enshrining Islamic human rights within the constitution, creating legislation that directs the government's executive power to respect and implement those rights and activating the dormant Islamic doctrine of *Hosbah* that

---

[393] See, Brown v. Mississippi, 297 U.S. 278, (1936) The United States Supreme Court had concluded that the defendant's involuntary confession extracted by police violence, meaning that the defendant confessed after being subjected to brutal whippings by police officers, is inadmissible evidence because it violates the Due Process Clause of the Fourteenth Amendment.

[394] Daniel Price, "Islam and Human Rights: A case of Deceptive First Appearances", Journal for the Scientific Study of Religion 41:2 (2002) ,213-225. See also Conway Henderson, "Conditions Affecting the Use of Political Repression", Journal of Conflict Resolution 35:120–42., David Cingranelli, "Measuring the Level, Pattern, and Sequence of Government Respect for Physical Integrity Rights", International Studies Quarterly 43:407–25., Steven Poe and Neal Tate, "Repression of human rights to personal integrity in the 1980's", American Political Science Review 88:853–72.

encourages every citizen of the Muslim-majority states to guard Islamic human rights.[395]

---

[395] Indeed, in the early years of Islam, when Muslims practiced their rights freely including the right of Hosbah, citizens of the Islamic state monitored the States' actions to the minute detail. When the well-regarded Islamic States ruler, *Caliph* Umar Ibn Khattab dressed in a long coat, a sign of spending a moderate amount of money on clothing, the people exercised Hosbah and questioned him about the source of his earnings. Auditing government's actions was understood not only as a right but also a duty upon every citizen of the Islamic state.

CHAPTER 7

Misapplication of Islamic Self-Governing Theory in Contemporary Practice

————— ༷ᩒᩕ —————

7.1   Introduction: Causes for Suppressing The Islamic System of Governance: The Struggle For Islamic Identity

By the second half of the nineteenth century and through the first half of the twentieth century, most Muslim-majority states had been subject to conquest by various Western imperial powers. The invading forces attempted to eradicate the identity of the conquered nations by devaluing their religion, language and laws.[396] As these Muslim-majority states regained their independence from the

---

[396] See Nathan Nunn. 2010. "Religious Conversion in Colonial Africa." American Economic Review, 100 (2): 147-52. See also Robert Phillipson, *Linguistic Imperialism*, (Oxford University Press 1992).

colonial powers, a struggle ensued between the forces that represented the traditions of the Muslim nations and forces that preferred Western culture. Traditionalists sought the immediate resurrection of local culture, religious directives, language, and law while opposing forces favored –what some have referred to as—"Westernized" economics, political institutions, and secularism.[397]

Islam was at the core of the struggle between these competing forces. This dominant religion in Muslim-majority states shaped the consciousness, traditions, and history of these societies. To be sure, this identity struggle was not between Islamic and secular identities; instead, it was a struggle between Islamic and anti-Islamic identities. For Muslims, Islam is a not a religion that can be applied arbitrarily, nor is it limited to a particular day of worship for prayers and social gatherings. It is the most decisive factor that defines Muslims' lives. Anti-Islamic identities, as distinguished from secular identities, refers to any religious or non-religious identity that is hostile to Islam. In contrast, a secular identity refers to a religiously neutral tendency that neither favors nor disfavors Islam. For example, Ataturk the former President of Turkey, embodied an anti-Islamic identity, not a secularist identity, since he devoted most of his presidency to erasing Islamic identity in Turkey.[398] This is distinguishable from the American approach to Islam, at least in theory, that neither favors nor disfavors the religion.

---

[397] Hugh Roberts, "Doctrinaire Economics and political opportunism in the strategy of Algerian Islamism, in John Ruedy (ed.), *Islamism and Secularism in North Africa*, (Palgrave Macmillan 1994), 123-142.

[398] Tariq Ramadan, *Islam and the Arab Awakening*, (Oxford University Press 2012).

Islam defines the moral standard for Muslims. Islam sets rules of conduct that control everyday transactions. In the mind of religious Muslims, legality or illegality of a particular action is not the decisive criterion for right and wrong. An action is right if it is permissible under Islamic law and it is wrong if it is prohibited under Islamic law. Legality or illegality of an action is of secondary significance and might be considered by religious Muslims to avoid sanctions. The *Qur'an* summarizes the role of Islam in Muslim life as follows: "Say (O Muhammad): 'Verily, my prayer, my sacrifice, my living, and my dying are for Allah (God).'"[399] Thus, if Muslims live their entire life for God, any intervention to limit, change or alter the Islamic lifestyle shall be understood by Muslims as anti-Islamic.

Anti-Islamic groups are fully aware that a direct attack on ideologies, philosophies or the social structure of Islam is ideological suicide. Muslims will not listen to advice from those who attempt to stigmatize their most precious ideal, Islam. Consequently, anti-Islamic forces have utilized several strategies and have worn many masks to undermine Islamic forces. For example, dictatorial regimes in many Muslim-majority states cooperate with Western states based on shared economic or political interests, thus gaining international recognition and support. This strategy started in the twentieth century when numerous Muslim-majority states gained independence from colonial powers.[400] Tyrannical ruling regimes, typically quasi-military regimes or absolute monarchies, suppressed Islamic forces with the full blessing of Western states and the Soviet

---

[399] Qur'an 6:162.

[400] See "Middle East: David Cameron says West was wrong to back dictators", The Telegraph 22 Feb. 2011.see also Mahmood Mamdani, "Indirect Rule, Civil Society, and Ethnicity: The African Dilemma". Social Justice. 23 (1/2 (63-64)), 145–150.

Union.[401] For example, declassified British documents revealed that Israel orchestrated the installment of Uganda's dictator, Idi Amin, in a military coup in order to destabilize Islamist Sudan.[402] To be precise, sometimes Western states criticize tyrannical regimes, including those in Muslim-majority states, and enumerate human rights violations in these countries, but only when it serves Western states' interests.

The suppression of Islamic forces is of mutual interest to—and is, indeed, an essential goal—for tyrannical regimes and many Western states, given that Islam advocates for the eradication of tyranny. Deposing these regimes may not serve Western interests, at least in the short term. Other strategies that tyrannical regimes utilize to suppress Islamic forces include the creation of puppet parliaments that are never freely elected, the appointment of anti-Islamic judiciaries, and the employment of police and military generals who are loyal only to those in power. The ultimate checkmate used to suppress any democratic process that could lead to an Islamic government is the military coup d'état.

In recent years, when terrorist acts were committed by ignorant Muslims deviating from true Islam, as understood by vast majority of Muslims, the Western political sphere became noxious enough to tolerate systematic, fundamental human rights violations in Muslim-majority states and elsewhere in the name of fighting terrorism.[403]

---

[401] Richard Dowden, Africa: Altered States, Ordinary Miracles, (Public Affairs 2008), 42-43.

[402] "Revealed: How Israel helped Amin to take power", The Independent, 17 August 2003.

[403] See fact sheet No. 32, Office of the United Nations High Commissioner for Human Rights Human Rights, Terrorism and Counter-terrorism. The report

Many Western countries, along with dictatorial regimes in Muslim-majority states, classified Muslims into self-serving categories. Muslims who advocated the full integration of their religious beliefs into political life were labeled Islamists, a term linked to terrorism in popular Western vernacular. Others who stand for very unpopular views towards the West were loosely branded as extremists, fundamentalists, Islamist extremists, radical Islamists, or Wahhabi to suit the political needs of the brander, be it a Western state or a totalitarian Muslim-majority state. In contrast, those Muslims who promoted the agenda of the Western states or the totalitarian Muslim-majority regime were labeled as moderate Islamists, notwithstanding that these moderate Islamists may act against the obvious interests of their own country and the clear directives of their religion.[404] The call to support moderate Islamist groups is loud and clear to ensure that the interests of Western states and tyrannical regimes in the Muslim-majority states continue to be served.

In the midst of this political struggle within Muslim-majority states, several political forces such as liberals, human rights advocates,

---

concludes "the measures adopted by States to counter terrorism have themselves often posed serious challenges to human rights and the rule of law. Some States have engaged in torture and other ill-treatment to counter terrorism, while the legal and practical safeguards available to prevent torture, such as regular and independent monitoring of detention centers, have often been disregarded."

[404] For example, see Abdullahi Ahmed An-Na'im, *Toward an Islamic Reformation: Civil Liberties, Human Rights, and International Law*, (Syracuse University Press 1996). See also, Ali Abdul Razik, *Al-Islam Wa-Usul al-Hukm* (Cairo, Mat'ba Misr 1925), Recent translation of the book is "Islam and the Foundations of Political Power", Abdou Filali-Ansary (ed.), Maryam Loutfi (Trans.) (Edinburgh University Press 2012). To be sure, the vast majority of Muslims believe that the "reformers" agenda contradicts basic Islamic teachings.

and patriots, who are either without strong Islamic religious beliefs or possess other non-Islamic beliefs, advocate their views with little or no impact on political life.[405] Perhaps the reason these groups fails to make a real impact is because Islam is the most crucial force that shapes all aspects life in Muslim societies. Taking Islam out the equation in Muslim-majority states renders any political power feeble.

Conceivably, uniting these forces with Islamic movements on the common ground of universal Islamic human rights and Islamic democratic principles would enhance the effectiveness of all these forces in the political sphere. For example, both liberal and Islamic movements appreciate fundamental rights such as the right to vote and the right to dignified human treatment. If these forces united and gained international support, they would have a chance to elevate the status of human rights in numerous Muslim societies. By contrast, any attempt to align these forces with dictatorial regimes, based on the common ground that both dislike Islamic principles, will not last, given that authoritarian regimes do not tolerate any ideology that does not serve the regime's interests, including human rights. Recent Egyptian history provides an example. Many non-Islamic political forces, including secularists and liberals, joined the military coup of 2013 against the duly-elected Islamist President Muhammad Morsi. After the military regime had fully grasped power, it persecuted all of its rivals mercilessly, including the non-Islamic political forces who were against Morsi in spite of their support of the coup.

Notably, the struggle for Islamic identity in Muslim societies is not new and has strong historical roots. Many Muslim societies in the

---

[405] For example, Amr Hamzawy, a contemporary Egyptian political scientist and human rights activist, has no real impact on the Egyptian society.

nineteenth century admired the scientific and industrial revolution in Europe. A number of Muslim societies attempted to replicate the scientifically advanced Western model of academics in their home countries. In the process of doing so, Western values were imported incidentally and were found to be frequently at odds with Islamic values. For example, while Muslim societies generally dress modestly and do not consume alcohol, many in Muslims societies refuse to dress modestly and consume alcohol in order to assimilate Western culture.

Those who embrace Western culture and values, sometimes supported by Western religious and political powers, as well as by the dictators of some Muslim-majority states have influenced the legal and political struggle for Islamic identity. Laws, especially French and British laws, were imported and substituted for Islamic law in most Muslim-majority states. Foreign arts and languages were widely introduced and presented as modernity. Conformity to Islamic traditions that had lasted for centuries were labeled archaic and therefore undesirable in the new modern age.

While the previous chapter attempted to illustrate the essence of an Islamic system of governance in theory, the following discussion shall capture the practical misapplication, or refusal to apply, the Islamic governance theory in a number of Muslim-majority states. Though each Muslim-majority state has had different circumstances shaping its politics in the twentieth century, the common determinative causes for misapplication or refusal to apply Islamic democratic system of governance are oppression and dictatorship.

7.2   Saudi Arabia - A Burden on The Image of Islamic System of Governance: Anti-Shura, Absolute Monarchy

Peculiarly, the constitution of Saudi Arabia emphasizes the supremacy of Islamic law but violates Islamic principles in numerous provisions. Section 1 of the constitution declares that the constitution of the Kingdom of Saudi Arabia is based on the *Qur'an* and *Sunnah*, the primary sources of Islamic law. The constitution elsewhere emphasizes many Islamic law principles: Article 26 guarantees Islamic human rights. Article 23 affirms the kingdom's duty to protect the creed of Islam, apply Islamic law, and propagate Islam. Article 34 concludes that the defense of the creed of Islam is every citizen's duty.

Nevertheless, the constitution is filled with provisions that are contrary to Islamic law. For example, Section 5 of the constitution maintains that the system of governance is an absolute monarchy, whereby the King and Crown Prince are the descendants of the founding King, Abd-Al Aziz Al-Saud. Citizens must confirm their allegiance to the King and are obligated to follow his commands under all circumstances.[406] These provisions are contrary to Islamic principles because they preclude the application of the Islamic principle of *shura* to select a head of state. Respected Islamic law scholars, apart from tyrants' supporters, have unanimously agreed that rulership or any position of public office is not subject to inheritance.[407] Absolute monarchy or sham republics, where no free elections take place, is contrary to the principles of Islamic governance. The Prophet Muhammad himself provides a clear

---

[406] Saudi Arabia Constitution, Section 6.

[407] Ibn Hazm, Kitab al-fasl fi al-milal wa-al-ahwa' wa-al-nihal, (Wentworth Press 2016).

example: he was cognizant of his imminent death yet refused to appoint a successor. Instead, he left the issue to the Muslim community to utilize Islamic principles to elect a leader. The issue of Saudi regime noncompliance with Islamic law has been discussed in detail in Chapter Six.

In fact, the Saudi regime's drawbacks extend beyond the Islamic system of governance. Islamic law principles, especially those aimed to combat tyranny are either poorly drafted or omitted to protect the ruling authoritarian regime. For example, while Article 26 of the Constitution affirms the state's obligation to protect fundamental Islamic human rights, it falls short of enumerating those rights and explaining them adequately. Thus the legislature has broad discretion to define and illustrate the protected human rights. This approach opens the door for the State to ignore many fundamental Islamic legal rights, such as citizenship rights. Citizenship under Islamic law is earned either by declaring adherence to Islam or accepting the social contract of *dhimmah* for non-Muslims.[408] Saudi Arabia has never followed such a rule. Not every Muslim can gain Saudi citizenship. In fact, foreigners are rarely awarded citizenship even if they are Muslims. Regarding non-Muslims, seeking a *dhimmah* contract under Islamic law, which would result in the attainment of citizenship, has never occurred under the Saudi regime.

The Constitution also allows the State to violate numerous Islamic human rights. For instance, equality under Islamic law is not upheld. Basic rules of equality under Islamic law demand equal pay for equal work, notwithstanding the ethnic background, gender, religion, etc.

---

[408] *Dhimmah* is the social contract between non-Muslims and the Islamic state upon which non-Muslims express an interest to be a citizen, reside permanently in the Islamic state, and intend to accept the general covenant/social contract terms.

Yet non-citizens in Saudi Arabia typically receive less compensation than their citizen counterparts. Frequently, wages are determined according to employee citizenship.

Unfortunately, while many Saudi intellectuals propagate the regime as a model for an Islamic regime, they turn a blind eye to steady violations of Islamic law. Frequently they amalgamate Islamic law with Saudi practices to provide themselves with unparalleled justification for Saudi regime practices. For instance, Professor al-Hageel rightly concluded that "Islam defined the relationship between Man and his brethren according to the principles of equality and justice: piety and righteousness are the only real criteria for nobility."[409] al-Hageel also concluded that equality is a component of the governing system in Saudi Arabia.[410] What al-Hageel and many Saudi intellectuals fail to acknowledge is that Saudi Arabia does not practice equality as mandated by Islamic law. There is no equality in wages, rights of citizenship or rights of any Muslim to be head of state. By mixing un-Islamic Saudi regime practices with the principles of Islam, Saudi Arabia has effectually become a bad example for the Islamic system of governance.

7.3 Pakistan: Islamic Law Defines a System of Governance Yet Unfortunate Practices Lead to Adverse Outcomes

In contrast to many Muslim-majority states, Pakistan's laws seem much closer to Islamic principles, at least in theory. The first

---

[409] Suleiman Bin Abdul Rahman Al-Hageel, *Human Rights in Islam and Their Applications in the Kingdom of Saudi Arabia*, (Mataba' Al-Hamidee 2001), 33 & 61.

[410] Id.

constitution of Pakistan, passed in 1956, did not declare Pakistan as an Islamic state. However, in 1970, a large number of pro-Islamic system of governance political leaders were elected. The democratic process reflected the people's will: to revert to their faith, traditions, and lifestyle norms, and lean towards Islamic law to the exclusion of alternatives. As a result, a few years later, Pakistan passed a new constitution in 1973. A conglomerate of pro-Islamic and other political parties agreed to produce a "consensus constitution" that would reflect the views and priorities of all parties. The pro-Islamic political parties insisted on naming Islam as the state religion. This action changed Pakistan's legal norms for years to come.

When Article 2 of the 1973 Pakistani constitution declared Islam to be the state religion, Pakistani courts took this provision seriously, concluding that all Islamic rulings and jurisprudence are binding.[411] Accordingly, English common law, the colonial origin of the current laws of Pakistan, was progressively eliminated in favor of Islamic law. A court noted that Islamic law — based on equity, justice, and good conscience — should be applied instead of the English rules of equality.[412]

Moreover, when Article 227 of the constitution instructed all legislative bodies to create legislation only in conformity with Islam, Pakistani courts adopted a liberal interpretation and expanded the scope of Article 227 to include all branches of government, including the executive branch. [413] In this context, any regulation, decree, or rule

---

[411] Pakistan constitution 2012, Article 2.

[412] Abdur Rehaman Mubbasher v. Ameer Ali Shah Bukhari, NLR 1978, civil p.6.

[413] Section 227 provisions relating to the Qur'an and Sunnah.

(1) All existing laws shall be brought in conformity with the Injunctions of Islam as laid down in the Holy Quran and Sunnah, in this Part referred to as the

made by the state that carries the force of law must conform with Islam. Any gaps in legislation must be filled with Islamic rulings. It was held that "it was not only open for courts, but they were duty bound to apply Common Law of Islam, its jurisprudence, and philosophy, in fields which were not occupied by statutory dispensation."[414] It follows that if Islamic law is silent or there is no clear Islamic injunction regarding a matter, then the Pakistani courts would have no power to intervene between contracting parties.[415] Moreover, it seems to suggest that the terms of contracts shall prevail so long Islamic law is silent.

To advance the application of Islamic law and philosophy, Article 228 of the Pakistani constitution establishes a Council of Islamic Ideology to act as an advisory body to Parliament, provincial assemblies, the President and provincial governors.[416] To emphasize Islamic identity, Article 40 of the constitution commands the state to strengthen bonds with the Muslim world and to promote international peace. The Pakistani courts utilized Article 40 to justify the deployment of Pakistani troops in Saudi Arabia. The courts also

---

Injunctions of Islam, and no law shall be enacted which is repugnant to such Injunctions. [Explanation: In the application of this clause to the personal law of any Muslim sect, the expression "Quran and Sunnah" shall mean the Quran and Sunnah as interpreted by that sect.

(2) Effect shall be given to the provisions of clause (1) only in the manner provided in this Part.

(3) Nothing in this Part shall affect the personal laws of non-Muslim citizens or their status as citizens.

[414] Aziz A. Sheikh v. The Commissioner of Income-Tax, PLD 1989 SC 613.

[415] Commissioner of the Income Tax v. Siemens, PLD 1991 SC 368.

[416] See Section 230 of the Pakistan Constitution. See also, Mst. Sakina Bibi v. Federation of Pakistan, PLD 1992 Lhr.99.

concluded that giving the Sultan of Oman a piece of land in Pakistan to construct a residence and offices was in harmony with this Article.

> Pakistan has conformed to various Islamic principles of governance, such as shura. An election takes place for the head of the state, the President. The Parliament, which is vested in lawmaking and supervising the executive branch of government, also comes to power through free elections by the citizens.

The 1973 Constitution of Pakistan enumerated various Islamic human rights that were promoted enthusiastically by the courts. For instance, a Pakistani court was petitioned concerning the public hanging of individuals sentenced to death. The court determined that public hanging violates the "dignity of man" provision enshrined in Article 14 of the Constitution and Article 7 of 1980 universal declaration of human rights in Islam.[417] Similarly, the Pakistani court invalidated the educational institution's quota-admission system that accepted students in the ratio 4:1 for males to females, concluding that such a quota system violates equality provisions in the constitution.[418]

However, as in other states' constitutions, some principles of Islamic law were omitted in Pakistan's constitution. For example, the Islamic law of citizenship, which allows any Muslim, or non-Muslim under a *Dhimmah* contract, to be a citizen of the Islamic state does not exist in Pakistan's constitution.

The rise of Pakistan's Islamic identity and its determination to follow Islamic law, is best explained by reviewing the recent history of Muslims in the Indian subcontinent. In 1935, the British government passed the Government of India Act in response to the people's

---

[417] Suo Motu Constitutional petition 1994 S.C.M.R. 1028.
[418] Shrin Munir v Government of the Punjab. P.L.D. 1990 S.C. 295.

demand for more sovereignty over their affairs. The legislation created a federation. In the meantime, Muslims who resided in Hindu-majority provinces suffered from systemic and continuous undignified treatment. Accordingly, in 1940, the All-India Muslim League passed the Lahore Resolution, which demanded independent sovereign states for Muslims in areas where Muslims constituted the majority. Later, in 1946, the elected representatives of Muslims of India modified the 1940 resolution, calling for one independent Islamic state: Pakistan.

In 1947, the British government agreed to partition the Indian subcontinent into Muslim India and non-Muslim India. As a result, in that same year, the All India Congress Committee approved the plan to partition India, which took effect by virtue of the Indian Independence Act. When non-Muslims in India became aware that India, especially Punjab and Bengal, were about to be partitioned, a massive massacre of minority Muslims was committed in those provinces aimed at driving Muslims out of those regions towards Pakistan. The number of Muslims massacred is estimated to be at least one million. Several million Muslims fled to Pakistan to escape the indiscriminate killing. Adding fuel to the fire, a much fewer number of Hindu had been subject to violence or death. All these circumstances formed the foundation for the establishment of an independent Pakistan with a strong Islamic identity.[419]

---

[419] The first prime minister of Pakistan, Liaquat Ali Khan, gave a famous speech that defined the Islamic identity of Pakistan in the following terms: "We as Pakistanis, are not ashamed of the fact that we are overwhelmingly Muslims and we believe that it is by adhering to our faith and ideals that we can make a genuine contribution to the welfare of the world. …. All authority must be subservient to God…… the state [of Pakistan] shall exercise all its powers and authority through the chosen representative of the people. This is the very essence of Democracy….I

However, any theory of governance, even a divine one, cannot establish a successfully functional state if its application is incorrect. Pakistan is plagued by numerous problems arising from the incorrect application of Islamic law. Several military coups have occurred in which the generals leading the coup seemed mainly interested in strengthening their grip on power at the expense implementing Islamic principles of governance or advancing the state's economic and social interests. What's more, while Islam, as a religion, is widely practiced in Pakistan, Islamic moral code, beyond acts of worship, are not regularly exercised. For example, while Islam has forbidden *fasad* "corruption" it is a widespread problem in Pakistan.[420] Such a state of affairs, including lack of proper application of Islamic law or an alternative impartial and practiced system of governance, has significantly contributed to countless political and social problems, such as political assassinations, the lack of tolerance to different religious opinions, poverty, poor education, and terrorism.

---

just now said that the people are the real recipients of power. This eliminates any danger of the establishment of theocracy. In the technical sense, theocracy has come to mean a Government by those who claim to drive their rights from their sacerdotal position. I cannot overemphasize the fact that such an idea is absolutely foreign to Islam, Islam does not recognize either priesthood or any sacred authority: and therefore, the question of theocracy does not arise in Islam. If there are any who still use the word theocracy in the same breath as policy of Pakistan, they are either laboring under a grave misapprehension or indulging in mischievous propaganda."

[420] And when it is said to them, "Do not cause corruption on the earth," they say, "We are but reformers." Qur'an 2:11. See 1997 UNDP report "Corruption and Good Governance".

7.4   Sudan: Ambitious, Erroneous, Self-Centered and Conflicting Movements

The trajectory of the Sudanese Islamic movement can be adequately summarized in one sentence. While the Islamic movements succeeded in gathering momentum toward ruling the country, it failed to unite and achieve the selflessness required to govern successfully, adhering to true Islamic principles. Principally, the failings of the leaders of the Islamic movements, sometime associated with greed and unintelligent choices, are the prime causes for the unfortunate state of affairs in Sudan.

The Islamic political movement in Sudan began in the 1940s. Initially, it was modeled after the Muslim Brotherhood in Egypt. However, the youth involved in the Sudanese Islamic movement refused to follow the Muslim Brotherhood blindly. Instead, they studied various Islamic movements worldwide for guidance and borrowed the organizational models of communist movements. The movement had to determine the best approach to apply Islamic law in Sudan. There were two options; either the gradual implementation of Islamic law or swift and complete Islamization of the legal and governance systems of Sudan. The movement opted for the latter, although achieving this goal was far beyond its immediate capabilities.

In the meantime, Sudan was experiencing significant political change. Sudan gained independence from the UK in 1956 after which a civil government assumed authority. However, the political parties failed to achieve the harmonious relationship necessary to govern and deal with tenacious social, economic, and political problems. This era of independent, civil rule ended with a military coup in 1958 led by

General Ibrahim Abboud. The military ruled until 1964 when a significant uprising by civilian political forces compelled the government to relinquish power to civilian authorities. A few years later, in 1969, General Gaafar An-Nimeiry led a successful second coup and became President.

The Islamic political movements superficially allied with Sudan's second successful coup leader, President Gaafar An-Nimeiry to implement Islamic law. As a result, Islamic law was imposed in Sudan in 1983. Perhaps the An-Nimeiry- Islamic movement alliance was motivated by Islamic political movements' eagerness to implement Islamic law, which had been delayed by adverse circumstances, such as colonization of Sudan, and An-Nimeiry's attempts to gain popularity. Despite implementing Islamic law, the An-Nimeiry regime was not popular with many of the Islamic movements. In 1985, a popular uprising fueled by social, political and economic discontent forced the military to intervene and oust An-Nimeiry, transferring power to an elected government in 1986. Nevertheless, this civilian government did not last long due to a third military coup in 1989, which was orchestrated by the Islamic movements, with the understanding that the movements would have real power to rule. However, the military leaders subsequently refused to hand over power to their Islamic backers and remained in control of Sudan until April 2019 when the most recent coup d'état deposed President Umar al-Bashir.

The Sudanese experience demonstrates the failure of the Islamic movements to achieve their goals due to both external and internal difficulties, despite their popularity. The Islamic movements' failure to equitably resolve the problems in southern Sudan and Darfur led to trouble with many foreign powers resulting in catastrophic social, economic and political effects on the state. Sudan was partitioned into two states, Sudan and South Sudan. Sudan was subject to economic sanctions because of atrocities committed in Darfur and allegations of supporting terrorism. The internal obstacles before the Islamic movements included (1) the movements' lack of a clear vision of the appropriate methods to achieve their goals, i.e. implementing Islamic law correctly and an Islamic system of governance; and (2) the movements' defiance of Islamic law principles they themselves propagated. To be sure, these Islamic movements have utilized un-Islamic means to reach their goals. Since the military coup of 1958, Sudan has been ruled mostly by oppressive military authorities. Gaining power through a military coup, capturing power by force, and imposing custodianship on oppressed peoples is utterly indefensible under Islamic law since Islam mandates *Shura* and the right to be free from oppression.[421] In Islam, the ends never justify the means; both the means and the ends must be correct. Islamic movements should have political legitimacy that is not based on *de facto* force and coercion. Calling for a general and free election, as mandated under *shura* doctrine, is the first step. Islamic movements should realize that the ideal Islamic system of governance tolerates various ideologies, political movements, and religions. Failure to maintain a diversified and plural society results in the systemic exclusion of meritorious citizens and their contributions to the state, which impedes the state's ability to make changes for the better. Ultimately, Islamic movements must realize their critical position as representatives of the Islamic system of governance model to the

---

[421] And fight them on until there is no more tumult or oppression, and there prevail justice and faith in Allah; but if they cease, let there be no hostility (and aggression) except to those who practice oppression. Qur'an 2:193.

international community. The long history of negative propaganda on Islam and the misrepresentation of the ideal Islamic system of governance by misguided Islamic movements have forced the Islamic movements to fight an uphill battle to gain the trust of ignorant politicians from non-Muslim-majority states. Needless to say, as a matter of foreign policy, Islamic movements wielding power have to mature and act as a unified state that avoids uncalculated adventures, unnecessary arguments and unwarranted involvement in non-state problems.

The Sudanese Islamic movements also failed to achieve social cohesion based upon Islamic law principles. At a grass-roots level, different Islamic groups, especially the Muslim brotherhood, Sufi and Salafi movements, have engaged in lengthy, exhausting conflicts with each other. As early as 1954, disputes arose between university students belonging to the Muslim Brotherhood and those students belonging to different Islamic groups at the University of Khartoum. Apart from the university setting, the Sufi Islamic movement has a long history of clashes with Sunni, non-Sufi movements. The Salafi movement in Sudan, like other Salafi movements elsewhere, branded itself as the sole representative of true Islam and protector of the faith, and failed to propose Islamic solutions to the existing dire problems. Most of their agenda is filled with issues that were either irrelevant to current challenges in society or trivial in comparison to crushing crises such as war, famine, poverty, lack of education, and corruption that threaten the existence of Muslims. Until now, many Salafi's vigorously propagate the view that all male Muslims should sport a beard while they are silent in addressing the un-Islamic dictatorial system of governance in their country.

Within the Islamic movements, leaders have failed to be selfless, as Islamic law requires, not resigning and calling for open and free elections when necessary.[422] They could have utilized Islamic law principles of unity, justice and compassion in leadership but they did not. Umar al-Bashir, the former Sudanese president came to power in a military coup with the blessing of several Islamic movements to "optimistically" implement Islamic law in Sudan. After al-Bashir implemented an inferior and false version of Islamic law, he became a dictator, contrary to the Islamic system of governance, and remained in power through sham elections. His presidency was marked by genocide in Darfur and war with the south.

The Sudanese Islamic movement failed to reach out, understand, and cooperate with other ideologies, including secular socialists, communists, and non-Muslims. All of these groups were fearful of the idea of imposing Islamic law in Sudan. The extensive negative propaganda about Islam, reinforced by the un-Islamic practices of the so-called Islamic movements, and failure to implement and propagate Islamic human rights likely contributed to magnifying these groups' fears.

The Islamic movement's failures in governance created many socioeconomic problems. Among the worst outcomes were the civil war in South Sudan, which resulted in the division of the country, and the war in Darfur. Had the Islamic movement succeeded in transmitting a message of unity throughout the state, adopted true Islamic ideals as its system of governance, and upheld Islamic human rights, the outcome might have differed. Furthermore, employing the Islamic doctrine of *shura* would have solved many intrinsic problems

---

[422] And whoever is protected from the avarice of his self, then those are they who are the successful. Qur'an 59:9.

within the Islamic movements. Islamic groups could have collaborated with each other to reach either a consensus or majority opinion in decision-making, instead of implementing the authoritarian practices of the groups' leaders.

Unfortunately, the Islamic movement did not appreciate the depth of social, economic and political problems in Sudan and thus did not act upon them. An Islamic movement that took power, for instance the military coup of 1989, had substantial political and ethical encumbrances. The Islamic movement should have refrained from acting as a movement and instead behaved as responsible state agents. The movement should have adopted a meritocratic system of governance, appointing the best candidate for the government job, not merely elevating the movement's members or supporters at the expense of better performance. The movement ought to have strived to provide basic human needs to all Sudanese, including food, shelter, medicine, and security, thus giving every citizen the hope for a brighter prosperous future. Societal problems should have been addressed with intelligent solutions based on Islamic law principles.

7.5 Algeria: Oppressing Islamic Movements May Breed Violence

Without a doubt, Abdelhamid Ben Badis (1889–1940) is the father of the modern Islamic movements in Algeria. In 1931, he founded the Association of Algerian Muslim *Ulema* (scholars), which had a significant influence on Algerian Muslim politics throughout the twentieth century. Initially, the association focused on religious issues, such as cleansing Islam of various non-Islamic practices that had become dominant in Algerian society. Later, the Association actively opposed the intrusion of French language and culture into

Algerian society because of the gradually changing fabric of Algerian Islamic identity. As a result, the association fought successfully for the mandatory instruction of Arabic in elementary schools.

The rise of the Association alarmed the French colonizers, who implemented numerous strategies designed to oppress it, including banning preaching by Association members at government-controlled mosques. The Association survived the oppression. However, when World War II erupted, it refused to support France in the war. Perhaps the Association may have taken this step for fear that endorsing France would open the door for Algerian youth to join the French army. In response, the government closed the Association in 1940 and it remained closed until 1946. In 1947, the Association changed its focus and became more involved in Algerian politics.

By November 1954, a number of attacks took place against French interests in Algeria, marking the beginning of the Algerian revolution and the creation of the National Liberation Front. The Association supported such developments and, in January 1955, published a statement condemning the French occupation. Notably, some historians have concluded that, in the wake of violent acts by revolutionary forces and the heinous French actions against Algerians, the Association decided to take a neutral position, neither supporting nor condemning the revolutionary forces.[423] Regardless of the truthfulness of such claims, the Association's formal stance did not discourage enthusiastic members of the Islamic movement, including many members of the Association and several Islamic scholars, from participating in the revolution. Eventually, the

---

[423] Michael Willis, The Islamist Challenge in Algeria: A Political History, (New York University Press 1997).

revolution succeeded with unequivocal support from the voluminous members of the Islamic movements.

When Algeria gained independence in 1963, Ahmed Ben Bella was elected the first Algerian president. He attempted to merge his socialist agenda with Islamic values. However, Ben Bella's socialist values were neither fully compatible with nor a viable alternative to Islamic values. Also, the overwhelmingly influential French/western culture and norms in Algeria were not at ease with Islamic values. For example, sales and consumption of alcohol and extramarital sexual relationships, common practices in French culture, are forbidden for Muslims. Thus, allowing or banning such practices would definitely anger either religious Muslims or pro French culture advocates respectively. This political atmosphere created the perfect environment for the formation of the Association of *al-Qiyam* (values/morals) in 1964 with the aim to endorse and promote Islamic values in society and eradicate French cultural influence. The Association of *al-Qiyam* gained more followers over time while the President gradually became alienated from Algerian society. In 1965, Houari Boumediene seized power in a bloodless coup and became the second President. Boumediene utilized an ingenious approach to eliminate the Islamic movement's influence on Algerian politics. He asserted his loyalty to Islamic teachings, an approach attractive to Islamic movements, and from 1966 to 1970, gradually banned the Association of *al-Qiyam*.[424]

---

[424] Boumediene said: "Islam is not only a spiritual path but a social and political program. It exceeds all other religions in its struggle for the liberty of man" see the New York Times editorial Houari Boumediene, President of Algeria, Dies After Long Coma, Dec. 27, 1978.

In the early 1980s, Mustapha Boyali formed the Islamic Armed Movement out of desperation that the government failed to take substantial steps to implement Islamic law in full. This movement was involved in some violent acts that culminated in the death of Boyali and five followers at the hands of security forces in 1987. However, killing Boyali did not bring peace and order to Algerian society. People were not satisfied with the social, political, and economic environment; in 1988, massive protests erupted. As a result, a new constitution was adopted that introduced a few democratic features, including free, multiparty elections and the right to form non-state-sponsored political parties.

In December 1991, Algeria conducted its first parliamentary elections. The Islamic Salvation Front scored 82 percent of the congressional seats in the first round of elections. Newsweek magazine described the election outcome as "The Victory of God" and predicted that Algeria would be radicalized and become a fundamental Islamic state like Saudi Arabia.[425]

The results of the election were shocking for the Algerian military generals and Western states alike. Many Muslim-majority regimes — such as Egypt, Tunisia, Morocco, and Turkey — as well as France were terrified by the Algerian election outcome. Muslim-majority states' governments were afraid that their local Islamic movements would become revitalized and demand free elections in the wake of their counterparts' success in Algeria. France and many non-Muslim-majority states were worried about losing their economic interests and political influence in Algeria.

---

[425] See Newsweek Editorial, In Algeria, 'The Victory Of God' (1/12/1992 Issue), http://www.newsweek.com/algeria-victory-god-197554.

In the wake of this political unrest, in January 1992, the Algerian President resigned. The High Security Council, which was run by the army generals, assumed power, cancelled the election results, and banned the Islamic party. Secularists in Algeria and the political parties that had been trounced in the elections were thrilled at this development, although it was clear that voiding the election results would result in slaying the newly born Algerian democracy. Violent social unrest erupted, resulting in an open war between the government and armed Islamic groups resulting in a death toll of more than 60,000. To be sure, the lesson to be learned from these unfortunate events is that oppression shall always breed terrorism and violence as the only possible means of change. John F. Kennedy once summarized this particular state of affairs as follows: "Those who make peaceful revolution impossible will make violent revolution inevitable."

Nowadays, the Islamic State of Iraq and the Levant (ISIS) in Algeria Province and al-Qaeda continue their violent acts in Algeria. Perhaps some join these groups as a result of frustration caused by the military domination of political life. Conceivably Algerian society has mixed feelings of disappointment, shock, anger, and disbelief. On one hand, military generals commit various crimes to prevent a free and open election; while, on the other hand, violent groups may be perceived to have noble goals but employ heinous means to achieve them. As noted earlier, Muslims have been taught throughout their lives that the ends never justify the means. Accordingly, these groups' violent actions are surely not justifiable under Islamic law. Nevertheless, oppression may induce some individuals to forget or ignore their most important values to eradicate tyranny. Perhaps it is wise for the Western world to uphold their democratic values and never tolerate oppression, even if they dislike the elected Islamic parties, in order to prevent unjustifiable violence and terrorism. This is important because while Islamic political movements are almost dormant in Algeria nowadays, the possibility of new acts of violence are still real so long as oppression persists.

7.6 Turkey: Military Generals Suppress Islamic Law

The struggle between secular and Islamic identities in Turkey dates back to the late nineteenth century. The significant European influence on the feeble Ottoman Empire led to the first Ottoman constitution of 1876 which was modeled after Western constitutions. Sultan Abdul Hamid II testified in his memoirs that those who championed the making of the constitution, such as Midhat Pasha and his political comrades, owed their allegiance exclusively to the Masons and the British embassy. He believed that they used the constitution and the Parliament as a shelter to propagate secularism at the expense of Islamic culture.[426] Accordingly, Sultan Abdul Hamid II dismissed Midhat Pasha from his official post and suspended the Parliament and the Constitution.

In 1923, the identity struggle tilted in favor of the anti-Islamic movement at the hands of Mustafa Kemal Ataturk. Ataturk was an army officer who achieved some victories for the weakened Ottoman army and founded the Republic of Turkey from the remnants of the Ottoman Empire. Ataturk not only transformed the Ottoman Empire into a secular nation-state but also shrank the role of Islam in public

---

[426] *Mozakrat al-Sultan Abdul Hamid al Thani: Akhr al-Salateen al othmaneen Al kobar*, (Muhammed Harb trans.), (Dar al-Halal publishing 1985).

life and ended the *Caliphate*, the unified Muslim state, in favor of an authoritarian and militarized political system. He also marginalized Islamic law in favor of Western law. Ataturk formally instituted a set of principles that would define modern Turkey, known as Kemalism. Many of these principles targeted the heart of Islamic identity in Turkey. These principles are:

1. Nationalism: Nationalism was introduced as an alternative to Islamism. It emphasized the new Turkey as a nation-state that was independent and distinct from the Islamic world.

2. Secularism: Ataturk believed that his people were imprisoned by religion, specifically Islam. Although he declared Turkey a secular state, this was a stance against Islam rather than a move to implement true secularism. True secularism is neutral to religion. Thus, it does not favor or disfavor any religion. Ataturk attempted to reduce the presence of Islam in public and private life as much as possible.

3. Populism: Populism was mainly meant to be another label for democracy. However, the implemented democracy was only nominal. Ataturk utilized an authoritarian hand to silence any opposition, especially Islamic opposition.

4. Reformism/Revolutionism: Ataturk's so-called revolutionary system was a smoke screen to deeply root his ideologies and crush any opposition, including Islamic opposition.

Ataturk strived to annihilate the Islamic cultural face of Turkey. In 1926, he introduced the Gregorian calendar as the official calendar of Turkey to replace the *Hijri*/Islamic calendar. In 1928, Ataturk abolished the constitutional provisions that declared Islam to be the religion of the state and replaced the Arabic alphabet in the Turkish language with the Latin alphabet. In 1935, Ataturk changed the work week to include Friday, the day that Muslims gather in congregational prayer, thus rendering Friday weekly prayers difficult, if not impossible, for many to attend. He also introduced a Turkish-language *azan* (the Muslim call to prayer) and *Qur'an*, to be used instead of the original Arabic book.

Ismet Inonu, the second Turkish President, who assumed power in 1938 after Ataturk's death, continued his predecessor's legacy of anti-Islamism. Later, a significant shift in Turkish politics occurred in 1950 when Adnan Menderes' party, the Democrat Party, achieved a landslide victory in the first free election in Turkey in over 25 years. Although Prime Minister Menderes emphasized the separation of religion and state as the cornerstone of modern Turkey, he lessened the official state hostility towards Islam. He developed better relationships with Muslim-majority states, allowing Islamic religious programs to be broadcast openly on public radio and Islam to be taught in public schools.

Menderes' policies were viewed by the military generals, an elite group of self-proclaimed guardians of Ataturk's ideals, as a direct threat to Kemalism. Thus, in 1960, the Menderes' government was ousted in a military coup. Menderes was arrested and faced an unfair military trial that sentenced him to death.[427] The National Unity Committee (NUC), a group of military officers who seized power after the coup, realized that Islam was an indispensable component in Turkish identity and that any attempt to eradicate Islamic teaching was political suicide. Accordingly, the NUC adopted a less restrictive approach than ideal Kemalism towards Islam in Turkey. They tolerated a number of the state's institutional changes from the 1950s

---

[427] See Şaban Halis Çalış, Turkey's Cold War: Foreign Policy and Western Alignment in the Modern Republic, (I.B.Tauris 2017).

and established schools for *Imams* and a Higher Institute of Islam to promote Islam. However, the NUC stressed the political principle that parties should refrain from employing Islam in political campaigns in future elections.

A new constitution passed in 1961 that reinstated democratic life in Turkey. From 1961 to 1965, several coalition governments assumed power but none was successful in dealing with Turkey's sociopolitical and economic problems. In 1965, the Justice Party, a descendant of the Democrat Party, won an election with a clear majority of 53 percent and its leader, Suleyman Demirel, became Prime Minister.

In 1970, the National Order Party was formed and openly propagated Islamic values as an alternative to the secular political and social norms that had been mandated by the Turkish constitution. Turkish generals did not tolerate National Order Party policies. They led the military coup of 1971. After the coup, the Turkish Constitutional Court banned the National Order Party, concluding that the propagation of Islam violated the Turkish secular system of governance. In 1972, the National Salvation Party (NSP) arose from the remnants of the National Order Party. The NSP had a clear Islamic identity and engaged in a cultural war with secularism. The NSP openly criticized Turkish secularism and Kemalism, pointing out that religion is an indispensable part of Western states.[428] Accordingly, in Turkey, where 98 percent of the population is Muslim, Islamic values must have a place in the public consciousness.

---

[428] In fact, many Western countries are not genuinely secular. For example, in Denmark the constitution prescribes that the Evangelical Lutheran Church is the state church of Denmark. Even the purported secular ones, such as the United States, still value religion in private and public life.

With the election of 1973, the NSP formed a coalition government with the secularist Republican People's Party. However, another military coup occurred in 1980, and the NSP, a party with a clear Islamic identity was closed down. This latest coup was orchestrated by the National Security Council, under the leadership of Army General Kenan Evren who became President in 1982 and ruled Turkey with an iron fist. His presidency was marked by the total denial of civil and human rights. Hundreds of thousands were detained, hundreds were tortured to death, and many were executed or simply disappeared.

The military gave up power in 1983 to an elected government run by the Motherland Party, which governed Turkey until 1989. There was tension between military leaders and the Motherland Party's leader, Turgut Ozal, concerning the Islamic movements. Ozal was tolerant of the systemic increase of the Islamic movements' influence in public life. In fact, the majority of government ministers were members of various Islamic parties. On the other hand, military leaders were intolerant to the Islamization of Turkey, and they initiated a purge within the Turkish military. Any military personnel suspected of being a religious Muslim was automatically dismissed from the military. Unhappy with these military policies, Ozal succeeded in replacing the chief of the general staff who had championed these exclusionary policies.

More broadly, Ozal attempted to end religious intolerance towards religious Muslims. For instance, many Turkish universities expelled female students for wearing the Muslim headscarf (*hijab*), in conformity with a provision in Turkish law. This issue was brought before the Constitutional Court which upheld the universities' decision. In response, Ozal overruled the court's decision and reinstated the students in the universities. Citizens were able to practice Islam freely. Truly, forced secularism/anti-Islam ideologies were greatly weakened under Ozal's leadership. Ozal did the unthinkable in Turkey. He was the first Prime Minister to perform the *Hajj*, pilgrimage to Mecca, while in office.

In the early 1990s, Islamically inclined voters divided their votes between the True Path Party (later called the Democrat Party) and the Welfare Party. Consecutive governments ruling Turkey in early 1990s were more tolerant, than the strict Kemalism principles, of the free exercise of religion/Islam. After the Welfare Party's surprise success in the 1995 general election, it formed a coalition government with the True Path Party. The Welfare Party leader, Necmettin Erbakan, became the Prime Minister of Turkey until the military forced him to step down in 1997, alleging that he was advancing an Islamist agenda. Erbakan, indeed, had taken several steps to facilitate the exercise of Islam in Turkey. His party succeeded in passing legislation guaranteeing Muslim women the right to wear *hijab* in universities and governmental sectors. He changed working hours during the month of Ramadan, in which Muslims fast from dawn to sunset, to ease the fast. He also permitted the construction of mosques in affluent neighborhoods in Istanbul and Ankara. Later, the Constitutional Court banned the Welfare Party for violating the constitutional principle of separation of religion and state.

Subsequently, President Suleyman Demirel, elected in 1993, asked Mesut Yılmaz, the then-leader of the Motherland Party, to form a new government. In the Yilmaz era, military generals continued to express hostility towards Islamic parties. The deputy chief of the general staff publicly declared that the armed forces would never allow the Welfare Party to return to power, even if the party won the election. In January

1999, the Yılmaz government collapsed in the wake of the Susurluk scandal, which revealed connections between the government, the armed forces, and organized crime. Bulent Ecevit, leader of the Democratic Left Party, formed a new government. In the same year, Ecevit's party won a plurality of votes and Ecevit was sworn in as the Prime Minister.

The Virtue Party was established in 1998 as the successor to the banned Welfare Party. Although the Virtue Party ranked third in the 1999 election, secularist forces united to suppress Islamic parties by every means possible. For example, Ecevit led a successful campaign to prevent Merve Kavakçı from swearing her parliamentary oath while wearing a *hijab* and convinced the President to have her stripped of her Turkish citizenship. Apart from its hostility toward the Islamic movement, Ecevit's government failed the people economically and socially. For instance, in 1999 when a powerful earthquake struck Turkey, the government was unable to provide sufficient relief to the devastated areas. The Turkish economy became stagnant and slid into a deep recession.

In 2001, the Justice and Development Party (JDP) was formed by members of the Islamic movement. Since its establishment, the party has won the last five general elections: 2002, 2007, 2011, June 2015, and November 2015. The JDP has brought social stability and extraordinary economic growth to Turkey. Notably, while the JDP is seemingly committed to the secular principles mandated by the Turkish constitution, its heart and members belong unmistakably to the Islamic movements.

Yet the power struggle between anti-Islamic forces in the Turkish military and the Islamic movement seem endless. On July 15, 2016, a faction within the Turkish military attempted a coup against the governing regime, led by President Recep Tayyip Erdoğan. The attempt immediately failed due to heroic acts of many Turkish citizens who stood fast against the coup conspirators. Unfortunately, at least 300 died in the process and several thousand were injured.

7.7 Egypt: Authoritarianism Subdues Islamic Movements

Since ancient Egyptian times, religion has been the most potent force that has shaped the social and political life of Egyptians. When the majority of Egyptians converted to Islam, the preeminence of religion in political and social life continued, and Islam became the cornerstone of people's lives. Consecutive governments throughout the centuries had been very attentive to Islam because of the enormous moral and spiritual power that Islam enjoys in Egypt. Indeed, this power can lead to wars, change governments or build peace and prosperity.

For example, in 1805, a group of Islamic scholars succeeded in forcing the Ottoman Empire to replace the incumbent governor of Egypt with a popular public figure, Muhammad Ali Pasha. Muhammad Ali internalized the lesson of his predecessor's dismissal. He understood the moral power of Islamic scholars over the people, and sometimes over authorities, and thus exiled numerous Islamic scholars — even those who were responsible for his rise to power — without meaningful opposition.

Muhammad Ali and his successors, his ruling family, maintained a firm grip on all political opponents including Islamic speech to ensure there was no real challenge to the monarchical, non-Islamic, system of governance. However, the very essence of Islamic teaching, including the Islamic political system of governance, was honored and taught at Al-Azhar, the most influential Islamic institution in Egypt. The seed of the Islamic political movement was alive but dormant.

In 1952, a group of army officers, known as the Free Officers' Movement (FOM), ousted the government in a military coup. The FOM represented various incompatible ideologies, including liberalism, socialism, communism, and Islamism. Members also had different political strategies. General Muhammad Naguib, the FOM's leader and the first President of Egypt after the coup, preferred to implement democracy in Egypt, while low-ranking officers, including Gamal Abdel Nasser (then, a lieutenant colonel), refused to relinquish power to the people.

The Muslim Brotherhood, the most organized Islamic movement in Egypt, allegedly formed an agreement with Nasser before the 1952 coup, in which they gave their support to the coup in return for the promise of implementation of Islamic law and an Islamic system of governance in Egypt once the coup succeed. This political deal fueled violent clashes between the Muslim Brotherhood and Nasser, given that Nasser had never intended to implement an Islamic system of governance or give up power. Nasser eliminated all active political players to create his absolute dictatorship in Egypt. Communists were persecuted, and Naguib was placed under house arrest. In 1954, there was a dubious assassination attempt on Nasser, supposedly by a rogue member of the Muslim Brotherhood acting on his own. Nasser subsequently cracked down on the Muslim Brotherhood, detaining many of them while prosecuting many others; brief trials led to several executions. The Muslim Brotherhood claimed the assassination attempt was false and staged by Nasser to justify the killing and imprisonment of his opponents.

Once Nasser was officially named President in 1956, he further diminished Islam's role in public life. Although many mosques were built during his rule (perhaps to accommodate the natural increase of the population), he abolished *Shari'a* courts in Egypt. In order to curtail the power of Islamic scholars to oppose his regime, top Islamic religious positions in Egypt, such as the Rector and administrators of Al-Azhar, became government-appointed positions, and the customary practice of elections for these jobs by Islamic scholars was abandoned. Other Islamic public figures not affiliated with Al-Azhar were either silenced or imprisoned. All Islamic organizations that were engaged in charitable activities became subject to the state's mandatory supervision. In reality, this meant that army officers who demonstrated unquestionable loyalty to Nasser's regime supervised the organizations to prevent any meaningful Islamic opposition to Nasser's dictatorial regime.

After Nasser's death in 1970, Muhammad Anwar El Sadat was sworn in as the third President of Egypt. Until his assassination by army officers in 1981, he demonstrated a more lenient approach towards the Islamic movements, perhaps to counter the expansion of communist political trends in Egypt. He released Islamic political prisoners, including former President Naguib, from house arrest, and allowed the Muslim Brotherhood to officially re-engage in politics. The Muslim Brotherhood was allowed to run in parliamentary elections and gained limited representation.

Sadat's successor, President Muhammad Hosni Mubarak, allowed various political ideologies to have parliamentary representation, including Islamic groups like the Muslim Brotherhood, while maintaining a firm grip on power. Indeed, during the Sadat and Mubarak regimes, Islamic groups were never allowed to have a significant role. The parliamentary and presidential elections were nothing but a theatrical show of democracy. A limited number seats in Parliament were offered to various political parties to lend credence to the claim that the Egyptian government was democratically elected and not authoritarian.

In 2011, Egyptians revolted against the stagnant authoritarian regime of Mubarak, who had been in power for over 30 years. The popular uprising was a big surprise to Mubarak's government. While the Western and Arab states that had significant interests in Egypt were caught off guard, many sympathized with the popular revolt.

In 2012, parliamentary and presidential elections took place in which the Islamist parties scored a clear majority in the Parliament, and the Muslim Brotherhood candidate, Muhammad Morsi, won a tough presidential race. It was the first free parliamentary election since the military coup of 1952 and was the first time the Egyptian people had ever had a true, free choice of a ruler. However, dictatorial regimes like the Mubarak regime are always supported by a large, corrupt foundation of businessmen and state officials. Unsurprisingly, the new Islamist-led government faced massive economic and social challenges that were either naturally unmasked by the uprising or created by Mubarak's corrupt foundation. Moreover, an organized media campaign incited people to revolt against President Morsi, claiming that the Muslim Brotherhood had a hidden agenda that conflicted with the national interest, and that the Muslim Brotherhood cared only for its members at the expense of the general population. None of these allegations were ever proven to be true.

On June 30, 2013, a disputed number of Egyptians gathered in Tahrir Square in central Cairo, demanding an early presidential election, which Morsi refused. On July 3, 2013, General Abdul Fatah al-Sisi ousted and detained President Morsi. In 2014, General al-Sisi was elected President, in an election that lacked any real competitiveness. al-Sisi was supported by the former Mubarak regime's supporters, as well as by Saudi Arabia and the United Arab Emirates, which were terrified of political change in Egypt, because any democratic change, especially if it resulted in the rise to power of an Islamic political party, posed a real threat to their dictatorial system of governance.

The al-Sisi regime to date brands any opposition as traitorous and accuses them of engaging in a global conspiracy against Egypt using the government-controlled Egyptian media for propaganda. The neutrality of the judiciary is also called into question after sentencing thousands of members of the Muslim Brotherhood to death in trials that appeared to lack due process.[429]

---

[429] See International Commission of Jurists report: Egypt's Judiciary: A Tool of Repression, Lack of Effective Guarantees of Independence and Accountability, September 2016. https://www.icj.org/wp-content/uploads/2016/10/Egypt-Tool-of-repression-Publications-Reports-Thematic-reports-2016-ENG-1.pdf (uploaded Nov.1, 2018).

CHAPTER 8

Islamic State Between Realities and Myth

———————— ꙩꙅꙩꙅ ————————

8.1   Introduction

The phrases "Islamic State" or "Islamic government" nowadays have negative connotations. Media, politicians and ill practices from self-branded "Islamic" groups have contributed to the demonization of the Islamic system of governance. Contrary to common belief, Muslims believe that the ideal Islamic state, which is not currently in existence, is a superlative, moral and civil state. Anyone who believes that 1.9 billion Muslims would agree that their religion, religious law or system of governance is intrinsically evil needs to reconsider his beliefs. Truly, non-Muslims may agree or disagree with Muslims on issue(s) but wholesale demonization of 1.9 billion persons is a matter that ought to be subject to scrutiny.

Notwithstanding negative propaganda, it is imperative to investigate Muslims' thoughts about the ideal Muslim state in theory; an issue hardly discussed in Muslim-majority states or in the Western world for a variety of reasons in spite of its importance. Politicians and groups, good or bad, utilize the concept of the ideal Muslim state to promote their actions and ideologies. In view of that, the following discussion sheds light on the Ideal Muslim state model and its characteristics from a historical and Islamic perspective. Two questions shall be answered: what rules of conduct are taught to Muslims in relation to their ideal state and to the rest of the world? What are the basic features of the Ideal Muslim state? These questions will be answered from a Muslim perspective irrespective of commonly held beliefs at the present time. Finally, it should be noted that this chapter is not intended to promote any specific idea but to uncover Muslim ideologies and debunk misunderstandings.

8.2 The Origins of The Aspiration for An Ideal Muslim State

Recently, many Muslims have been reflecting upon the past glory of Islam in light of current oppressive regimes, failing Muslim-majority states and the apparently dim foreseeable future with mixed feelings of sorrow and hope. Memories of glory days when the newly emerging Islamic State had conquered the contemporary world superpowers, the Roman and the Persian empires, are still vivid. They also remember when Saladin defeated the Crusaders, restored religious freedom in Jerusalem and permitted all Abrahamic religions - Islam, Christianity, and Judaism - to be practiced freely. They recall the days when Muslims led the world in scientific advances while Europe remained mired in the ignorance of the medieval period. The economy had flourished to such an extent that all prospered. No needy person was left behind without financial aid from the state.[430]

Presently, most of the Muslim-majority states citizens cry for relief from their oppressive regimes. These regimes brand themselves 'democratic,' 'Islamic' or 'hybrid Islamic-democratic' in an attempt to throw a cloak of righteousness over oppression. Sometimes the labels such as "Islamic system," is invoked to justify the worst of their Counter-Islamic law actions. It is quite natural for many citizens of the Muslim-majority states not to seek succor from Western democracies because, as they believe, the West only serves its own interests which may or may not coincide with Muslim interests. The bitter memories of Western colonization and imperialism in Muslim-majority states remain vivid in their collective consciousness. Moreover, Muslims have never appreciated Western democracies' support of their dictatorial regimes.

Oppressed by dictatorial regimes and dissatisfied with Western models of governance that are at odds with their history, customs, and beliefs, many Muslims search for a solution that is compatible with their values. It is natural under these circumstances to seek divine wisdom. Such wisdom is not farfetched; it is rooted in the Muslims' belief system, providing a promising model of governance that is expounded in the basic sources of Islamic law, *Qur'an* and *Sunnah*, and had been successfully implemented during the golden era of the Islamic State. This model is not just a theory or a piece of irrelevant

---

[430] During the reign of the second *Caliph*, Umar Ibn al-Khattab, Bayt al-mal, "treasury", was so full of gold and silver that Umar ordered that all citizens' debts shall be paid and that for every person wishing to marry, the state shall bear the expenses of marriage.

ancient history; rather, Muslims believe it to be destined. It is the prophesied future Ideal Islamic State. The Prophet Muhammad said:

> "Prophethood (meaning Muhammad: himself) will remain with you for as long as Allah (God) wills it to remain, then Allah will raise it up whenever he wills to raise it up. Afterwards, there will be a Caliphate that follows the guidance of Prophethood remaining with you for as long as Allah wills it to remain. Then, He will raise it up whenever He wills to raise it up. Afterwards, there will be a biting monarchy (referring to people's anger toward the regime to the extent of biting their fingers from the prejudice and injustice), and it will remain with you for as long as Allah wills it to remain. Then, there will be a reign of tyrannical, oppressive and forceful monarchy and it will remain for as long as Allah wills it to remain. Then, Allah will raise it up whenever He wills to raise it up. Then, there will be a Caliphate that follows the guidance of Prophethood."[431]

Here, the Prophet Muhammad predicted four periods Muslims would encounter after his death. Initially, the emergence of an ideal Islamic State would follow prophetic tradition. Then two periods of unjust and oppressive regimes would take hold. Ultimately, the ideal State would rise again and reinstate the true Islamic /prophetic tradition of governance.

Sunni Muslims agree that the Islamic regime of the first four *Caliphs*, Abu Bakr, Umar, 'Uthman, and Ali, following the death of the Prophet Mohammed, was the golden era that strictly followed the footsteps of the Prophet Muhammad. Accordingly, the first part of the prophecy has been fulfilled. From the time of the death of the fourth *Caliph*, Ali, until the current time, history shows that unjust regimes have been established either in the form of absolute

---

[431] Musnad Ahmed Hadith Collection

monarchies, or as comparable dictatorial regimes that have aimed to keep authority and power within one family. This lengthy period extending for more than thirteen hundred years yielded a drastic change in Islamic State identity. The Muslim-majority state was primarily subject to the individual righteousness of the ruler. When the ruler was impartial and competent, the Muslim majority state blossomed. When the ruler was either incompetent or unfair, the Muslim state suffered greatly.

After the golden era, two distinctive periods marked the Muslim state. The first period began with the death of *Imam* Ali and the rise of the Umayyad dynasty in 661 and ended with the collapse of the Ottoman Empire in 1922. Two fundamental features dominated this period: upholding Islamic law as the supreme law of the land and unifying various cultures and ethnicities into one federal Islamic State. It is, indeed, beyond question that Islam in this era was not only a religion but also *the* unifying factor, the melting pot where distinctive cultures and nationalities were integrated to form one single identity, the Islamic identity. The collapse of the Ottoman Empire in the early twentieth century combined with European colonization in the Muslim-majority states resulted in a repudiation of Islamic law as the supreme law of the land and as the system of governance. English Common law and French Civil Law replaced Islamic law to varying degrees, depending on the circumstances. Islamic identity was eroded and replaced with the concept of nationalism which, in turn, resulted in creating states of various sizes and populations ranging from hundreds of millions as in Indonesia to the microstates of the Persian Gulf region. These dictatorial regimes nourished the concept of nationalism, at the expense of Islamic identity, to maintain the grip of power on their newly emerged states and to defeat any call for unification under Islamic identity. Apparently Muslims' awareness that their Islamic identity had served their collective interest very well for more than thirteen hundred years is the ultimate threat facing the rulers of newly emerged Muslim-majority states. As a result, in the interest of self-preservation, each state propagated nationalism and silenced those who called for a unified Islamic state or raised the idea of Islamic identity.

The second period began when the two crucial features of the Muslim state(s), i.e., upholding Islamic law as the supreme law of the land and a unified federal Islamic State, vanished. This period manifested the beginning of a more oppressive era of European colonization, imperialism, and tyrannical post-colonial regimes. This period is currently ongoing. Recognizing such a change in the Islamic State's political structure, represented in the two periods formerly discussed, invites one to believe that the second portion of the prophecy has been fulfilled. The remainder of the prophecy is the foretold re-establishment of the Islamic State. This prediction/prophecy is rooted in the Islamic faith and often invoked by Islamic movements, politicians or even terrorist organizations self-branding as Islamic to gain public support and recruits. It is presented as an opportunity to establish a just state that is virtuous for its citizens and to the world.

8.3. Features Of Ideal Islamic State

8.3.1 The Islamic State as A Civil State

Perhaps the initial impression of a state with a religious label indicates a theocratic form of government. This impression is not accurate given that the Islamic State, from its inception, was founded by the

Prophet Muhammad as a civil state with an Islamic law background. Theocracy is best defined as a form of government in which a state is ruled by religious leaders. The Prophet Muhammad, as Islamic history testifies, acted in a dual capacity; as a Prophet and as a ruler of the Islamic State. As a Prophet, he made no consultation with Muslims in religious matters; Muslims followed the divine commands without hesitation. In all other affairs involving governance of the State, the Prophet Muhammad systematically consulted Muslims, as the *Qur'an* mandates.[432] If Islam had recognized the theocratic State as an ideal, then the Prophet Muhammad would not have consulted Muslims in state affairs or followed their opinions, which were sometimes contrary to his, since, in a theocratic state, the religious leader is empowered to act by divine right with no public consultation. In this sense, Prophet Muhammad is viewed, from the Muslim perspective, as the founder of a civil state.

By way of illustration, in the Battle of Badr, the Prophet Muhammad, as the leader of the Islamic State and the Muslim army, had ordered the army to make camp upon arrival at Badr. A Muslim, al-Hubab Ibn al Mundhir, asked the Prophet whether the suggested site of the camp was a command from God or a matter of opinion. The Prophet replied that it was his own opinion. al-Hubab Ibn al Mundhir then suggested that it would be better to camp at the furthest well which would be the closest to the advancing Makkan Army. Accordingly, the Muslim army could build a water reservoir to utilize for drinking while the enemies would not have any access to water during battle. The Prophet followed this advice immediately. The advice was an excellent strategic move that aided Muslims in the battle. Again, in the battle of Uhud, the Prophet consulted Muslims

---

[432] Qur'an 3:159 & 42:36.

regarding the best technique to confront the incoming enemy army. In the course of the consultation, two contradicting opinions appeared regarding the desired location of the battle. One opinion was that the Muslims should fortify themselves within the buildings of the city of Medina. The other opinion was that the Muslims should fight outside the zone of Medina. The Prophet followed the first opinion which in retrospect was less favorable to the Muslims in battle.

With the death of the Prophet Muhammad, no further divine commands would be revealed. The Prophet's legacy was the *Shura* principles and civil nature of the Islamic State. As a result, the vast majority of Sunni Muslim scholars followed in the footsteps of the Prophet Muhammad and did not intervene in the governance of the Islamic State in their religious capacity. Of course, this does not preclude the scholars from expressing a religious opinion, a *Fatwa,* in matters related to Muslims' affairs including issues relating to the State's legal and political system. Islamic religious opinions, especially under Sunni Islamic theology, should be understood in the correct framework to evaluate their impact on the civil nature of the Islamic State. Religious opinions in Sunni theology are only opinions and are subject to discussion, analysis, and rebuttal. There is no mandatory obligation on the State whatsoever to favor a particular opinion. Islamic scholars may adopt various methodologies and reach different conclusions. However, no scholar can claim superiority of his opinion over others. This approach is a direct application of the universally accepted rule in Sunni Islamic scholarship that all statements of opinions that are not explicitly expressed in the *Qur'an* or *Sunnah* are subject to rebuttal. To be sure, this is distinctly different from the role of the clergy during the European Middle Ages, in which the church intervened massively in State affairs, burdening offenders and shaping state policies.

In fact, the practices of the Islamic State from its inception has evidenced the civil nature of the State. Shortly after the death of the Prophet Muhammad, the newborn Islamic State elected the first ruler, Abu Bakr. Ordinary Muslims had a meeting and elected him. Neither Abu Bakr nor any subsequent rulers ever claimed that they had any divine authority to rule. Indeed, Abu Bakr utterly dismissed divine authority in his inaugural speech as the first Islamic ruler. He stated, "Obey me so long as I obey Allah (God) and his messenger. If I disobey Allah (God) and his messenger, do not obey me."

To Arabs, the Arabic language is considered a language of precise meanings and thus the terminology used to describe the ruler of the Islamic State is particularly suggestive of his limited, non-divine authority within the Islamic State. During the life of the Prophet, Muslims addressed him as the "Prophet of Allah." After the Prophet's death, Abu Bakr was addressed as "Khalifat Allah" (God's *Caliph*/Successor). Rightly, Abu Bakr renounced this title, instead, accepting the title of "Khalifat Rasul Allah," the successor of God's messenger (Muhammad). The difference between the two titles is indeed fundamental. "Successor of Allah" suggests that the ruler speaks in the name of God with full divine authority. He should then be able to change any rule, law or otherwise without question including changing the *Qur'an* and *Sunnah*. That might be the reason that Abu Bakr rejected the title "Successor of Allah." When Umar Ibn Khattab succeeded Abu Bakr, he approved a new title, "Amir Al Mu'minin," Prince of Believers, as awarded by Muslims. "Prince of Believers" (of Muslims) is less authoritative than the "Successor of the Prophet of God." The term "Prince of Believers" is not used in Arabic to refer to royal status; rather it is used to refer to the leader of the Muslims. The use of the term "Prince of Believers" hints that the leadership is not speaking in the name of Islam, but rather is subject to Islamic laws. While the term "Successor of the Messenger of God" might indicate some special status among Muslims such that he may not be subject to questioning in matters of State governance, the term "Prince of Believers/Leader of Muslims" indicates no special status whatsoever. He is subject to the law of the land, questioning, and impeachment if the circumstances so require.

Perhaps the main differences between the Islamic State and secular states are the sources of legislation and the concept of citizenship. In the Islamic State, Islam is the source of all laws, and any Muslim is automatically eligible to become a citizen of the State. The door is open for non-Muslims to become Islamic State citizens as well, if they join the Islamic State's social contract, *Dhimmah* contract, as explained in the previous chapters. In a secular state, people make their laws without reference, at least in theory, to any religion; thus religion is not determinative concerning the state's citizenship. However, while Islam is the State's official religion, the State is not under the control of scholars of Islam nor is Islamic interpretation and application or any other religion, under the control of the State. Only in dictatorial systems of Muslim-majority states, does the State aim to control religious speech through governmental bodies that seek to eliminate religious rhetoric that challenges dictatorship.

8.3.2   Supremacy of Islamic Law

Islam as the defining mark of the Islamic State necessitates the imposition of Islamic law as the supreme law of the land. The theoretical foundation for imposing Islamic law on the citizens differs depending on the religion of the citizen. For Muslims, the theoretical foundation for imposing Islamic law on Muslims rests on the premise that entering into a faith necessitates unconditional acceptance of the fundamental, core values of that faith. These fundamentals of Islamic faith are the basic sources of Islamic law, i.e., the *Qur'an* and *Sunnah.* These fundamentals unequivocally declare their supremacy over other laws. Any person that rejects the supremacy of these fundamentals, by virtue of the *Qur'an*, is either an unjust Muslim, a disobedient Muslim, a non-Muslim or just a Muslim ignorant of the directives of Islam. The *Qur'an* declares that if a Muslim expresses a preference to non-Islamic rule over Islamic rule s/he is disobedient;[433] if a Muslim makes a judgment between individuals utilizing non-Islamic law s/he is unjust/a wrongdoer;[434] if a well-educated person of the Islamic faith rejects Islamic fundamentals, believing that secular laws are superior to Islamic law, s/he is not a Muslim.[435]

On the other hand, the Islamic philosophical perspective has concluded that Islam, in contrast to secularism, refuses to create a distinction between the physical and spiritual aspects of life. The notion of God is central to all aspects of life including the norms, customs, and laws. All these aspects must conform with God's guidance which reflects the ultimate truth: oneness of God, the truth, all-knowing. Because there is only one God, who is all knowing, He knows what laws best govern His creations. Levels of knowledge vary

---

[433] And whosoever does not judge by what Allah has revealed (then) such (people) are the Fasiqun (the rebellious i.e. disobedient (of a lesser degree) to Allah. Qur'an 5:47.

[434] And whosoever does not judge by that which Allah has revealed, such are the *Zalimun* (wrong-doers). Qur'an 5:45.

[435] The Qur'an declares: Whosoever does not judge by what Allah (God) has revealed, such are the disbelievers. Qur'an 5:44.

between God and humans. Human knowledge is typically limited to acquired knowledge and learned experiences while God's knowledge is limitless and includes knowledge of the future and how various creatures will act in the future. If religion is not part of human thinking, the truth becomes a relative concept that depends upon what a human believes to be the truth. For instance, Western societies for many years believed that equality meant equality among white males only. Suffrage for women or people of color was not accepted generally as a truth. Only as recently as in the twentieth century did the Western mode of thinking change gradually, and past concepts that were purported as truth were accepted to be false.

In contrast, truth in Islam is only based on one notion, that God is the ultimate truth. In this context, there should not be any contradictions between human-made laws and God's laws. If any contradiction exists, it stems from humanity's ignorance of human nature and of what is best for humanity in general.

Attempts to exclude faith from law-making, initiated by the colonial powers, have created absurd results; presumably, Muslims can believe in Islam but should not follow its commands. Not surprisingly those Islamic societies, e.g., in Egypt, Libya and Tunisia, who were forced to accept this ideological schizophrenia, to believe in Islam but not to follow it, have fallen victim to long-term dictatorships. Once those societies rose up against these dictatorships, they uprooted oppression and attempted to end the ideological schizophrenia by reverting almost immediately to a law representing their faith, Islamic law.

Dissenters of Islam may reside within the Islamic State and become citizens. Non-Muslim membership in the Islamic State entails benefits and obligations. Chief among these obligations is respecting and obeying the law of the land that the majority has accepted, i.e., Islamic law. Becoming a member of a group, organization, social club, or in broader terms, a State, necessities giving up part of one's autonomy manifested in a pledge to accept and obey the rules of conduct that govern the relationship among members of the group. The rules of conduct within the Islamic State constitute Islamic law. From a social theory perspective, non-Muslims become members of the Islamic State by joining the social contract/*Dhimmah* contract.

In sum, Muslims, by definition, accept the Islamic faith and Islamic law including its benefits and obligations. Similarly, dissenters of Islam/non-Muslims, although they do not accept the Islamic faith, become members of the Islamic State when they accept the benefits and obligations of citizenship in a State that recognizes the supremacy of Islamic law.

Analogously, in the international law arena when sovereign States join a treaty, they give up part of their sovereignty to gain benefits. Indeed, the universal doctrine holds both in national and in international spheres; benefits reciprocate, obligations burden. A nonviable alternative approach would present itself if non-Muslims were allowed to reject the majority rules of conduct, i.e., Islamic law; it would lead to lawlessness and disorder in which each dissident creates his own, self-interest driven, rules of conduct. There is a necessity to have norms that constitute the nucleus of the legal system. These norms must also reflect the culture, beliefs, and values of the majority of the population while protecting the rights of the minority group(s). In the Islamic State where the majority is Muslim, the only plausible norms that undoubtedly serve this purpose are the norms of Islam. Remarkably, in existing Muslim-majority states, even without full application of Islamic law, non-Muslim culture and values have been profoundly influenced by the norms of Islam. For instance, Muslims and non-Muslims in the Middle-East share the same values relating to sexual relationships. Sex outside of marriage is taboo. Value similarities between Muslims and non-Muslims within Muslim-majority states evince that Islamic norms have become more acceptable; therefore, its implementation in Muslims-majority states should not create uncomfortable situations for non-Muslims. However, it does not follow that non-Muslims in the Islamic State have no rights. On the contrary, Islam has maintained a longstanding tradition, from the moment of its inception, in theory, and in practice, of respecting minorities' rights including those of non-Muslims. Perhaps the most significant Islamic bill of rights for non-Muslims is the Constitution of Medina and the Najran treaty. Although the treaty was originally made between the Prophet Muhammad and the Christians of Najran, the preamble of the treaty indicates that the treaty applies to all sects of Christianity. Most significantly, it is interminable which simply means that it still governs the relationship between Muslims and Christians to this day and until the end of time. It explains relationship fundamentals such as religious and administrative autonomy for non-Muslim citizens of the Islamic State. Fundamentals, including equal enjoyment of the right of legal and factual perfection, free exercise of religious worship, the right of non-Muslims not to be exiled from the Islamic State and the right to receive the bountiful gratuitous help needed in their religious and worldly affairs. The Constitution of Medina, a treaty between Muslims and the Jews of Medina, asserted the same concept; non-Muslims shall receive fair and equal treatment in the Islamic State and become partners in creating a pluralistic society consisting of different religions and standing for peace, equality, justice, and freedom. These documents represent a fraction of the non-Muslim's rights in the Islamic State, an issue that has been discussed previously in detail in this volume. However, the significance lies in the premise that a social contract was instituted very early in the creation of the Islamic State. Notably, although some rulers of Muslim-majority states did not follow the footsteps of the Prophet or the first four *Caliphs* in full, most of them did adhere to the founding principles of these treaties in managing the affairs of non-Muslims. Some exceptions are easily identified such as al-Mutawakel and al-Hakim bi-Amr Allah, historically known as the Mad, who were cruel to Muslims and non-Muslims alike.

A comparative analysis of the role of religion as the nucleus of the state in non-Muslim society is useful in understanding the Islamic State's position within the international community. It is a fact that faith-based state laws are not unique to the Islamic State; indeed, it has been widely adopted, explicitly or implicitly, in many democratic societies. For instance, the intermingling of principles of Christianity and law runs deep in common law from as early as the thirteen century. Henry de Bracton's famous manuscript, *On the Laws and Customs of England*, which became the flower of English common law, was infused with the language of God and the principles of Christianity. Throughout the eighteenth century, the Christian legacy of common law continued to be undoubtedly visible. Renowned jurist William Blackstone's commentaries on the laws of England are notable for the language of God that was a chief driving force in his writing. Most of his analyses are filled with Judeo-Christian principles. This religiously influenced manuscript became the foundation for all common law countries including the United Kingdom, Canada, the United States, Australia and New Zealand.

Similarly, the vast majority of European states still claim an official religion, to the extent that citizens must pay taxes to support the official state religion. For instance, the tax authorities in Sweden levy municipal taxes on citizens that support the Lutheran Church of Sweden. If a citizen is not a member of that Church, he might be entitled to a reduction of the church tax under the Swedish Dissenter Tax Act, paid to parishes, in an amount corresponding to 25% of the amount he would have had to pay had he been a member of the Church of Sweden. In Spain, taxpayers are given a choice between allocating part of their income tax to financial support for the Catholic Church or other charitable purposes. Other churches are not given the advantage of automatic financial support by their followers on their tax return unless they had brokered an agreement with the government of Spain. The followers of a church that fails to strike an agreement with the Spanish government will be at a disadvantage in comparison to the followers of the Catholic Church.

Nowadays, Western secular states such as the United States have abandoned the religious basis for law, at least in theory. Nevertheless, the origin of United States law is common law which, as explained earlier was profoundly influenced by Judeo-Christian teachings. Many judges, typically labeled as conservative, lean towards the Judeo-Christian interpretation of the law, though they may deny that officially. A total and absolute separation between law and religion, in Western democracies is a myth. There will always be at least the residue of religion hidden beneath the law. Separation of law and religion, if it ever occurs, would take a long time.

Skepticism towards Islamic law as the supreme law of the land might be understandable from the Western perspective given that European civilization flourished only after the enlightenment years when the state succeeded, at least partially, in escaping the grip of the Church and established expressly or implicitly the doctrine of separation of Church and State. In contrast, Islamic civilization has flourished only under an Islamic form of governance. Indeed, while Europe was still in the Dark Ages, Muslim scientists without a doubt led the world, both in science and prosperity, for an appreciable length of time. al-Razi (Razes), Abulcasis (Bucasis, Alzahravius), Ibn-Sina (Avicenna), Ibn-Rushd (Averroes), and Ibn El- Nafis were leaders in the science of medicine for centuries. al-Haitham (Alhazen) pioneered the science of modern optics. al-Khwarazmi (Algorizm) is one of the founders of algebra. Jabir-bin-Hayyan is the father of chemistry. During the reign of the first four *Caliphs*, the Islamic State enjoyed power and wealth beyond any other state in the history of humanity. For instance, during the reign of Umar Ibn Khattab, the Islamic State treasury was filled with gold and silver, and not a single poor person could be found to receive charity funds. Medicine was very advanced for that era, and citizens of the Islamic State enjoyed excellent medical care. The crime rate was very low, perhaps the lowest in history. Without a doubt, the inescapable conclusion is that Islam is not responsible for the current regressive state of affairs of Muslim-majority states. No parallel comparison can or should be drawn between the European experience with Christianity and the Muslim-majority states with Islam given the significant differences between the role of Islamic scholars and Christian clergy in their respective states and the inherent nature of the Islamic state as a civil state, though governed by Islamic law.

8.3.3   Unified Universal Nation

Unity of Muslims, as one nation, has been emphasized in the *Qur'an* and in the Prophet Muhammad's actions.[436] Prophet Muhammad described the role of Muslims within the nation as that of bricks forming a wall, reinforcing each other.[437] He affirmed the necessity of unity of the nation and warned of division.[438] The act of unity among Muslims does not recognize racial, cultural or geographic limitations. There exists only one nation, one culture, one moral standard in which all Muslims shall fulfill their obligations towards society and enjoy their rights. Islam, from its inception, sought to destroy all barriers to create a unified nation. When Muslims immigrated from Mecca to Medina, the Prophet Muhammad established a fraternity among the immigrants from Mecca and the welcoming Muslims of Medina. Soon after, the Prophet Muhammad drafted a document commonly known as the Constitution of Medina in which he emphasized the concept of the Muslim *Umma* (nation) as a distinct society that is liable collectively for their actions and enjoys the same rights. Later, the *Qur'an* marked the end of one era and the beginning of a new one, the official rise of the Islamic State as a unified nation governed by social contract.[439] The *Qur'an* revoked all open-ended conventions with non-Muslims and awarded a grace period for up to four months during which non-Muslims would have the choice to either enter Islam, integrate into the Islamic social contract becoming *dhimmi* or depart the Islamic State safely. Lastly, the Prophet Muhammad affirmed the foundations of the Islamic State in his

---

[436] See Qur'an 21:92.
[437] See Sahih Al-Bukhari.
[438] See Sahih Muslim.
[439] Qur'an 9:1-4.

farewell. He asserted that all pre-Islamic practices contradictory to Islam have ceased to exist. He assured the sanctity of life, the protection of wealth and equality, and affirmed the unity of the Muslim *Umma*, proclaiming the supremacy of the *Qur'an* and *Sunnah* as the Constitution of the Islamic State.

The first four *Caliphs* followed the footsteps of the Prophet in solidifying a unified Islamic State. All citizens of the Islamic State enjoyed the same rights and obligations including the freedom of movement between Islamic provinces, a State-wide welfare system, and a uniform tax system. Several historical incidents attest to the unity of the Islamic State in its rights and obligations. In a year of famine, Muslim *Caliph* Umar Ibn Khattab brought food supplies from Egypt, Syria, and Palestine to feed the hungry and distressed Arabia. When some provinces refused to pay Zakat (obligatory charity) the Muslim *Caliph*, Abu Bakr, fought them fiercely.

Unification, as thought of in the Islamic state requires the State's adoption of a broader perspective of citizenship. This comes naturally because the Islamic state encompasses diverse ethnic, cultural and racial backgrounds which require a broader concept of citizenship that differs significantly from contemporary views. In contemporary societies, individuals typically gain citizenship of a State either by place of birth, citizenship of a parent(s) or by fulfilling immigration regulations such as residing in the State legally for some years. Apart from the Israeli governing system, religion is not a factor in determining citizenship. In contrast, in the Islamic state, confessing Islam is a decisive factor in determining the citizenship of the Islamic State. Although this proposition seems impractical given the cultural, geographical, educational and urban disparity of Muslims in our time, it is the uncontested underpinning of the Islamic State. The current practice of Muslim-majority states, whether labeled Islamic States such as Saudi Arabia or secular states such as Turkey, never follows the Islamic law of citizenship for numerous political, economic and prejudicial reasons. Wealthier Muslim-majority states refuse to accept the influx of predominantly poor Muslim refugees from war-torn countries under temporary residence status or to accept these refugees as citizens. Nowadays, millions of Syrian refugees cannot find a host Muslim-majority state although many Muslim-majority states are wealthy and strive to enlarge their populations. The wealthy Gulf States refuse to share their wealth with other Muslims although these Muslims might be starving to death, an ongoing issue in Africa. Moreover, as Muslims societies distance themselves from Islamic culture and become more associated with their regional cultures, it might become more difficult for them to accept Muslims from other regions. Dissimilarity in culture and customs between the Turks and the Nigerians, the Egyptians and the Indonesians, the Pakistanis and the Algerians is a noticeable obstacle to enforcement of the Islamic law of citizenship. Perhaps the long and dreadful history of colonialism of Muslim societies is to blame for fragmenting Islamic unity. Perhaps the blame lies with the systematic oppression of the Muslim people by their corrupt rulers whose highest objective is to rule a fragment of Muslim lands as monarchs or under the label of a Republic, Emirate or absolute monarchy. It matters not who is responsible for the current state of affairs; what matters is the current state of affairs of Muslim-majority states: the corrupt application of Islamic Law, which has significantly deviated from its true meaning and application demonstrated at the time of Prophet and first four *Caliphs.*

A logical inference is that all current Muslim-majority states, even if they are labeled Islamic states, are not, in fact, real Islamic States because they have failed, or have intentionally refused, to implement the concept of citizenship in Islam. Perhaps the tendency to ignore the principle of Islamic state unity along with the rise of the notion of nationalism emerged recently after the demonstrated frailty and collapse of the Ottoman Empire, which was the last, albeit imperfect, Islamic state. Shortly before the collapse of the Ottoman Empire, Muhammad Ali, the Ottoman governor in Egypt, gained Egyptian independence from the empire as a reward for exceptional services rendered to the Empire. Meanwhile, the house of Saud fought the Empire to gain independence supposedly with the help of British intelligence to establish their kingdom. When the Empire collapsed, Ataturk vigorously fought the notion of Islamic state unity and reshaped the remainder of the Empire into a new country named after him. In these examples, the recurring theme is very similar in essence and outcome: rulers discounted the well-established principle of Islamic state unity in favor of personal gain, to institute a country they factually own.

Sometimes Muslims societies fail to recognize the Principle of Unity due to ignorance, corruption or political unrest. Pakistan was initially established to unify Muslims into one country and to protect Muslims from the constant maltreatment by the Hindu government of India. However, the Constitution of Pakistan never mentioned the Principle of Unity which would allow *any* Muslim to become a citizen of Pakistan. Some other Muslim-majority states such as the central Asian nations of Kazakhstan, Kyrgyzstan, Tajikistan, and Turkmenistan were forced to join the Soviet Union which ensured that the rulers of these states remained loyal only to the union exclusive of other ideology. After the collapse of the Soviet Union, political life in these states was too corrupt to allow the state to breathe and rediscover its real soul. Only the Afghans fought the Soviet Union for years, to perhaps rediscover their Islamic identity; however, their aim was not realized due to a host of political issues.

Apart from internal problems that plagued the Islamic principle of unity, external forces have been and remain significant factors that oppose the principle. Historically, colonial powers such as France and the United Kingdom have adopted the philosophy of divide and rule to maintain power over colonial lands, including Muslim lands. The UK and France created the Sykes-Picot agreement in 1916 for the dismemberment of the Ottoman Empire. The agreement effectively created new states including Syria, Iraq, and Lebanon with Britain 'acquiring' Iraq and France 'acquiring' Lebanon and Syria. Nowadays, Muslim-majority states in central Asia such as Kyrgyzstan and Tajikistan cannot escape Russian influence over their political life. Notably, some of the current crises in Muslim-majority states are the legacy of the colonial policy of divide and rule; a policy designed to defy the principle of Muslim unity. For example, after the partition of British India into Pakistan and India, the ruler of the independent state of Jammu and Kashmir, Maharaja Hari Singh, joined India despite the fact that the majority of Kashmir is Muslim. He was a Hindu ruler supported by the UK and viewed by the majority of Muslims as a tyrannical oppressor. Pakistan was not satisfied and asserted that the people of Kashmir have the right of self-determination and that they should not be forced to join India against their will. India refused to grant the people of Kashmir the right of self-determination for fear that it would lead to full independence or joining Pakistan. A series of wars erupted between Pakistan and India along with social unrest in Kashmir to settle this issue; as yet no satisfactory bilateral agreement has been achieved.

Apart from the reasons for the divisions within Muslim-majority states or the assertion that Islamic state unity is a must, the critical question is this. Do the facts, recognized by the *Qur'an*, that humanity is so diverse and that people possess such different habits and customs, justify different legal systems and laws and thereby necessitate the existence of more than one Islamic State?[440] In fact, some scholars have suggested that there can be more than one Islamic State especially because Muslim territories are vast and people from various regions possess different customs, language, and heritage. Thus, according to this approach, it would be proper to label Pakistan, Saudi Arabia or Sudan as the Islamic States. Irrefutably this perspective violates the indispensable Islamic rule of governance listed in the *Qur'an* that Muslims are one indivisible nation.[441] The Islamic State, as governed during the reign of the first four *Caliphs*, was so vast that Muslims spoke many languages and enjoyed different cultures and values. There was no scholarly proposal to divide the Islamic State into several small states. Those *Caliphs* overcame the problem of expanded Muslim territories by establishing a form of a federal state that emphasized the central authority and leadership of the Islamic state. Uniform laws represented the immutable rules of Islamic law; however, various Islamic provinces adopted, when permitted by Islamic law, mutable laws that reflected the cultural individuality of the provinces.

Notably, any Muslim, whether he intended to be a citizen of the Islamic State or not enjoyed automatic rights of protection afforded

---

[440] Qur'an 49:13.
[441] Qur'an 21:92.

by the Islamic State. This general obligation upon the Islamic State to help Muslims, whether citizens or not, was established in the basic sources of Islamic law. In a famous *Hadith*, the Prophet Muhammad addressed Muslims, "Help your brother whether he is an oppressor or the oppressed."[442] A man responded, "I will help him if he is oppressed, but if he is an oppressor, how shall I help him?" The Prophet said, "By preventing him from oppressing (others), for that is how to help him." The authority of this *Hadith* establishes dual obligations on the Islamic State. There is an obligation to help Muslims unjustly threatened and to protect others from being threatened or harmed by Muslims unjustifiably. Incidents triggered by the so-called war on terror provide an exemplary application of the Islamic State's obligation to protect Muslims and to protect non-Muslim states from deviant Muslims' actions. When a Muslim poses an illegitimate threat to non-Muslim States, the Islamic State is under obligation to prevent such harm by every means possible including arrest, interrogation or even detention of the Muslim(s), in accordance with Islamic law. An extradition treaty between the Islamic State and the non-Muslim State must be honored, and criminals must be extradited if their guilt has been established. Similarly, a Muslim who is unjustly threatened because of suspicious unfounded allegations such as possible links to terrorist organizations, by a Muslim or a non-Muslim, shall enjoy the Islamic State's protection guarantee. Logically, mere unsubstantiated allegations are never sufficient to trigger the Islamic State's obligation to protect Muslims and to provide protection from Muslims' actions.

---

[442] Sahih Al-Bukhari.

8.3.4   Autonomous Nation

Over the centuries, Islamic scholars have extensively invoked a prophetic *Hadith* affirming that Islamic rules prevail over others and that nothing supersedes Islam to emphasize the independence, uniqueness, and supremacy of Islamic law and culture in the Islamic State.[443] The Islamic State, especially during the life of the Prophet Muhammad and the reign of the first four *Caliphs*, was never a blind follower of norms of other nations, the existing superpowers, nor was it subject to any influence contrary to Islamic principles. Instead, the Prophet Muhammad and the first four *Caliphs* created rules and made judgments only in light of the *Qur'an* and *Sunnah*. In this context, the *Qur'an* has defined the Islamic State's relationship with the world regarding the supremacy of Allah's (God) commands over other norms and laws, forbidding blind following of non-Muslims.[444] Most significantly, the *Qur'an* explains the relationship between Muslims and Non-Muslims as follows:

> *Allah does not forbid you to deal justly and kindly with those who fought not against you on account of religion nor drove you out of your homes. Verily, Allah loves those who deal with equity. It is only as regards those who fought against you on account of religion, and have driven you out of your homes, and helped to drive you out, that Allah forbids you to befriend them. And whosoever will befriend them; then such are the wrong-doers.*[445]

Obviously, these verses define the interaction between the Islamic State and non-Islamic States regarding maintaining a just and kind

---

[443]   Al-Bayhaqi, Al-Sunan al-Kubra.

[444]   Qur'an 6:57, 42:10 &5:51.

[445]   Qur'an 60:8&9.

relationship so long as non-Muslims do not attack, or aid in attacking Muslim territories or fight Islam in any manner. These verses open the door for mutual understanding and cooperation with non-Muslims, both in domestic and international arenas, so long as such cooperation is in harmony with Islamic principles and promotes general good to humanity. Of note, the pre-Islamic world had many good traits that promoted cooperation for the general welfare. Islam was not founded to demolish all traits, good or bad, or to establish its own version of conduct and manners. Instead, Islam aims to elevate the best of humanity's characteristics. Prophet Muhammad acknowledged that he

'was only sent to complete the noblest character traits.'[446]

The implication of this approach is far-reaching. In the domestic sphere, within the Islamic State, Muslims and non-Muslims alike may cooperate to enjoin good and forbid evil. In the international arena, the Islamic State may cooperate with the international community to advance peace and justice and to join treaties and conventions that promote humanity's well-being and happiness. Multiple historical incidents, as well as the *Qur'an*, support this proposition. The *Qur'an* indicates:

'Help you one another in virtue, righteousness, and piety; but do not help one another in sin and transgression.'

[447] The Prophet Muhammad, before the revelation of the message of Islam, had witnessed the pact of justice, *Hilf al-Fudul*, which aimed to uphold justice and aid the oppressed. After Prophet Muhammad received the message of Islam, he spoke highly of such alliances,

---

[446] Sahih Muslim.
[447] Qur'an 5:2.

indicating that if he were called to it in the time of Islam, he would have joined it. The Prophet did not find any problem in allying with non-Muslims so long as the aim was to uphold justice and aid the oppressed. The legacy continued throughout the centuries as Muslim-majority states joined numerous international accords that promoted human security, well-being, and prosperity.[448] A proper Islamic state would be expected to continue this legacy and cooperate with the international community aiming for justice and prosperity of all of humanity.

8.3.5 Sovereign Nation

While upholding the supremacy of Islamic law, the Islamic State enjoys absolute sovereignty manifest in holding elections, legislating, choosing a form of government, and establishing political, economic and social relationships with other nations. The Islamic state, to achieve absolute sovereignty, ought to liberate itself from the foreign, imperialistic, colonial ideological heritage that has been forced upon it during the past two centuries. This colonial heritage includes the imposition of language, culture, and laws of the colonial powers upon Muslim societies, as noted in the historical imposition of the French language, culture, and laws upon northwestern African nations and that of English law and language upon the Indian subcontinent. Such liberation might be challenging at present because, although Muslim-majority states have gained independence from the imperialistic colonial powers, the influence of the colonial period remains robust.

---

[448] For example, most of Muslim Majority States joined international instruments that promoted Human prosperity including the Universal Declaration of Human Rights (UDHR), the International Covenant on Economic, Social and Cultural Rights (ICESCR) and the International Covenant on Civil and Political Rights (ICCPR).

For a variety of reasons, many Muslim decision-makers remain loyal to Western ideologies even when such ideologies contradict the foundations of Islam. Similarly, a segment of non-Muslim minorities in Muslim-majority states may also prefer Western heritage over Islamic State values. Such a preference is a direct threat to the Islamic State's social contract. Here it is essential to distinguish between the freedom to believe and the freedom to act. Every individual in the Islamic State, whether Muslim or non-Muslim, is free to believe in any ideology, norm or value. However, every individual member of the Islamic State is bound to act within the social contract of the nation. Again, allowing individuals to act contrary to the collective social contract is an invitation to lawlessness and disorder. To achieve absolute sovereignty that is free from direct and indirect foreign influence, the Islamic State must act on dual fronts, domestic and global. On the domestic front, a new social contract is needed in which Muslims and non-Muslims agree upon fundamental issues and create a new Islamic constitution that guarantees minority rights. The process might be somewhat lengthy because it would involve educating non-Muslims on Islamic law principles so they would feel secure under the Islamic regime. Also, many Muslims have to be educated on the real Islamic spirit of tolerance and the acceptance of the "other". Suppression of freedom of thought and expression, both during the colonial periods and later by dictatorial regimes, did not permit the true teaching of Islam to prevail over the erroneous teachings. Both the colonial powers and the dictatorial successors in many Muslim-majority states were interested in manipulating Islamic teaching to serve their agendas. Inciting intolerance among various religious groups is a successful technique used to create divisiveness within society and thus facilitate rule, a classic divide and conquer method. The British colonial legacy of generating religious intolerance in the sub-Indian continent within a single nation is an example. Currently, the extreme ideologies and intolerance of ISIS towards others is evidence that some Muslims need to re-educate themselves regarding correct Islamic practices. In the international arena, the Islamic State must alleviate the international community's fears by asserting its respect for international law and customs including international humanitarian law. Consequently, the international community would not feel the need to circumvent an emerging sovereign Islamic State. In this context, it is important to emphasize that asserting the Islamic State's sovereign power does not necessitate wholesale rejection of humanitarian laws and social values. Only those laws and values that contradict Islam are subject to revision.

The Islamic State is continually monitored by its citizens when exercising its sovereignty by passing legislation and engaging in international conventions or otherwise. Citizens obey the laws of the nation so long as they conform with Islamic law. The *Qur'an*, *Hadith* and the practices of the first four *Caliphs* have emphasized this fundamental doctrine.[449] The Prophet Muhammad concluded that

> "A Muslim has to listen and obey (the commands of his Muslim ruler) whether he likes it or not, as long as it does not constitute a sin. If the ruler commands making a sin, a Muslim should neither listen nor obey".[450]

In his inaugural speech, Abu Bakr, the first rightly guided *Caliph*, asserted that a citizen's obedience to the ruler is limited by Islamic law. Accordingly, laws and commands contrary to Islam are per se of no force and without effect on Muslims. The application of this

---

[449] Quran 4:59.
[450] Sahih Muslim.

doctrine is indeed all-encompassing. A citizen may refuse to join a military action, where he might be ordered to kill innocents or if there is no just cause for the war under Islamic law. A citizen may challenge, by every legal means, under the Islamic doctrine of *Hosbah*, any law, practice or command contrary to Islamic law whether the violation of Islamic law is due to the State or private individuals. The *Hosbah* doctrine allows any citizen to challenge any governmental action or law in the courts if it contradicts Islamic law. The unity of the Muslim nation doctrine clarifies the rationale for *Hosbah*: Islamic society is one entity, whatever harms the society or deprives it of lawful gain affects every citizen regardless of whether a citizen is directly or indirectly benefited or harmed by the wrongdoing. Accordingly, it is a citizen's encourageable right to enjoin good and forbid evil. In fact, the Prophet Muhammad explicitly recognized the doctrine of *Hosbah* in the following terms:

> *Whoever of you witnesses the wrong, let him correct it with his hand; and if he cannot then with his tongue (deny the practice verbally and advise the practicing person, gently, to stop what he/she is doing]); and if he cannot, let him abhor it in his heart; this reflects the weakest level of Iman (faith).*[451]

Islamic state expressive sovereign acts such as legislating based on Islamic law tolerates individuality and encourages freedom of thought. It respects dissenting views provided all individuals confine their *actions* to the collective social contract. Invariably and across various systems of governance in ancient and modern worlds, all states must have some form of a social contract in which individuals fulfill basic obligations such as paying taxes and refraining from committing crimes that threaten the well-being of humans such as

---

[451] Sahih Muslim.

killing, assault and the like. Individuality while typically tolerated, especially in democratic societies, is not encouraged at the expense of the social contract. For example, those who refuse to pay taxes or who assault others based on the racial discrimination are not tolerated because not only do their actions pose harm to others but they also constitute a direct threat to the collective socially acceptable norms of behavior enumerated in the social contract.

When exercising the sovereign power of legislating, if a contradiction arises between an individual's interest and the State's interest, Islamic law is the decisive factor in settling the dispute without preference to the State or the individual. An excellent historical example of this ideal practice of Islamic law follows. When the Tartars attacked the Abbasside dynasty killing millions and annihilating societies, the Islamic State in Egypt needed money to raise an army capable of defending the nation from the incoming threat. Sultan Aa-Muzaffar Saifuddin Qutuz, the ruler of Egypt at that time, needed a *fatwa*, a religious opinion under Islamic law, as Islamically required, that would justify imposing further taxation on the people to fund the army. The Islamic law scholar, Izz Ibn 'Abd al-Salam, refused to issue this *fatwa*, refusing to burden the public until all the Mamluk Princes, the top government officials at that time, spent all of their wealth that had been generated by their official status, to fund the army. Sultan Qutuz followed Izz Ibn 'Abd al-Salam's *fatwa* and ordered all the Mamluk Princes to sell all their properties to fund the army. It turned out that the money collected from the Mamluk Princes was sufficient to fund the army and there was no need to impose further taxation on the public. This demonstrates that legislating as an act of sovereignty is not absolute; it is constrained by

Islamic law limits, even under extreme circumstances when the state may be threatened with extinction.

Following the same line of analysis that Islamic State's Parliament does not enjoy absolute sovereignty, it is imperative to note that parliamentary sovereignty is restricted by the immutable tenets listed in the *Qur'an* and *Sunnah*. Islamic law includes mutable and immutable rules. The immutable rules are constitutional limitations whose validity cannot be challenged because they constitute the creed of Islam. The immutable rules are prefixed resolutions and general guidelines that aid the Islamic legislature in crafting mutable rules that address ever-changing social needs. The Islamic State's Parliament may exercise its power to legislate in light of the general guidelines in the immutable text. If the Parliament exceeds its power and passes legislation in violation of the immutable tenets that enjoy constitutional status, such legislation would be of no force or effect from the moment of its inception. Notably, Islamic law's self-characterized classification serves many desirable goals including maintenance of a minimum human rights standard as declared in the *Qur'an* and *Sunnah*, protecting minorities and non-Muslims from the tyranny of the majority. It is a historical fact that sometimes under the guise of 'democracy,' the majority have enjoyed unlimited privileges while suppressing minorities' basic human rights.[452] Islam has crafted an expansive list of human rights including minorities' rights that has been entrenched into the mutable tenants in the *Qur'an* and *Sunnah*.

---

[452] For example, historically in ancient Rome, where Rome presented itself as a democratic State, individuals were entitled to their human rights based upon their status; i.e. Roman Citizen, Roman woman, freedman or client state citizen. Nowadays, many States discriminate against minorities such as Kuwait's discriminatory treatment towards the Bedouins.

Ultimately, it is vital to stress that citizens cannot challenge the government's actions or that of an individual under the doctrine of *Hosbah* unless the law violates an immutable tenet listed in the *Quran, Sunnah* or *Ijma* (consensus). A scholarly opinion that did not achieve consensus is not a valid excuse to violate a State 's commands. Logically, a citizen's own interpretation of the *Qur'an* or *Sunnah* shall not avail the violator from legal consequences. As a result, whenever a citizen violates a State's law claiming *Hosbah*, he is taking the risk that he may bear the legal consequences if he is wrong.

Because Islamic scholarly opinion, *Ijtihad/fatwa,* is determinative in law making, an act of sovereignty, there has been an attempt to better regulate *Ijtihad* since the time of the Ottoman Empire. In 1876, the Ottoman Empire issued a *Majalla Ahkam Adliyyah* containing the most critical *fatwas* and *Ijtihad* of Hanafi scholars, the officially adopted Ottoman school of thought. Currently, other models of practice exist in some Muslim-majority states, such as in Egypt, where the authority to issue a religious opinion or *fatwa* is assigned to a governmental agency. Although the *fatwa* may not be legally binding to the courts or the government, courts and governmental agencies find it nearly impossible to ignore any *fatwa* given that the majority of the population is Muslim. This practice is meritorious given that it provides a natural, systemic, uniform and harmonious interpretation of Islamic law. However, it can be problematic when dictatorial governments influence the *fatwa*-making process by various means to serve their interests.

8.3.6   Moral Nation

The maxim, the ends justify the means, is a standard state policy that drives nations to commit horrendous acts such as enslaving other nations, annihilating a race or usurping other nations' natural resources. The Islamic state does not recognize the behavioral model of 'the ends justify the means.' Islamic law, as religious law, requires that both the ends and the means be justifiable as expected in an Islamic moral society. This rule applies to both times of war and of peace without exception.

Prophet Muhammad ordered Muslims to seek peace as feasible.[453] Indeed, justice and peace are Islamic goals that the Islamic state strives to spread universally notwithstanding people's religion, or its lack thereof, or the state's conflicting political and economic interests with others so long as the others do not fight Muslims because of their religion, or drive Muslims out of their lands.[454] Nonetheless, war might be inevitable in order to fight injustice and oppression.[455] When war becomes fact, the Islamic state is restrained by Islamic law which permits the Islamic state, as a general rule, to provide reciprocal treatment to other nations. However, if a nation at war with the Islamic state commits unethical acts that are impermissible under the Islamic code of war ethics, the Islamic state cannot reciprocally

---

[453] The Prophet Said (O people! Do not wish to face the enemy (in a battle) and ask Allah (God) to save you (from calamities)...) Sahih al-Bukhari.

[454] Allah (God) does not forbid you to deal justly and kindly with those who fought not against you on account of religion and did not drive you out of your homes. Verily, Allah loves those who deal with equity. It is only as regards those who fought against you on account of religion, and have driven you out of your homes, and helped to drive you out, that Allah forbids you to befriend them. And whosoever will befriend them, then such are the Zalimun (wrong-doers). Quran 60:8-9.

[455] (And what is wrong with you that you fight not in the Cause of Allah, and for those weak, ill-treated and oppressed among men, women, and children, whose cry is: "Our Lord! Rescue us from this town whose people are oppressors; and raise for us from You one who will protect, and raise for us from You one who will help.) Qur'an 4:75.

commit the same acts against that nation.[456] Accordingly, if a nation at war with the Islamic state targets civilians or employs weapons of mass destruction that inevitably cause death or bodily harm to non-combatants, the Islamic state cannot utilize the same war practice. Without a doubt, Islamic law forbids treachery and transgression.[457] Transgression includes harming non-combatants and civilians such as women, children or monks in monasteries.[458] Even non-combatant citizens of a transgressor nation that are unjustly fighting the Islamic state shall receive dignified and humane treatment from the Islamic state. The rights of the citizens of the transgressor nation who reside or are visiting the Islamic state during wartime shall remain intact notwithstanding the war between their home state and the Islamic state.[459] These rights include the right to life, liberty, and personal

---

[456] See, (The sacred month is for the sacred month, and for the prohibited things, there is the Law of Equality (Qisas). Then whoever transgresses the prohibition against you, you transgress likewise against him. And fear Allah, and know that Allah is with the pious.) Qur'an 2:194.

[457] (If you (O Muhammad) fear treachery from any people throw back (their covenant) to them (so as to be) on equal terms (that there will be no more covenant between you and them). Certainly Allah likes not the treacherous.) Qur'an 8:58. See also, (Fight in the way of Allah those who fight you but do not transgress. Indeed. Allah does not like transgressors). Qur'an 2:190. It should be noted that while Peace is a supreme goal in Islam, it does not follow that Islamic state should be unprepared for war. Qur'an ordered Muslims to be prepared for the worst scenario that is war. See (And make ready against them all you can of power, including steeds of war (tanks, planes, missiles, artillery, etc.) to threaten the enemy of Allah and your enemy, and others besides whom, you may not know but whom Allah does know. And whatever you shall spend in the Cause of Allah shall be repaid unto you, and you shall not be treated unjustly. But if they incline to peace, you also incline to it, and (put your) trust in Allah. Verily, He is the All-Hearer, the All-Knower. Qur'an (8:60-61).

[458] Musnad Imam Ahmad.

[459] (And if anyone of the Mushrikun (disbelievers in the Oneness of Allah) seeks your protection then grant him protection, so that he may hear the Word of

security.   Prisoners of war are treated with dignity and kindness.[460] All means to ensure human prosperity and livelihood should be kept intact during wartime. Therefore, it is a prohibited transgression to destroy anything, such as roads, waterways or agriculture, that is set to the benefit of humans or animals during wartime except in circumstances of extreme necessity.[461] Indeed, the *Qur'an* commands that permissible war in Islam occurs only *"fi Sabil Allah / for the sake of God."*[462] This verse suggests that war is justified only for the benefit of humanity under strict Islamic standards. It also means that wars cannot be launched for economic gain, to usurp another nation's resources, to extinguish existing civilizations, to build occupiers' civilizations or even to diminish human prosperity.[463] Eventually, when an aggressor nation inclines towards peace, the Islamic state is commanded to seek peace and end hostilities.[464] The Islamic state is

---

Allah (the Qur'an), and then escort him to where he can be secure, that is because they are men who know not.) Qur'an 9:6.

[460] (And they give food, in spite of their love for it (or for the love of Him), to Miskin (poor), the orphan, and the captive, (Saying): "We feed you seeking Allah's Countenance only. We wish for no reward, nor thanks from you.) Qur'an, 76:8-9.

[461] (And do not do mischief on the earth, after it has been set in order, and invoke Him with fear and hope; Surely, Allah's Mercy is (ever) near unto the good-doers.) Quran 7:56

[462] (And those who believed, and emigrated and strove hard in the Cause of Allah, as well as those who gave (them) asylum and aid; - these are the believers in truth, for them is forgiveness and Rizqun Karim (a generous provision i.e. Paradise) Qur'an 8: 74.

[463] For example, Islam never justified launching unfair wars such as the first Opium war (1839–42) that erupted between Chinese Qing dynasty and UK over the UK's insistence to sell products such as Opium to China against the interest of China.

[464] (But if they incline to peace, you also incline to it, and (put your) trust in Allah. Verily, He is the All-Hearer, the All-Knower.) Qur'an 8:61.

commanded to fulfill the terms of all peace treaties made with the other nation(s).[465]

On the other hand, during peacetime, the Islamic State and its citizens owe a duty to promote the highest standard of morality. Muslims are required to follow the footsteps of the Prophet emulating his great moral character.[466] The Prophet Muhammad's *Sunnah* shows a clear tendency to establish peace and prosperity in the world as much as possible. Prophet Muhammad commanded every Muslim to fulfill his religious duty to do good deeds towards others in need.[467] Following in his footsteps, the *Caliph*, Umar Ibn al-Khattab, guaranteed welfare for those incapable of providing for themselves regardless of their religion.[468] Prophet Muhammad, in an example of international cooperation for peace and justice, had expressed admiration for the pre-Islamic treaty of *Hilf al-Fudul* (Alliance of al-Fudul), which aimed to uphold justice and aid the oppressed. He

---

[465] (O you who believe! Fulfill (your) obligations....) Qur'an 5:1.

[466] And verily, you (O Muhammad) are on an exalted standard of character. Qur'an 68:4. The Prophet Muhammad said "The best of you (O Muslims) is the best among you in conduct." Sahih Al-Bukhari and Sahih Muslim. The Prophet Muhammad said: "I have only been sent to perfect good characteristics" Musnad Ahmed.

[467] See (The prophet Muhammad said: Giving charity is obligatory upon each Muslim. It was asked: What do you say of him who does not find (the means) to do so? He said: Let him do manual work, thus doing benefit to himself and give charity. It was asked: What about one who does not have (the means) to do so? He said: Then let him assist the needy, the aggrieved. It was asked: What do you say of one who cannot even do this? He said: Then he should enjoin what is reputable or what is good. He asked: What if he cannot do that? He (the Prophet) said: He should then abstain from evil, for verily that is charity on his behalf.) Sahih Muslim explained by Nawawi Hadith # 1676.

[468] The *Caliph*, Umar Ibn Al-Khattab, had ordered payments to a destitute Jewish citizen of the Islamic state and condemned the officials who failed to recognize the deprived status of that citizen.

stated that he would have joined such an alliance if it had occurred after the revelation of the message of Islam. Prophet Muhammad made the Constitution of Medina that included the organization and promulgation of the relationship between the newly emerging Islamic state and non-Muslim nations (at that time, Jewish tribes). The constitution laid the foundation for social welfare and guaranteed the Islamic state's protection of non-Muslims from external aggression. The Islamic State, under the leadership of the Prophet, joined peace treaties, such as the Treaty of Hudaybiyyah, whenever feasible to end conflicts. Correspondingly, the *Qur'an* commands numerous good traits including honesty, humane treatment of prisoners of war, supporting the welfare of the poor and the orphans, rendering excellent care to parents, relatives, and neighbors.[469] At the state level, the *Qur'an* and *Sunnah* have drawn clear guidelines for an Islamic state code of conduct. The *Qur'an* directs the Islamic state to deal kindly even with its enemies in the hope that animosity, over time,

---

[469] O you who believe! Be afraid of Allah, and be with those who are true (in words and deeds). Qur'an 9:119, And they give food, in spite of their love for it (or for the love of Him), to Miskin (poor), the orphan, and the captive, (Saying): "We feed you seeking Allah's Countenance only. We wish for no reward, nor thanks from you. Qur'an 76:8-9, And your Lord has decreed that you worship none but Him. And that you be dutiful to your parents. If one of them or both of them attain old age in your life, say not to them a word of disrespect, nor shout at them but address them in terms of honour. And lower unto them the wing of submission and humility through mercy, and say: "My Lord! Bestow on them Your Mercy as they did bring me up when I was small." Quran 17:23-4., Worship Allah and join none with Him in worship, and do good to parents, kinsfolk, orphans, Al-Masakin (the poor), the neighbour who is near of kin, the neighbour who is a stranger, the companion by your side, the wayfarer (you meet), and those (slaves) whom your right hands possess. Verily, Allah does not like such as are proud and boastful. Qur'an 4:36.

might be transformed into friendship with kind treatment.[470]   A mutual peaceful relationship, between the Islamic state and other states, is the norm. The only exception to the norm that is mentioned in the *Qur'an* is in the case of the state(s) that is at war with the Islamic state seeking to capture its land or to fight the Islamic religion.[471] The *Qur'an* also lists numerous human rights that shall be maintained in the Islamic state including: the right of asylum, punishment is person-specific, no crime and no punishment except in accordance with predetermined law and honorable and dignified treatment to every human being.[472]

---

[470] Perhaps Allah will make friendship between you and those whom you hold as enemies. And Allah has power (over all things), and Allah is Oft-Forgiving, Most Merciful. Qur'an 60:7.

[471] Allah does not forbid you to deal justly and kindly with those who fought not against you on account of religion and did not drive you out of your homes. Verily, Allah loves those who deal with equity. It is only as regards those who fought against you on account of religion, and have driven you out of your homes, and helped to drive you out, that Allah forbids you to befriend them. And whosoever will befriend them, then such are the unjust. Qur'an 60: 8-9.

[472] With respect to right to asylum, see, And if anyone of the Mushrikun (disbelievers in the Oneness of Allah) seeks your protection then grant him protection, so that he may hear the Word of Allah (the Qur'an), and then escort him to where he can be secure, that is because they are men who know not. Quran 9:6. Several verses in Quran have repeatedly emphasized that punishment is personal and that there is no punishment or crime without predetermined law. See "Who receives guidance, receives it for his own benefit: who goes astray doth so to his own loss: no bearer of burdens can bear the burden of another: nor would We visit with Our Wrath until We had sent a Messenger (to give warning)." Quran 17:15; "Verily We have sent thee in Truth, as a bearer of glad tidings, and as a Warner: and there never was a people, without a Warner having lived among them (in the past)." Quran 35:24; "Nor was thy Lord the one to destroy a population until He had sent to its centre a Messenger, rehearsing to them Our Signs: nor are We going to destroy a population except when its members practice iniquity." Quran 28:59; "Of some Messenger We have already told thee the story;

One significant aspect of morality in the Islamic state is the concept of *Ihsan* which roughly translated means perfection in acting with the highest standard of ethics and skillfulness. *Ihsan* also denotes the bountiful philanthropic acts that fall beyond justice to include conscientious behavior, generosity, forgiveness, tolerance and merciful treatment of all creatures. *Ihsan* as a sense of generosity, mercy, forgiveness, and tolerance has been articulated several times in the *Qur'an*.[473] The *Qur'an* seemingly suggests the favored behavioral code for Muslims - while justice is guaranteed if demanded by the victim(s); nevertheless, it is highly recommended for the victim(s) to demonstrate *Ihsan* and forgive the offender. The *Qur'an* outlines the recommended logical and natural steps to attain *Ihsan* in the sense of generosity and forgiveness.[474] Initially, the victim should restrain his anger, pardon those who have harmed him unjustly and

---

of others We have not, and to Musa Allah spoke direct. Messengers who gave good news as well as warning, that mankind, after (the coming) of the Messengers, should have no plea against Allah: for Allah is Exalted in Power, Wise." Quran 4:164-5. As God honored mankind, every human is command to offer honorable and dignified treatment to his fellow human. See, (And indeed We have honored the Children of Adam, and We have carried them on land and sea, and have provided them with At-Taiyibat (lawful good things), and have preferred them above many of those whom We have created with a marked preference. Qur'an 17:70.

[473] For example, see, (Verily, Allah enjoins justice and al-ihsan, and giving (help) to kith and kin, and forbids al-fahsha' (i.e all evil deeds), and al-munkar (i.e all that is prohibited by Islamic law), and al-baghi (i.e. all kinds of oppression). He admonishes you, that you may take heed). Qur'an 16:90. The role model for all Muslims, the prophet Muhammad, was an exemplary in showing mercy to friends and foes. (And We have not sent you (O Muhammad) except as a mercy to mankind) Qur'an 21:107.

[474] (Those (believers) ...who repress anger, and who pardon men; verily, Allah loves al-muhsinun [the good-doers who act in accordance of ihsan].) Qur'an 3:134.

finally perform *Ihsan* by bestowing forgiveness and generosity upon the offender. The practice of numerous Muslims has demonstrated the application of *Ihsan*. In one incident during the early years of Islam, a Muslim was severely aggravated by his slave. When the slave realized his master's anger, he started reciting the *Qur'anic* verses alluding to "those who repress anger"; the master responded with the verse, "I restrain my anger"; then the slave recited "those who pardon men," and the master responded, "I have granted you a pardon." Finally, the slave recited "Allah loves those who perform *Ihsan*." The master responded, "Go, you are a free man."

Ihsan, in the sense of forgiveness and generosity, is different from mutual fair treatment among individuals. It is a victim's generous act in response to the aggravation. The renowned Islamic scholar al-Alusi in his commentary of the *Qur'an*, Ruh al-Ma'ani, concluded that 'Isa [Jesus, son of Mary] said that *Ihsan* occurs when you present it to the one who harms you, not to the one who is good to you. Nevertheless, attainment of *Ihsan* is a level of such lofty spiritual superiority that many cannot achieve it. For those who seek justice and cannot reach the superior *Ihsan*, their right to justice is guaranteed. The *Qur'an* lists justice before *Ihsan* to explain that justice is assured.[475]

Ihsan in the sense of being conscientious was explained in the Prophet Muhammad's famous *hadith* that describes *Ihsan* - it is that you should serve Allah as though you could see Him, for though you cannot see Him yet (know that) He sees you.[476] Being conscientious with attention to the slightest detail in all actions to ensure full compliance with the Islamic code of conduct is a duty upon every Muslim in the Islamic State, whether he is an average citizen or an

---

[475] Qur'an 16:90.

[476] This is an excerpt from a hadith mentioned in the forty Nawawi hadith.

official. This mode of behavior is a great formula to combat human infirmities and social problems such as corruption, greed, dishonesty, and deceitfulness that lead to the erosion of a healthy productive and prosperous society. The application of *Ihsan* reaches far beyond domestic rules of conduct in the Islamic State. The Islamic State ought to treat other nations with *Ihsan*. Accordingly, the Islamic state is under an obligation not to violate treaties or Islamic Human rights when dealing with foreign nationals. Furthermore, the Islamic state is required to offer all humanitarian aid possible to other nations in need and to encourage universally responsible environmental policies.

It should be noted that the Islamic code of morality does not coincide with the ever-changing, undefined Western moral standards. The Islamic code of morality, as delineated by the *Qur'an* and *Sunnah*, is fixed and unresponsive to human whim.

CONCLUSION

Looking Forward: The Road to Peace and Prosperity

Introducing Islamic law and its system of governance for educational purposes to Western readers is a difficult task given that Western readers enjoy a different mindset that measures right and wrong according to their own customs, norms and laws. The average Western reader is unlikely to spend a great deal of time searching for Islamic law rationales, norms, justifications and Islamic ethical standards especially if they do not share the faith. Islamic law and its system of governance are usually presented as an alien force, archaic laws, a cause of oppression and terrorism, which is mostly applied in third world countries or in dictatorships. As a result, the task of introducing Islamic law and its system of governance to Western readers in a single concise volume, is an uphill battle. Nevertheless, it is important that the Western reader understand Islamic law and its system of governance properly, as distinguished from Islamophobic propaganda, because lack of such understanding induces the West to support oppressive authoritarian regimes in Muslim-majority states and can ultimately lead to terrorism. There is a complex relationship between the lack of proper understanding, misapplication of Islamic law and its system of governance, oppression and terrorism.

Two main groups of factors shape political, social and economic life in Muslim-majority states: oppression and foreign intervention, usually harmful and Western. Oppression can be traced to colonialism's legacy of creating government branches subservient to the colonial regime notwithstanding notions of impartiality, democracy, independence or justice. Nowadays, many dictators in Muslim-majority states, under the guise of a democratic Republic or Kingdom, have inherited the colonial powers role. As explained previously in this volume, dictators minimize or eliminate, the role of Islamic law, Islamic human rights and Islamic system of governance because its resurrection poses a great threat to any authoritarian regime. To do so, regimes utilize subservient, corrupt and oppressive branches of the government. Both history and current practice testify to this fact: For instance, historically, the Egyptian judiciary favored Westerners during British colonial role. Mixed courts, established in 1874 in Egypt under the British colonial regime, in which the majority of sitting judges were non-Egyptians, were notoriously known for their bias against Egyptians.[477] After Egypt's independence, the Egyptian judiciary, except for a few brave judgments, continued to follow the ruler's whims.[478] As explained previously, the

---

[477] See, Hisham Ramadan "Conflicts of rights: free speech freedom to practice a religion and the social phobia mighty machine", in Hisham Ramadan and Jeff Shantz (ed.), *Manufacturing Phobias: The Political Production of Fear in Theory and in Practice*, (Toronto University Press 2016), 40-41.

[478] Id.

Constitutional Court of Egypt, to comply with the political will, had issued judgments that stood at odds with the Egyptian Constitution in order to suppress the application of Islamic law. Similarly, though constitutionally obliged to create legislation compatible with Islamic law, the Moroccan legislature, under political pressure, passed numerous legislations utterly incompatible with Islamic law. The military in Egypt, Turkey and Sudan overthrew duly elected governments even after the people deposed previous militarized dictatorial regimes. To maintain the tyrannical grip of power over states' agencies, authoritarian regimes in Muslim-majority states appointed only loyal individuals to public offices. These loyalists were not necessarily the best or most qualified. This state of affairs led not only to an oppressive environment but also poor economic performance, corruption and a general state of helplessness, desperation, and anger among the people.

Moreover, all Islamic movements in the Sunni world were subject to oppression. The following are the major Islamic movements in Sunni Muslim-majority states.[479]

A. The traditional Salafi movement that was revitalized by Muhammad Ibn 'Abd al-Wahhab and adopted in Saudi Arabia.

B. The Reformist Salafi movement / Modernist Salafism led by Mohammed Abduh, Jamal ad-Din al-Afghani, Muhammad Rashid Rida in Egypt and followed by Ben Badis in Algeria.

C. The Muslim Brotherhood movement founded in Egypt by Hassan Al banna.

---

[479] See, Pierre Dévoluy, La Poudrière Algérienne: Histoire Secrète d'une République Sous Influence, (France, Calmann-Lévy 1994).

D. Islamic movements in Pakistan and India led by Abul Ala
Maududi and Abul Hasan Ali Hasani Nadwi.

Although these four factions have achieved very different
outcomes under the current state of affairs they share one common
feature: all have been subject to oppression. The traditional Salafi
movement in Saudi Arabia is turning a blind eye to homegrown
oppression to survive. The Reformist Salafi movement after
producing a duly elected Islamic government was overthrown in a
violent military coup in Algeria. Similarly, when the Muslim
Brotherhood movement took power in a democratic process, it was
ousted in a violent military coup in Egypt. Finally, Islamic movements
in Pakistan and India led by Abul Ala Maududi were marginalized by
the state, and some followers of these movements adopted extreme
non-Islamic violent means to change the status quo.

The relationship between oppression in Muslim-majority states
and the misrepresentation and misapplication of Islamic law and its
system of governance is conspicuous. A negative view of Islamic law
and its system of governance is produced by many channels including
lobbies with political or economic interests, Christian religious
leaders engaged in a mass media war against Islam, misrepresentation
of Islam by some Orientalists and misapplication of Islam by several
dictatorships in Muslim-majority states. This negative view in the
West may have driven general public opinion to pressure politicians
to make decisions averse to Muslims. It also provides the West with
the moral ground for supporting the authoritarian regimes in
Muslim-majority states.

On the other hand, the authoritarian regimes in Muslim-majority
states exploit the negative view of Islamic law and its system to gain
legitimacy and support from the West. These authoritarian regimes

present themselves as the only viable alternative to the "malevolent" Islam. These regimes also show their willingness to grant political and economic favors that may conflict with Muslim-majority states' interests in return for the West's support. The West, to gain moral ground, occasionally criticizes these dictatorial regimes but time and again exploits the situation and supports the dictatorial regimes for gain. However, when the West pursues its interests, regardless of morality or cost to Muslim lives and reaps obvious substantial benefits, it has also incurred undesired side effects. The veiled side effect is violence, motivated by hatred of the oppression and its supporters; the West. This state of affairs begs the question: what is the West's *real* interest? Is it the immediate, readily apparent interest such as the privilege of allowing passage of American warships through the Suez Canal at the cost of supporting the dictatorial regime in Egypt? Is it the French, British and American arms sales to the Middle East in return for ignoring blatant massive human rights violations? Certainly, these may be the Western States' genuine interests. However, when the West betrays its principles of democracy and human rights by ignoring them in international relations to gain short-term returns, long-term unforeseeable negative consequences may follow. The West runs the risk of a backlash of terrorism as a byproduct of condoning oppression in Muslim-majority states. Many Muslims are angry at their corrupt dictatorial governments and at the countries that support and empower these dictatorships including Western states. These angry Muslims may unjustifiably seek mental relief in joining terrorist organizations. They may join terrorist organizations wrongfully believing that terrorism is the only way to defeat oppression. This marks the creation of armed terrorist movements, such as al-Qaeda and ISIS, that are rooted in the belief that oppressive regimes in the Muslim-majority states can only be removed by force and violent acts. Truly the acts of these armed movements, such as al-Qaeda and ISIS, are incomprehensible and violate every human rights code, including Islamic Human Rights but it is oppression and desperation that may incite individuals to do the most heinous acts. Numerous Islamic politicians have consistently warned that Muslims' anger may not observe the strict Islamic code of conduct that prohibits terrorism. Hassan al-Turabi, a Sudanese religious and political leader, and Rached Ghannouchi, the Tunisian political leader, have warned countless times that religious Muslim youth passionate about their religion are looking forward to making a meaningful change in their failed society.[480] They are striving to implement social justice, Islamic democratic principles, better education, and healthcare. If the road is not open for peaceful change within the political system, they may resort to violence. They may fall victim to the twisted interpretation of Islam such as that propagated by al-Qaeda. Some may ignore Islamic principles altogether and decide to take law and justice into their own hands to change the stagnant political environment in their countries. These possibilities are real. The rapid and unexpected rise of ISIS is the direct result of the lack of hope and lack of confidence in peaceful mechanisms of change within the Muslim-majority states. Many Sunni Muslims in Iraq were subject to ruthless persecution by the Shia in recent years. They were killed, raped and tortured with the full blessing or willful blindness of the West. Similarly, in Syria, the dictatorial regime's crimes are beyond comprehension. Bombs fall on the civilian population as rain falls in the West. Millions are killed and tortured with impunity. Given that, it is not surprising that ISIS recruits a large

---

[480] See Muhammad Mukhtar Ash-Shinqiti, *al-Haraka al-Islamiyya fi al-Sudan*, (Beirut, Mo'sesah al-Entashar al-Arbi, 2011), 21.

number of supporters from Iraq and Syria as well as garnering sympathizers from all around the globe who have witnessed the crimes against humanity committed without any world powers' real intention to stop it.

Nevertheless, there is a hope to change the status quo only if a political will is present to defeat extremism and open the road for peace and prosperity in Muslim-majority states. One must start with addressing the grievances caused by authoritarianism as well as eliminating harmful Western interventions.[481] Hurdles must be identified, and mechanisms to attain the goal must be created. The negative propaganda on Islam in the West that aggravates Muslims needs to be addressed. If the West's freedom of speech permits, for example, the offensive caricature of the Prophet Muhammad, which causes harm to 1.9 billion Muslims, then the West may consider not protecting such hate speech. The West may reconsider supporting authoritarian regimes in Muslim-majority states. The West can deprive terrorist organizations such as ISIS or al-Qaeda from gaining financial support and recruits from the Islamic world by addressing fair Muslim grievances. In balancing the interest of global security, Muslims' prosperity and fairness versus these hurdles, it seems that overcoming these hurdles is an inescapable task for the free world. The first step is true knowledge of Islam; most importantly Islamic law and its system of governance, not false Islamophobics' propaganda.

"The greatest enemy of knowledge is not ignorance; it is the illusion of knowledge".[482]

---

[481] See Robert Dreyfuss, Devil's Game: How the United States Helped Unleash Fundamentalist Islam, (Metropolitan Books 2006), 15.

[482] This quote is owed to Daniel Boorstin.

Index

human infirmity, 162

Human Rights

international standard, 65, 117

humanity's unity of origin, 57

I

Ibn Taymiyya, 176, 242

Ihsan, 332, 333

Ijma (consensus), 14, 29, 30, 31, 34, 35, 36, 38, 43, 119, 324

Imam, 28, 33, 40, 41, 64, 67, 90, 109, 134, 150, 175, 191, 217, 227, 228, 244, 296, 327

Imam al-Shaybānī, 175

impossible crime, 79, 82

in crime

mental element, 70, 71, 75, 77, 83, 84, 85, 86

physical element, 78

Preparatory acts, 79

in Muslim Majorty states

ill practices, 64, 92, 95, 100, 126, 158, 199, 292

in Muslim-majority states

Dictators, 201

Islam

Reformers, 110

Islamic human rights, 8, 56, 61, 62, 63, 64, 130, 132, 137, 139, 145, 172, 174, 179, 180, 194, 248, 249, 253, 259, 261, 262, 263, 266, 274, 336

Islamic legislature, 31, 40, 69, 73, 82, 84, 86, 87, 89, 148, 186, 323

Islamic movement, 102, 121, 122, 259, 269, 270, 271, 272, 273, 274, 275, 276, 277, 278, 284, 286, 288, 289, 297, 337, 338

Islamic scheme of

natural rights, 57

O

Orientalists, 55, 64, 65, 66, 147, 148, 155, 158, 167, 174, 192, 195,
197, 198, 227, 338
Ottoman Empire, 16, 95, 121, 132, 201, 279, 280, 287, 296, 312, 313,
325

P

parliament, 69, 134, 141
prisoners of war, 59, 161, 162, 176, 207, 330
Prohibition
intoxicants, 13, 21, 35, 36, 70, 160, 161, 183

Q

Qisas, 68, 74, 75, 80, 82, 83, 84, 88, 148, 149, 150, 152, 153, 154, 326

R

Rabbinical courts, 180
riba, 42, 135, 137, 142
rightly guided *Caliphs*, 63, 203, 208, 209, 239
Roman Empire, 178, 187, 246
rules
Immutable rules, 315, 323
mutable rules, 227, 324

S

separation of Church and State, 308
shura, 140, 141, 145, 261, 266, 272, 274

Made in the USA
Middletown, DE
20 June 2021